DANCING WITH THE DINOSAUR

HOW TO DO BUSINESS WITH MOD IN THE SMART PROCUREMENT WORLD

by

BILL KINCAID

Published by:

The UK Defence Forum, North House, 17, North Street East,
Newcastle-upon-Tyne, NE1 8DF

Enquiries to:

The Author, 10, Crutchfield Lane,
Walton-on-Thames, Surrey, KT12 2QZ

Tel: 01932-227827
Fax: 01932-269445

ISBN 0 9537483 0 8

Produced in Great Britain by

The Short Run Book Company Ltd
St Stephen's House
Arthur Road
Windsor
Berkshire SL4 1RY

ABOUT THE AUTHOR

Bill Kincaid served for 36 years in the Army, half of which period was spent in Ministry of Defence posts dealing with the procurement of equipment. His last job was as Director of Operational Requirements for all land systems equipment.

His sell-out book of 1997, *A Dinosaur in Whitehall,* was a hard-hitting, controversial criticism of what was then wrong with defence equipment procurement in the Ministry. Many of his recommendations for improvement subsequently found their way into the Government's Smart Procurement Initiative.

He has written and lectured widely on the subject and has spent much of the last year seeking the views of people in over 100 organisations in both Government and industry.

Tel: 01932-227827 Fax: 01932-269445
e-mail: billkincaid@tinyworld.co.uk

FOREWORD

by the
Rt Hon Dr David Clark MP

Picture the combat-ready British soldier.

He's in his armoured vehicle, waiting to go ashore from a landing craft, eating a sandwich, various types of ammunition ready for use while information and orders, updating his battle maps with new enemy positions and friendly force locations, are passed automatically in data format through his combat net radio. He has fuel, rations and spares to get him to his objective. Overhead, combat aircraft ensure that the enemy cannot disrupt his landing from the air, while out at sea lies the amphibious force which brought him here, complete with surface ships, submarines, helicopters, air defence and missiles of all sorts.

Everything that makes this landing, and all other types of operations, possible has to be purchased by the Ministry of Defence and manufactured by the defence industry. Their relationship is altering and it is this, and other changes taking place in the defence equipment procurement process, that concern this book.

In 1996, John Spellar MP, a member of my shadow defence team, addressed the UK Defence Forum on the need for a more cost-effective way for the MOD to spend its multi-billion pound equipment budget. The thoughts he outlined then have become known as the Smart Procurement Initiative, which is now being implemented.

At the same time I challenged the UK Defence Forum to "Think the Unthinkable". *Dancing with the Dinosaur* is part of that response. Its author, Bill Kincaid, has carried out extensive research with small, medium and large suppliers to the MOD, and with serving officers, civil servants, academics and observers.

The book reviews the evolution of the procurement processes; details how Smart Procurement is envisaged to work; reveals the hopes and fears of those for whom defence procurement is a central issue of their lives; and contains invaluable advice on the impact of these changes on all companies, large or small, who want to do business with the organisation which Bill Kincaid, in his earlier biting analysis, called *The Dinosaur in Whitehall.*

It makes lively, interesting and, no doubt, controversial reading. It is a comprehensive contribution to the evolving procurement story.

Rt Hon Dr David Clark MP

Patron, UK Defence Forum
Shadow Defence Secretary 1992-1997
Chancellor of the Duchy of Lancaster 1997-1998

PREFACE

The search for Smart Procurement was begun more than two years ago and, during that time, a great deal has been written about and spoken about what it consists of and how it is to be implemented. Despite this, very few people in either the Ministry of Defence or in the defence industry have a clear idea of what it is and, crucially, how it will affect them. Moreover, those that do know seem to be largely unaware of the many difficulties that are lurking in the undergrowth.

Having shot my mouth off (or should that be pen?) with my previous book about what was wrong with MOD equipment procurement, I felt that I ought to explore the whole subject of Smart Procurement and try and provide some suggestions as to how to overcome some of the major problems that are strewn along the implementation path. There are few easy answers and in some cases I have been unable to suggest any at all. Nevertheless, I have been able to propose some options for examination.

None of this would have been possible without the help of numerous people in both MOD and industry. Over the last twelve months, I have sought the opinion of some hundred individuals from all relevant parts of the Ministry and from large and small firms, both UK and foreign-owned. Almost all made the stipulation that what they said was a personal viewpoint and was non-attributable. I would like to thank them all, but I can only do so here without mentioning names. Nevertheless, my thanks are sincere and I hope that the views of others that are reflected in this book will be of interest to them all.

Any author who writes about defence procurement has to face the problem of abbreviations. Some readers will know the acronym but will be unfamiliar with what it means; others will not know the acronym and will need the full title spelt out. I have tried to spell out the full meaning, with the abbreviation, most of the time, resorting to just the acronym when it has been used in the previous couple of pages and should be fresh in the mind of the reader. This should mean that readers will not have to repeatedly look up meanings in a list. I hope I have not fallen between two stools!

There is a little duplication in places, but it is intentional as I wanted to pursue the main arguments in each chapter without making the reader refer to other chapters to make sense of it. It will also, I think, be useful if the book is used, after the first read, as an aide-memoire. And if it is thrown in the bin, it won't matter anyway.

But, however you use it, I hope that it will stimulate more ideas; ideas that are better than mine. If it does, I will feel justified in adding this book to the mountain of paper that already exists on Smart Procurement.

November 1999

CONTENTS

PART FOUR: WINNING PROPOSALS

PART FIVE: CONCLUSIONS

PART ONE:

THE COMING OF

SMART PROCUREMENT

INTRODUCTION

A DINOSAUR IN WHITEHALL

I wrote *A Dinosaur in Whitehall* [1] in 1995 at a time when there was huge pessimism at the working level in the Ministry of Defence in Whitehall about the possibility of improving a military equipment procurement system which was widely recognised as inefficient, bureaucratic, wasteful of taxpayers' money, and unable to deliver equipment until it had been overtaken by the increasing pace of technological change. The MOD battery-operated marionettes, engaged in a Downey stately dance to a Treasury tune, were running down and the pulse of the dance was stagnating.

This slowing down had, of course, one advantage in that it allowed funds to be repeatedly 'moved to the right' into later years to make way for the cost growth of projects and the cost of increasing bureaucracy and sterile scrutiny by a host of civil servants. This had been unnecessary in the early 1980s as the defence budget increased in real terms year on year but, with the stabilisation of the defence budget in the late 1980s and its significant reduction in the early 1990s, something had to give.

What gave was the schedule of projects. As Communism waned and finally disappeared, meeting the declared in-service date of equipment lost its importance. Projects 'moved to the right' continuously, many entering service in the field only after taking twice as long in the development and production cycle as originally envisaged. Time is money, so delay reinforced cost growth which was increasing alarmingly for other reasons, despite 'fixed price' contracts and fierce competitions.

Delay and cost growth attracted the attention of the National Audit Office, the Public Accounts Committee and the House of

---

[1] *A Dinosaur in Whitehall* by Bill Kincaid, Brassey's, September 1997.

Commons Defence Committee. Such attention brought more internal scrutiny. More scrutiny meant more delay. More delay brought more cost growth. A vicious circle.

When my book was finally published in September 1997, it brought an interesting reaction. Although the majority, particularly at the working level, were strongly supportive, many senior officers and officials were non-committal, and some extremely hostile. One went so far as to say he did not agree with a single idea in it. Another, with whom I had formerly been on friendly terms, continues to cut me dead.

In 1995, this would not have surprised me, but in the Autumn of 1997 it did, for the new Labour government had, a couple of months earlier, launched 'Smart Procurement' as a part of their Strategic Defence Review. It was clear that the old culture was deeply engrained at, and near, the top and that it would be a tough battle to change things.

It was. Nothing happened for six months. Then McKinsey and Company was brought in to produce a plan. After that it all went quiet for another eight months. It was only in September 1998 that action finally got under way.

A year later, much has changed or is slated to change. I have to admit that in July 1997, when 'Smart Procurement' was launched, I did not believe it possible that so much progress could have been made in just over two years and that attitudes at the top could have been transformed so radically. These changes have been spectacular and the credit must go to the Secretary of State for Defence, George Robertson, and his Under Secretary of State, John Spellar, for without their determination another initiative would have run into the sands.

Of course there is still time for that. Smart Procurement, despite all the paperwork and plans, has only just started out on its journey. The steps taken so far do not amount to a great deal in terms of equipment delivery in ten years' time, and it needs all the other measures, that have been announced, to be effectively implemented before real progress is assured. And there are worrying signs that many of these will be diluted or swept under the carpet. Will Robertson's and

Spellar's successors keep the pressure on or will other initiatives blur their vision?

But it's a start.

One of the most admirable aspects of the Smart Procurement Initiative has been the openness with which it has been conducted. Despite this, there is an amazing ignorance in many parts of the Ministry of Defence and throughout the defence industry. Three common questions crop up time and again:

- What is Smart Procurement?
- Will it actually happen?
- How will it affect me?

This book attempts to answer these questions. It looks at the Smart Procurement Initiative, at the changes that it will bring to the Ministry of Defence, and at the implications for industry, both for large prime contractors and for small and medium-sized enterprises (SMEs).

The Dinosaur in Whitehall is evolving. If industry is to continue to do business with it, it must get to know the new beast. It must dance with the new Dinosaur.

The Whitehall Dinosaur is evolving. Industry must dance with the new dinosaur.

CHAPTER ONE

A HISTORICAL PERSPECTIVE

In 1958, Ministry of Supply studies found that, on average, actual costs of defence equipment were 2.8 times those forecast.[2] The main causes are said to have been changes to operational requirements, inadequate understanding of the scope of work, and 'cost-plus' contracts. In 1965, the TSR-2 aircraft was cancelled partly because of rising costs:

'The cost of producing the first 150 TSR-2 planes had soared from the original £500 million to over £1000 million, and possibly as high as £2000 million'.[3]

> Procurement of military equipment is a most complex business.

More than forty years later, after repeated initiatives to cut out cost increases, there is a distinct whiff of déjà vu about all this. True, cost overruns have been reduced, although they are still high and, true, 'cost-plus' contracts have become the exception rather than the rule. Nevertheless, the situation today is distressingly similar to that which pertained then. Is this inevitable? Can the problems be overcome?

It must be stated at once that procurement of military equipment is a most complex business, aimed at the uncertainties of future warfare, harnessing advanced (often immature) technology to gain a leading edge, and paid for by the country's tax-payers, to whom value-for-money (however that is defined) must be demonstrated.

[2] House of Commons Defence Committee, Eighth Report 97/8, *SDR*, Volume 1, Paragraph 305

[3] *Defence by Ministry* by Franklyn A. Johnson, published by Duckworth, page 133

Procurement of military equipment bears as much relation to purchasing a new model from a car-dealer as does a dinosaur to a nuclear physicist. Procurement is complicated without doubt, but is the management of the procurement process, as practised by the Ministry of Defence and constrained by the Treasury, as effective as it should be?

A good question.

Gibb-Zuckerman

In 1961, the Gibb-Zuckerman report[4] answered growing parliamentary and press anger over fantastic research and weapons costs in the 1950s:

> *'The record from the early 'fifties was not good..... the rising costs of military equipment in Britain was staggering, much of it traceable to poor initial estimates..... aircraft carriers were slated to be built and were cancelled; missiles such as Blue Water, Blue Streak, Blue Steel and Skybolt were never produced in quantity; and aircraft such as the F-111, P-1154 and HS 681 remained only bad memories. The R and D costs alone for some aircraft rose 100 per cent.'*[5]

This report established an improved procurement process whereby every major project would include:

- A formal Staff Target to define the capability required.
- A Feasibility Study to identify the main technical risks.
- A Staff Requirement defining key performance parameters.
- A Project Study to resolve risks, define development and forecast costs and timescales.
- Full Development leading to Production.

Costs continued to rise. For example:

---

[4] Office of the Minister for Science, *Report on the Committee on the Management and Control of Research and Development*

[5] *Defence by Ministry* by Franklyn A. Johnson, published by Duckworth, page 158

'Seaslug, developed from a very modest naval anti-kamikaze missile of the 'forties, was first estimated to cost £1 million to £1.5 million, and actually soared in the end to £70 million at the very least. By 1966, after cruisers had been adapted as bases from which to fire it, the entire complex was pronounced obsolete and abandoned.'[6]

Downey

By the late 1960s, it was perceived that the Gibb-Zuckerman reforms had not gone far enough and William Downey chaired a Steering Group on Development Cost Estimates which reported in 1968. This report[7] established the 'Downey Cycle' which governed all significant projects for the next 30 years. It built on the Gibb-Zuckerman project milestones, but recommended replacement of the Project Study stage by a more detailed Project Definition stage, which for complex projects was to be divided into two parts.

More importantly, Downey recommended that each phase must be fully completed before the next phase began, and that 'sufficient technical work should be done in the early Feasibility Study and Project Definition phases (ideally absorbing about 15% of the total development cost) so that Full Development could be launched with confidence that projects would meet performance, cost and timescale targets.'[8]

The Downey Cycle was, in itself, a useful framework but failed to take into account that every project was different and, ideally, required different procedures to achieve optimal results. It was too slow and stately for small or less complex projects and it was not difficult to find good reasons (military, political, industrial) to depart from it or to move on to the next stage before the previous one had been satisfactorily concluded. Flouting Downey led to increased costs and delays more often than not. In 1975, the House of Commons Expenditure Committee, in examining the Statements on the Defence

---

[6] Ibid, page 87

[7] *Report of the Steering Group on Development Cost Estimating,* Ministry of Technology 1968

[8] House of Commons Defence Committee, 8th Report, *SDR,* Volume 1, Paragraph 307

Estimates, expressed concern about the cost of some equipment projects, including the Tornado aircraft, and delays in introducing new equipment into service.[9]

Much of the problem lay in the failure to implement the Downey recommendation to spend around 15% of the total development budget on the early stages of a project, thus making it impossible to define the technical risks and establish ways of managing them before the major expenditure began. Despite repeated evidence of the need, early investment has rarely approached and has usually fallen a long way short of the recommended 15%.

> *The problem lay in the failure to implement Downey recommendations.*

Formation of the Procurement Executive

In the 1950s and 1960s, military procurement was split variously between the three Service Ministries, the Ministry of Supply, the Aviation Ministry and, latterly, the Ministry of Technology. In 1971 the Rayner Report[10] recommended the establishment of a Procurement Executive as a sub-department of the Ministry of Defence to pursue improved value for money in defence procurement. A close but clear customer/supplier relationship between the Services and the Procurement Executive was to be established, as was an equally clear customer/supplier relationship between the Procurement Executive and industry. At the same time the high level equipment committee structure in the Ministry of Defence was overhauled and the new structure was designed:

> *'to prevent unwanted projects slipping through. It has been authoritatively stated that "the TSR-2 could not happen now".'*

---

9 Second Report from the Expenditure Committee, 1974-75, *The Defence Review Proposals, HC 259,* Paragraph 28

10 *Government Organisation for Defence Procurement and Civil Aerospace (Cmnd 4641) 1971*

11 National Audit Office, *Defence Procurement in the 1990s,* HC 390 of 93/4

Levene

The establishment of the Procurement Executive was revolutionary in the changes it made to the organisation and management practices of procurement but major changes to procurement methods had to await the arrival of Peter Levene in 1985 as Chief of Defence Procurement. He instigated a more commercial approach involving:

- Competition, involving foreign as well as UK contractors, for almost all defence contracts.
- Replacement of cost-plus contracts with fixed-price contracts with stage payments linked to specific milestones.
- Appointment of industrial prime contractors.

The Ministry of Defence has estimated[11] that competition saved £1 billion per year in procurement costs and was a major factor in improving the competitiveness of British industry.

Jordan, Lee, Cawsey

> *The costly demise of Nimrod AEW blew that out of the sky.*

'TSR-2 could not happen now', but only because it had been scrapped years before. The costly demise of the Nimrod Airborne Early Warning (AEW) aircraft blew that self-congratulatory view out of the sky. In its wake, a Ministry of Defence Working Party was set up in 1987 to examine the management of major defence programmes. It recommended[12] that:

- The Downey procedures be vigorously implemented.
- A professional project manager, with clear goals and authority, be given responsibility for each major project.
- Full Development be started only when all risks had been analysed.
- 'Learning from experience' be initiated by systematically reviewing performance of past projects.

---

[12] *Learning from Experience:* A report on the Arrangements for Managing Major Projects in the Procurement Executive, 1987

In 1988, the House of Commons Defence Committee reviewed a range of major equipment projects and noted time slippage and cost overruns on a number of them, although it did welcome improvement brought about by competition and incentive pricing.[13] However, it noted that only 8% of a project's total development cost had on average been spent on the feasibility and project definition stages, compared with the repeatedly recommended 15%.

Options for Change and the Defence Costs Study

In the wake of the disintegration of communism and the dissolution of the Warsaw Pact, the Options for Change exercise was initiated to determine the future shape of the UK's armed forces in the light of a defence budget drastically shorn of a huge and immediate 'peace dividend'. However, neither this nor the 1994 Defence Costs Study (DCS) or 'Front Line First', produced much in the way of procurement change, except for the reduction in numbers of some equipments, and the confirmation of the move of the Procurement Executive from its large number of disparate locations to a central powerhouse at Abbey Wood, near Bristol.

National Audit Office Reviews of Major Projects

If the Defence Costs Study failed to focus on cost overruns in procurement, the steadily accumulating National Audit Office reports on major projects slowly brought the spotlight to bear. These reports were introduced at the request of the Committee of Public Accounts in their 9th report of 1981/2. Each year it examines the 25 projects which are projected to have the largest expenditure over the following ten years. The 1998 report[14] shows that for the ten common projects in the 1993 and 1998 reports, cost overruns increased from an average of 3.2% to 13.7% (see Figure 1), and that delays grew from an average of 32 months in 1993 to 43 months in 1998 (see figure 2).

---

13 House of Commons Defence Committee, 1997/8, Fifth Report, *The Procurement of Major Defence Equipment,* HC 431

14 NAO, *Ministry of Defence: Major Projects Report* 1998, HC 519, 30 June 1999.

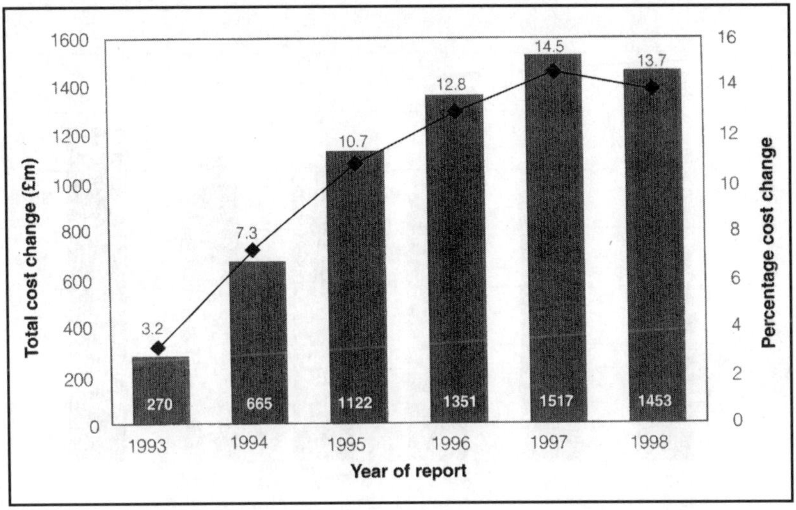

Figure 1: Cost Changes in the Ten Projects Common to the 1993 to 1998 Reports.

(Excluding Eurofighter. Source: NAO Major Projects Report 1998, Figure 11)

Together with the threat that inflexibly applied competition posed to the future viability of the UK defence industry, it was this worsening performance during a time when the defence budget was declining fast, that captured the attention of the Labour Party's Shadow Defence Team. Its 1995 report[15] attacked the 'Ministry of Waste' and, quoting NAO reports, said that it was:

> *'a national disgrace that the Ministry of Defence should be throwing away billions of pounds of taxpayers' money on vital projects which are hampered by lack of foresight and proper management control.'*

It promised that Labour, when elected, would carry out a strategic defence review, would initiate a partnership with industry and address the decline in research and development spending. How this was to be done was not spelt out.

---

[15] *Strategy for a Secure Future,* Labour's approach to the defence industry, October 1995

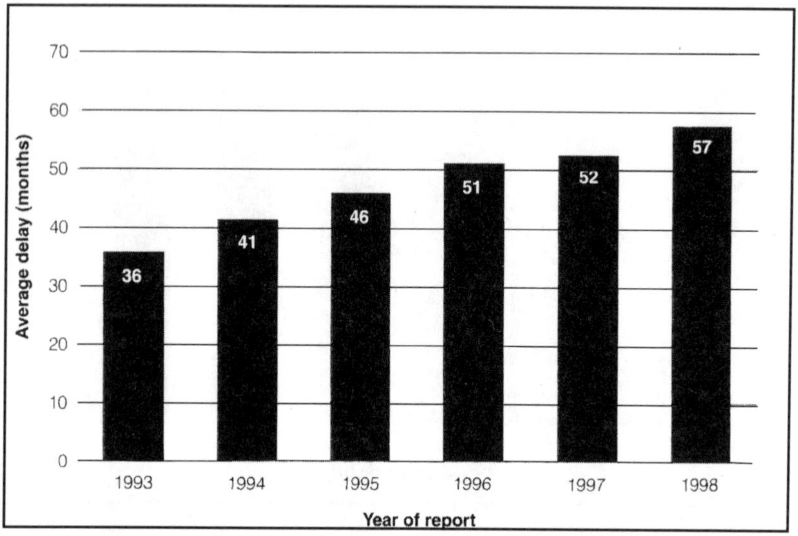

Figure 2: Average In-Service Date Delays for the Ten Projects Common to the 1993 to 1998 Reports.
(Source: NAO Major Project Report 1998, Table 14)

The National Audit Office has established an association between cost variance and In-Service Date (ISD) delay and this is shown at Figure 3. The relationship shown is reasonably consistent, except for three projects where delay was caused by factors which did not cause significant cost increases. The COBRA weapon locating radar suffered delays caused mainly by collaborative negotiations, while the future radio system BOWMAN was delayed by repeated changes to the MOD procurement strategy and industrial reorganisation.

But it would hardly be surprising if there was no correlation between cost escalation and delay, for time is money. What is perhaps more surprising, at least to the layman, is the increased cost of projects on fixed price contracts, but this is due either to increases before the main contract was let or because of changing quantities and/or specification after contract let.

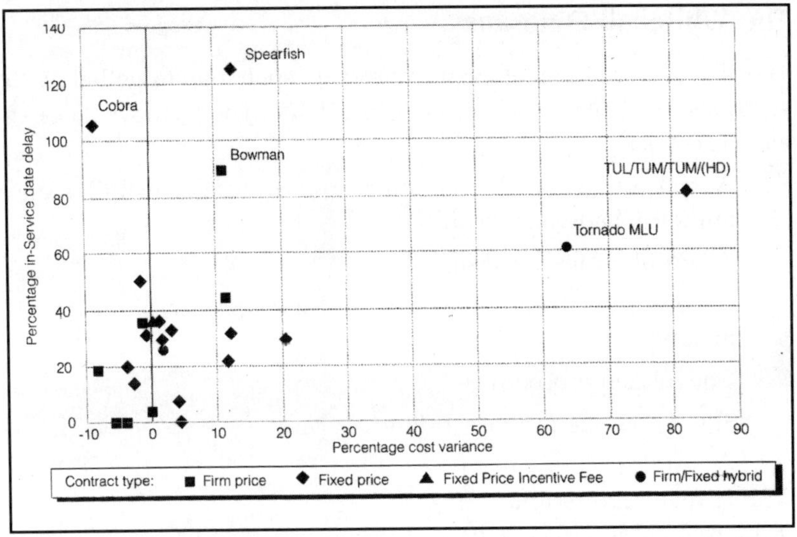

Figure 3. Relationship between Cost Variance and ISD Delay

(Source: NAO Report, *MOD: Major Projects Review 1997*, 13 May 1998, Figure 13.)

Causes of Cost Variance and Delay

According to the National Audit Office,[16] the main reasons for cost variance and ISD delay have not changed much over the last few years. The main contributors are:

Cost Variance	ISD Delay
Programme changes	Project Definition
Inflation adjustment	Technical difficulties
Specification changes	Budgetary constraints
	Collaborative processes

16 NAO Report, *MOD Major Projects Report 1998*, 30 June 1999, Part 2

The Whitehall Dinosaur

The ills of procurement were, however, spelt out (together with solutions) in *A Dinosaur in Whitehall* in 1997[17]. The main weaknesses were listed as:

- A lack of personal accountability, with responsibility and authority badly matched.
- A lack of professionalism.
- A consensus committee culture, leading to weak decision-making.
- Convoluted procedures.
- Stifling but ineffective scrutiny.

My analysis brought widespread condemnation from many MOD civilians (the military were by-and-large supportive, but felt that there was as much chance of introducing realistic solutions as there was of breeding flying pigs).

The key seemed to be a lack of personal accountability.

The key seemed to be personal accountability: from that everything else could flow; without it, nothing very useful was possible. It was recognised by the Efficiency Unit in its report *Improving Management in Government: The Next Steps*:

> *'At present the freedom of an individual manager to manage effectively and responsibly in the Civil Service is severely circumscribed. There are controls not only on resources and objectives, as there should be in any effective system, but also on the way in which resources can be managed..... the rules are seen as a constraint rather than as a support; and in no sense as a pressure on managers to manage effectively. Moreover, the task of changing rules is often seen as too great for one unit or one manager or indeed one department and is therefore assumed to be impossible.'*

[17] *A Dinosaur in Whitehall* by Bill Kincaid, Brassey's, September 1997

The perceived impossibility of changing the rules had, by 1996, become the main stumbling block to improved procurement. The faults in the system were widely perceived and possible solutions were dimly made out. But, to both internal and external eyes, the MOD had become about as stagnant as the Soviet Union in the Brezhnev era. But that system had thrown up Gorbachev and evolved. Where was our catalyst for change to come from if the Whitehall Dinosaur was to be exterminated, or at least metamorphosed?

It needed a change of government.

CHAPTER TWO

THE SMART PROCUREMENT INITIATIVE

The necessary change of government occurred when Labour swept to power in May 1997 and quickly announced that it would honour its commitment in its election manifesto and,

> *'conduct a strategic defence and security review to reassess our essential security and defence needs. It will consider how the roles, missions and capabilities of our armed forces should be adjusted to meet the new strategic realities. The review we propose will be foreign policy led, first assessing our likely overseas commitments and interests and then establishing how our forces should be deployed to meet them.'*[18]

Smart Procurement Launched

The Secretary of State for Defence launched the 'Smart Procurement' initiative when he appeared before the House of Commons Defence Committee in July 1997:

> *'The British people want strong defence for this country, but they do not want defence at any price and we must justify every pound that is spent in the defence budget. This review is going to include a ruthless examination of how value for money for defence procurement, one of the most important aspects of the review, can be improved. I am therefore launching a major initiative to try and eliminate the kind of cost overruns and delays that have characterised some equipment projects in the past..... by spreading best practice and learning from experience at home and abroad..... so we are looking for 'smart procurement.'*[19]

[18] *New Labour because Britain Deserves Better* p.38

[19] House of Commons Defence Committee, Eighth Report 1997/8, *SDR*, Volume 1, paragraph 333

The Main Problems

In November 1997, the consultants McKinsey were called in to advise on Smart Procurement. They found the major problems to be that:

- Early stages of the procurement cycle were ineffective, unproductive and under resourced.
- The process was over reliant on technical specifications.
- There was an over-reliance on competitive tendering.
- Project management was weak.
- There was too little delegation.
- Key people spent too short a period in post.
- There was low accountability.
- There was poor scrutiny.
- Carrots and sticks were too small.

> *Within MOD, there was no clear, single customer for equipment.*

Further work identified more significant problems, the chief of which were that, within MOD, there was no clear, single customer for equipment projects and that a number of processes were managed separately, making an effective whole life approach impossible.

These findings bore a striking resemblance to those discussed in *A Dinosaur in Whitehall,* which had been published a couple of months before, but this should have come as no surprise as the problems were clearly understood at the working level at least (further up there had been a determination not to recognise them) and had been endlessly discussed informally. It was, in effect, common ground.

---

[20] *Strategic Defence Review Report* Supporting Essay Ten, July 1998, paragraph 8

The Recommended Initiatives

If the problems were generally understood, the solutions were less clear. It was not until July 1998, when the Strategic Defence Review was published, that the recommended initiatives to achieve 'faster, cheaper and better'[20] Smart Procurement were defined:

- *A through-life systems approach*, taking decisions on a broader view of the equipment's life-cycle and making trade-offs between military requirements, costs and timescales.
- *Incremental acquisition* which would allow fielding of equipment of a less ambitious capability which would then be upgraded in several, lower-risk stages.
- *Partnering* to involve industry more closely in developing operational requirements and equipment designs.
- *Personal accountability* to improve time and cost estimating.
- *Integrated Project Teams (IPTs)* consisting of all stakeholders and scientific staff as well as industry when competition allows. IPTs would have a clear leader who would be given authority to make trade-off decisions and would remain responsible for equipment after it had entered service.
- *Streamlined procedures* including changes to the Downey Cycle and tailoring of procedures to project categories.

These initiatives were generally welcomed although, in the absence of any detail, there was a high degree of scepticism about whether, unlike all previous attempts, something useful would be the outcome, a scepticism that was re-inforced by the clear message that competition would remain a primary tool of Government procurement. Competition and partnering were clearly uneasy bedfellows.

Competition and partnering were clearly uneasy bedfellows.

But there were other indicators pointing at high level determination that perhaps went unperceived by many at that time: the Procurement Executive was to become an Agency; delegated financial powers were significantly increased to take effect immediately; and the three single-Service logistics organisations were to be merged under a single Chief of Defence Logistics.

Still cynicism was rife. Not surprisingly, perhaps, in view of the poor record of implementing most earlier initiatives. And the cynicism was re-inforced when the appointment of the Team Leader of the Implementation Team was repeatedly postponed and the start of the implementation phase delayed.

For implementation was all-important. Creating initiatives is easy; implementing them effectively is difficult and often requires very tricky decisions which can be blocked by little empire builders.

> *Creating initiatives is easy; implementing them effectively is more difficult.*

This is not a new phenomenon. In 1532, Machiavelli [21] wrote:

'There is nothing more difficult to take in hand, more perilous to conduct, or more uncertain in its success, than to take the lead in the introduction of a new order of things.'

The difficulty of implementation in the case of Smart Procurement is well illustrated by one person's view of the interfaces and interlinking dependencies which was produced in 1998 and is shown in Figure 4.

Crucially, effective implementation of such major changes clearly required a major change of culture and that can not happen overnight. Indeed, John Spellar, the Under Secretary of State given responsibility for Smart Procurement implementation, admitted that such a change of culture might take five years or even more. A key implementation measure was stated to be 'a continued Ministerial lead.'[22]

For all the 'wait-and-see' attitude of most people in MOD and the defence industry, it should have been quickly clear that Ministers were themselves setting the lead in the culture change, for never

[21] Niccolo Machiavelli, *The Prince,* 1532

[22] *Strategic Defence Review Report* Supporting Essay Ten, July 1998, Paragraph 25

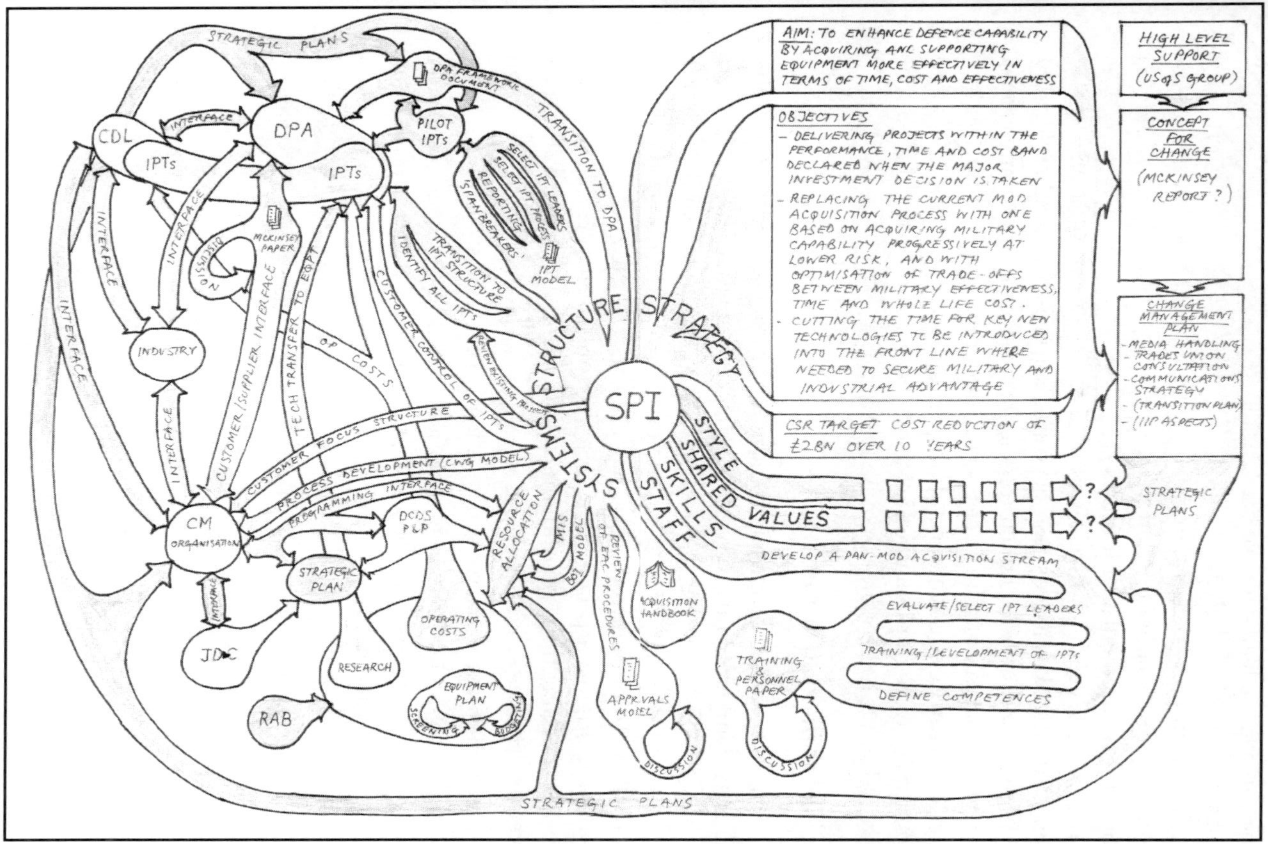

Figure 4: Interlinking Dependencies in Smart Procurement Implementation.

before had such an exercise been conducted so publicly, nor with so much emphasis on drawing in non-MOD personnel to sit on Smart Procurement Committees at all levels. This was encouraging. What was less encouraging was the number of very knotty issues that faced the Implementation Team. How many would prove intractable and be swept finally under the carpet, with a sigh of relief? How effective would implementation be if only some measures were implemented? Wasn't there a danger that half-a-loaf would prove to be worse than no loaf at all?

> *A danger that half a loaf would prove worse than no loaf at all.*

US Acquisition Reform

It was not that the proposals could not be implemented successfully. In the United States, a very similar reform had been pursued energetically for some five years, with very similar aims to Smart Procurement, including a reduction in procurement cycle times, creating new relationships with industry, moving to output contracting, empowerment, a whole-life-cycle approach, professionalisation, incremental acquisition, incentivisation and reward sharing.

Although there have been problems, several astonishing results have been reported:[23]

- Over 100 weapon systems are being introduced now after procurement cycles of under 2 years.
- 90% of all items costing less than $5000 are now purchased by credit card and this has spectacularly driven down instances of fraud.
- Pursuit of commonality has driven down component and sub-system prices (in one case from $20,000 to $5000).
- 50% of civilian posts in the Army have been cut.

---

[23] Presentations by Dr Ken Oscar and Mr Michael Chilworth to the conference on *Managing the Revolution in Military Affairs* at RMCS Shrivenham on 11 November 1998

- The cost of purchasing $1-worth of goods has been reduced to around 1c, i.e. 1%. (Although difficult to compare like with like, the UK figure is far higher: perhaps 50p for each £1 when all costs are included [24]).

Mr Stephen Conver, formerly a senior official in the US Department of Defense and now a Vice President of Lockheed Martin, has said:[25]

> *'There is no reason why you can't come down from a procurement cycle of 12 years from one of 3-5 years.'*

A key to achieving this is the removal of rules as far as is practical and consistent with the safeguarding of public funds. In the US,

> *'we had loaded our procurement system with so many rules that it raised barriers rather than beacons to the private sector, particularly for innovative newcomers whose talent we sought.'*

Implementation of Smart Procurement

The Smart Procurement Implementation Team was formed in September 1998 and very quickly showed it meant business. Conscious of the need for 'Quick Wins', it seized on IPTs as its vanguard. Eleven projects were selected to pilot the IPT concept from 1 November 1998, and included projects in all the phases of the procurement cycle from concept (pre-feasibility) to in-service. Notably, one pilot IPT is now led by an industrialist, selected from open competition.

A further 23 IPTs were formed in April 1999, around 40 more in September and the remainder of the total 145 IPTs will be 'rolled-out' in January and March 2000.

---

[24] This extremely approximate figure sets the cost of equipment bought against the operating costs of the procurement system (DPA + DERA + Systems etc). The figure is similar if you add in spares and DLO operating costs.

[25] Mr Stephen Conver to the RUSI seminar on *Smart Procurement*, 29 January 1998

Another 'Quick Win' was the transformation of the Procurement Executive to Agency status as the Defence Procurement Agency on 1 April 1999. It is claimed that this will enable MOD to provide a clearer customer focus for industry, that it will give greater delegated powers to its chief executive, CDP, that it will allow more freedom to shape policy to fit the business and to facilitate changes.

On the same date, the three single-Service logistics organisations came together to form the Defence Logistics Organisation (DLO) under a single head, the Chief of Defence Logistics (CDL), tasked to provide 3% efficiency savings per year. CDL has said that, with huge (35%) efficiencies already delivered over the last five to seven years, the formation of the DLO is the only way to achieve the further efficiency required.

But these 'Quick Wins' by themselves achieve little more than some short term savings. What they should do is to provide the organisational changes which will allow other measures (such as personal accountability and delegation, successful definition of the MOD customer, and creation of 'smart people') to achieve the improved effectiveness that is sought. Successful implementation across the board is therefore essential, and there are plenty of areas where little valid progress can be discerned. The hype over the changes made so far is obscuring the fact that change does not necessarily equal progress.

Smart Procurement and Phoenix

> *The hype is obscuring the fact that change does not necessarily equal progress.*

Although the Phoenix unmanned aerial vehicle is now in service and flying very successfully in the Balkans, its development was dogged by problems, both technical and managerial. Technical difficulties under a fixed price contract led to a contractual stand-off between the prime contractor, which had no incentive to remedy the problems at his own expense, and MOD which had paid the company a high percentage of the overall cost and was therefore unable to cancel and buy something else. The stand-off delayed the project, eventually doubling the originally envisaged procurement timescale, thus losing the company huge export opportunities.

It is interesting to speculate whether a Smart Procurement regime could have produced a better answer for Phoenix. Certainly a sensible partnering arrangement, whereby each side shared the penalties as well as the benefits, might well have avoided much of the time delay and resolved the technical difficulties more quickly. A through-life systems approach would have allowed trade-offs between procurement costs (the extra required being very small) and in-service support costs (which are much larger). Personal accountability, and delegation of authority within an IPT, would have given the Project Manager the ability to get on with an agreed programme of work.

So Smart Procurement would have produced a better answer. But only if it had been implemented effectively before the difficulties arose and, much more crucially, if a change of culture in both MOD and industry had been achieved.

Smart People and Culture

It is impossible to emphasise too strongly that the gains sought, and promised, by Smart Procurement will only be realised if the Ministry implements its 'Smart People' initiative, which is central to achieving a change of culture. It has been announced that a specialist Acquisition Stream will be created,

> *'for both civilian and military staff which would provide core personnel for the Integrated Project Teams. This will be supported by training and personal development and there will be increased interchanges with industry.'*[26]

There is a very strong view in industry and, indeed, within the MOD that too many military and civilian procurement staff (in all procurement areas – Operational Requirements, the Defence Procurement Agency, the Defence Logistics Organisation) are ill-

---

[26] *Strategic Defence Review,* Supporting Essay Ten, July 1998, Paragraph 25

equipped to carry out their responsibilities effectively. Many can be made much more effective by ensuring that:

- They have the right experience and expertise for the job.
- They have better and more relevant training both prior to, and during, their tour of duty.
- They have the best personal development opportunities.
- They stay in each job for much longer.

There will of course be a percentage (significant, but not a majority) who will not measure up to the new Smart World, who will not get promoted and who may leave. The worry is that there will be too many of them to allow all 145 IPTs to function as well as they should.

This will not be the case with the majority, provided empowerment becomes a reality for more than just the Pilot IPT leaders. Empowerment will motivate. Empowerment, or personal accountability, is the key.

The Time Factor Circle

Empowerment and more streamlined procedures should limit delays, but on their own will do little to reduce the overall procurement time cycle to 3-5 years as suggested by Stephen Conver; or even to 8-10 years. Major reductions need something more.

> *Empowerment will motivate.*
> *Empowerment is the key.*

It must be understood that the battlefield-winning technological advantage, sought by our much reduced armed forces, can only be provided by the incorporation of the latest technology. But advanced technology brings technical risk and, in its wake, cost and time risk. The less mature the technology incorporated, the greater the risk. Maturer technology will reduce the procurement risk but increase the risk of obsolescence on fielding.

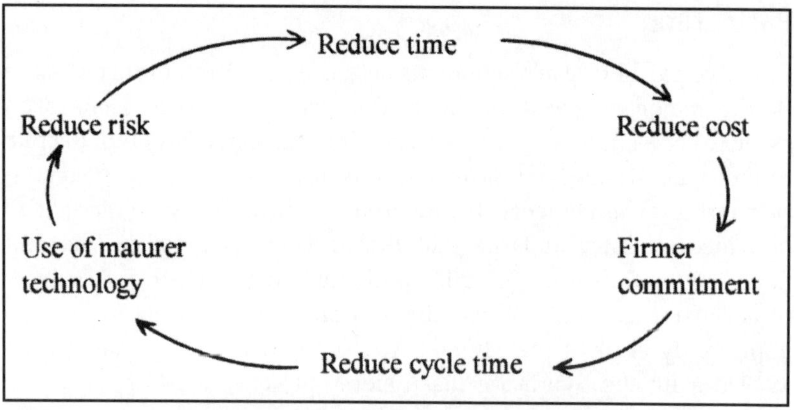

Figure 5 – The Time Factor Circle

So we have a magic circle which has to be broken into. But where to start? Not by reducing cost: the Treasury will not look kindly on numerous loss-leaders. Nor by reducing risk as this is not an independent parameter.

> *Immature technology increases risk; mature technology increases obsolescence.*

One possibility would be to use incremental acquisition to use maturer technology, but this will be of limited value if the initial equipment is still bound to a long procurement timescale. Reducing timescale by a large enough amount, as a starter, is likely to do nothing but import schedule risk. So we have to start with firmer project commitment. Firmer commitment will reduce decision-making hiatuses and overall timescale; a shorter procurement will allow more mature technology to be included from the start; more mature technology will reduce risk which in turn will reduce the procurement timescale still further; a reduction in timescale will reduce costs; cost reduction will lead to still firmer commitment which in turn will reduce timescales even further .... and so on. And it is firmer commitment which industry requires and which can form the incentive for true partnering arrangements between MOD and industry.

Partnering

Effective partnering arrangements between MOD and industry is one of the major elements of Smart Procurement and is seen as an essential prerequisite for real success. It is still early days but, in spite of the large number of words that have been written and spoken on partnering arrangements in procurement, little has yet emerged to convince industry at large that the Ministry is grasping the real nettles along the implementation path. Indeed, partnering is a subject of confusion amongst both industrial and MOD people as became abundantly clear at the MOD/DMA seminar at Didcot on 24 June 1999 during the Syndicate discussion. No-one knew its scope or application: Where does it begin and end? Does it apply to equipment projects? What are the objectives of each partner? We shall see in Chapter Five.

Getting the Message Across

MOD has made a huge effort to listen and to inform. It has produced a Smart Procurement handbook, a video, a website, and spent countless hours speaking at seminars and conferences. They are all to be congratulated..... so far.

However, the message will only strike home once the important elements are in place and seen to be working. Elements such as partnering; such as delegated decision making; such as smarter people. Until then, industrial (and some MOD) views will remain sceptical or worse. One senior defence industrialist may be an extreme example but, two years after the idea of Smart Procurement had been introduced, he said to me:

'I think they're all nuts.'

PART TWO:

THE MAJOR ELEMENTS OF SMART PROCUREMENT

CHAPTER THREE

THE INTERNAL MOD CUSTOMER-SUPPLIER RELATIONSHIP

On 1 April 1999, the Procurement Executive was converted to Agency status and became the Defence Procurement Agency (DPA). Various options had been considered, including leaving the whole procurement task to the private sector. However, it was concluded that, although many routine tasks could be out-sourced, the MOD needed to keep core management in-house.[27] Having established this,

> *'The aim was to achieve greater clarity in customer/supplier relationships within the rest of MOD.'*[28]

The MOD Central Customer

Although the detailed organisation of the MOD internal customer has taken a long time to reach approval, it has been clear for some time that the MOD Central Customer was to have greater powers than the existing operational requirements supremo, the Deputy Chief of the Defence Staff (Systems), including at least some responsibility for balance of investment in the equipment programme:

> *'A Central Customer within MOD headquarters, organised around capabilities, acting as customer for the IPT [Integrated Project Team] for all procurement phases of the project life cycle. This Central Customer to be capable of making well-founded balance of investment decisions and resource allocation decisions, and of providing clear and consistent direction to the IPT. The front line commands to act as customer for equipment in service.'*[29]

---

[27] Ibid, Paragraph 17

[28] Ibid, Paragraph 18

The new MOD Central Customer, sometimes known as Customer One, will take on the full responsibilities of the former Deputy Chief of the Defence Staff (Systems) – DCDS(S) – together with the programmes and plans responsibilities of the former Deputy Chief of the Defence Staff (Programmes and Personnel) – DCDS(P&P) and will become the Deputy Chief of the Defence Staff (Equipment Capability) – DCDS(EC). He will be,

> *'heftily empowered, will be accountable, will have the ability to make decisions and will have control of the equipment budget.'*[30]

If this is what actually happens, then it will be widely welcomed, for it is a huge step forward from what we had been left with ever since the Heseltine reorganisation: the senior operational requirements officer at three-star level with huge responsibility but minimal power.

Because it is so large a departure from the previous divorce of responsibility and authority (i.e. true accountability), it is difficult to believe this is actually happening. One senior officer in the MOD believes that the central MOD civil servants will seek to recover their former power so, he said:

> *'If you want anything done, you've got about three years to get it done.'*

Cynical? Of course. Accurate? There's no telling at the moment. But the long delay in identifying the role, organisation and authority of the MOD Central Customer suggests blood on the carpets of the Main Building..... and blood on the carpet generally leaves behind a thirst for future recovery.

The MOD Central Customer will now have responsibility for:[31, 32]

- Constructing and maintaining the 10-year Equipment Plan.

> *Blood on the carpet usually leaves behind a thirst for recovery.*

---

[29] MOD's Acquisition Handbook, *A Guide to Smart Procurement,* April 1999

[30] DCDS(P&P) to RUSI Seminar, *The Whitehall Machine,* 29 June 1999

- Establishing the basic future capability and setting it out in the User Requirement Document (URD).
- Making balance of investment decisions within, and across, capabilities.
- Obtaining approval to initiate projects and gaining approval for project continuation at the main approval stages.
- Tasking Integrated Project Team Leaders in the Defence Procurement Agency (DPA) and reviewing their work during the procurement phases of all projects.
- Accepting equipment into service.
- Directing the applied research and technical demonstrator programmes.

To carry out these responsibilities, he will be organised as shown in Figure 6.

Under each of the four two-star Capability Managers, will be 15 Directors of Equipment Capability (DECs) of either one-star or full-colonel equivalent rank, who will between them manage 19 capability areas, each with a number of Capability Working Groups under them. These DECs will be created during the winter of 1999/2000, and will not welcome Millenium Bug jokes.

One area of potential difficulty is the meshing of the long-term (10-year) Equipment Plan, which is the responsibility of the Central Customer – DCDS(EC) – with the shorter-term (4 year) plan, which is the responsibility of the Principal Finance Officer – PFO.

Clearly there will have to be very close links between the Director General Equipment (alias AUS (Systems)) and the Principal Finance Officer. But who will be ultimately responsible for what goes in and what comes out? There could be tension here: but will it be 'creative tension' or just destructive?

---

[31] MOD's Acquisition Handbook, *A Guide to Smart Procurement,* Volume 1, April 1999, page 7

[32] *A Guide to Smart Procurement,* MOD Video DO3/99

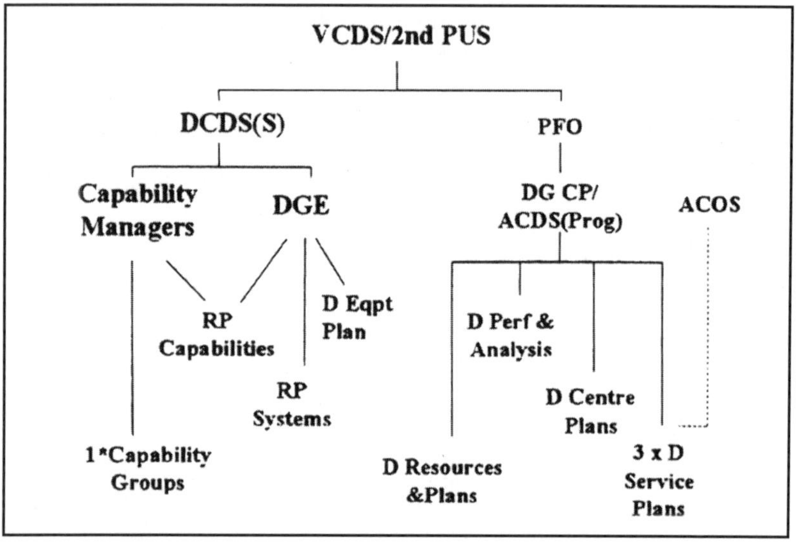

Figure 6: Central MOD Customer Organisation

DCDS(EC) will discharge his capability and IPT oversight responsibilities through four Capability Managers, one heading up each of the following capability areas: Strategic, Manoeuvre, Strike and C4I/ ISTAR. While this seems very similar to today's Sea, Land, Air and CIS divisions, there will be more purple-isation within the capability areas. Indeed, it is seen within MOD as very different, as the new divisions are based on balance of investment factors rather than on Service: for example, Manoeuvre will include all helicopters, Harrier and the Brimstone air-launched, anti-armour missile, while Strike will be responsible for Army air defence.

Will it be creative tension, or just destructive?

Beneath these four Capability Management areas, will be 13 Capability Areas each run by a Manager (at Colonel equivalent rank) who will report direct to the two-star Capability Manager without going through a one-star as before. As yet the scientific support to the Capability Management organisation is not yet finalised.

It is generally agreed throughout MOD that the Capability Management structure is under-resourced, although by how much is debatable, estimates ranging from 'nearly enough' to 'hopelessly inadequate'. It would seem to me that the latter is nearer the mark and, if so, will totally undermine the work done so far on establishing a taut internal customer-supplier relationship during the procurement phases, because the Defence Procurement Agency (DPA) will have to take a greater role in the Concept Phase as, indeed, it already is doing.

The Defence Procurement Agency

The Defence Procurement Agency (DPA) will be the MOD supplier to the Central MOD Customer during the procurement phases. The Agency, which like all Ministry of Defence Agencies will supply a service to the MOD (unlike Agencies of other government departments which supply a service directly to the public), will be headed by a chief executive, the Chief of Defence Procurement, who will be personally responsible to the Minister (Defence Procurement) for the management and performance of the Agency including:[33]

- The procurement of equipment within the performance, time and cost bands approved for individual projects.
- The provision to customers within MOD and elsewhere of certain specialist, professional, commercial, technical, intellectual property and safety services.
- The efficient and effective management of the Agency, its assets and resources.
- Ensuring that the requirements of Government Accounting are met.

Integrated Project Teams

The Defence Procurement Agency (DPA) is to be organised around a number (about 90 eventually) of Integrated Project Teams (IPT), which will include 'core members' from all necessary backgrounds and expertise, including operational requirements, project

[33] DPA Framework Document, Section 1, Page 1, April 1999

management, finance, contracts, logistics, DERA and industry (when competition allows), and may be swelled at certain points in the procurement cycle by 'associate members' such as financial and scientific scrutineers.

Core members, despite certain questions over 'solid' and 'dotted' lines of responsibility, will be under the line management of the IPT Leader who will be specially selected as the best man for the job from all walks of procurement life, including industry. While in the DPA,

> *'IPTs will receive support and guidance from senior members of the Agency, certain of whom will be on the DPA's Executive Board.'*[34]

Defence Procurement Agency Organisation

The IPTs are grouped into eleven 'Peer Groups' each under a 'Support Director'. These 'Peer Groups' do not recreate the former Business Unit approach, but link together projects at a similar stage in the procurement cycle, although some have a wide cross section of project maturity. Above them will sit six Executive Directors each of whom will take responsibility for one or more Peer Groups and who will have varying responsibilities including reviewing progress, appraisal of project leaders and cross-cutting responsibilities at Board level.[35]

Empowerment of IPT Leaders will, it is said, make the former systems of line managing directors and directors-general unnecessary. This is welcome as it will allow IPT Leaders to make the decisions without repeated reference up the chain of management, thus speeding up the whole process and reducing bureaucracy.

There must, however, be a concern that things will not work out this way and the Pilot IPTs give not only little clue, but also provide a small warning, as to how things will develop. The ten Pilot IPT Leaders have, indeed, been free of one-and two-star oversight and scrutiny, but that is because they have reported direct to the Chief of

---

[34] DPA Framework Document, Section 3, Page 1, April 1999

[35] John Howe, presentation on DPA Structure and Organisation at MOD/DMA Seminar, Didcot, 24 June 1999

Defence Procurement (CDP) and have, in effect, had their direction and decisions agreed or otherwise by him. It has worked a treat and all leaders have felt greater freedom and, consequently, been highly motivated.

But what is possible with ten pilot projects will be impossible with ninety. Who, then, will play the part that CDP has played with the pilots? Peer Group Support Directors? Executive Directors? If they do, will they then feel the need to clear decisions up the line? If they do not, what pressure will be brought to bear when things go wrong? And by whom? And on whom?

> *What is possible with ten pilot projects, will be impossible with ninety.*

These are valid questions, but will only be answered over the next few years as IPTs pass through all the phases of procurement, particularly Main Gate, final prime contractor selection and into production. It is to be hoped that the DPA follows its envisaged 'empowered' course and that pressure from outside (from the National Audit Office, the Public Accounts Committee, the House of Commons Defence Committee, Ministers, the Central MOD Customer and the MOD financial scrutineers) does not push 'empowerment' off-course. There are huge gains to be had by following the mapped-out course; there are plenty of escape routes back to the 'bad old days.'

The Customer-Supplier Relationship (One)

During the procurement phases, the greater clarity sought by Smart Procurement in the internal MOD customer-supplier relationship will be governed by a Customer Supplier Agreement (CSA) between the Central MOD Customer and the Defence Procurement Agency (DPA) which will,

> *'outline the working practices to be adopted between the IPT and the Customer and, typically record the performance, time and whole-life cost parameters the IPT has to work within, specify work plans including time and cost targets for completing the next project phase, set out equipment options to be investigated by the IPT, and the*

outputs to be provided for the support of the equipment when in-service.'[36]

As shown in Figure 7, the IPT Leader will be 'answerable' to the Central MOD Customer for delivering the equipment within time, cost and performance parameters set by the approving authorities, but also 'accountable' to the Chief of Defence Procurement for procedures, processes, propriety and best practice.

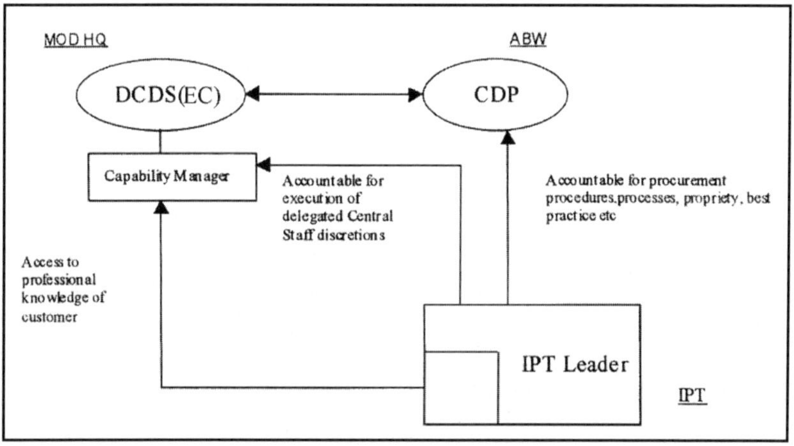

Figure 7: IPT Accountability

The question here is whether the Capability Managers have sufficient staff to carry out their increased responsibilities after their imposed 30% manpower cut. The consensus is that they do not. If this is so, then the DPA will have to take on the shortfall. Taking a greater share in the Concept Phase than originally envisaged may not be the end-of the-Smart-Procurement-world; after all, it is happening now in the absence of any CWGs. It will, however, distort the relationship.

Much more serious is the ability of the Capability Mangers to judge and accept the work of the IPTs against the User Requirement Document (URD). Without the requisite staff, they will not be able to do so, and this task will fall more and more to the requirements

[36] MOD's Acquisition Handbook, *A Guide to Smart Procurement*, April 1999, page 9

managers in the IPTs. And they are under the line management of the IPT leaders.

What price a taut customer-supplier relationship during the procurement phases?

The Defence Logistics Organisation

The Defence Logistics Organisation (DLO) was created in April 1999 by bringing together the three single-Service logistic organisations, headed respectively by the Chief of Fleet Support (CFS), the Quartermaster General (QMG) and the Air Member for Logistics (AML), and placing them under a new four-star post, the Chief of Defence Logistics (CDL). Its aims are to:

- Focus on its customers and provide effective logistics support to the front line on time, and at best value for money.
- Drive down through-life costs using Smart Procurement techniques and Integrated Project Teams.
- Achieve improvements and greater efficiency through converged business processes and IT systems.
- Provide sound strategic logistics policy advice.
- Identify and adopt best practices.
- Introduce effective output-based costing mechanisms.
- Invest in its people through the development of skills and career opportunities.
- Develop a learning culture that fosters continuous improvement.

Efficiency savings of 3% per year will be sought and these, despite the huge savings made by the three logistics organisations over the last half-dozen years (approximately 35%), should be possible in many areas. But the savings must take second place to effective service support:

> *'The need to deliver effective and responsive logistic support to our deployed forces will be the dominant consideration in all planning.'*[37]

[37] General Sir Sam Cowan, CDL: *Merger Mission,* Supply Management, 13 May 1999, Page 28

CDL will report direct to the Chief of the Defence Staff. Beyond that, the organisation and operation is still in the early stages of definition because the period April 1999 to April 2000 is a 'transition year', during which CDL will work through the existing logistics chiefs of the three services from a small headquarters, before turning the DLO into a fully unified structure from April 2000. The outline organisation of DLO is shown at Figure 8.

Current planning aims to form the DLO headquarters in Bath between November 1999 and March 2000 with a complement of around 280. It is expected that the three former single-Service logistics organisations will be formed along 'model lines' with one-star appointments having common titles.

Early identification of where major efficiencies can be found is a high priority. The adoption of best practice from the commercial world, the reduction of stock levels (the MOD holds stocks of missiles and ammunition to the value of £8 billion, and spares and repair equipment worth another £11 billion), and agency rationalisation are all early targets. But all those things that cross inter-Service boundaries are likely to yield savings.

The Service Customer

Once the equipment is in-service and the Integrated Project Team (IPT) has moved from the Defence Procurement Agency (DPA) to the Defence Logistics Organisation (DLO), the internal MOD customer function lead passes from the MOD Central Customer (i.e. Customer One) to the Service Customer (Customer Two). Definition of the Service Customer has lagged behind even that of the Central Customer, but it will be a 'representative of the user Top Level Budget Holder, normally the appropriate front-line Commander-in-Chief.'[38] Many projects will be clearly destined for one of the front line commands (Fleet, Land or Strike), but in many other cases they will cross two or even three. Presumably, the 'appropriate Commander-in-Chief' will be designated on a case-by-case basis.

---

[38] MOD's Acquisition Handbook, *A Guide to Smart Procurement*, Edition 1, April 1999

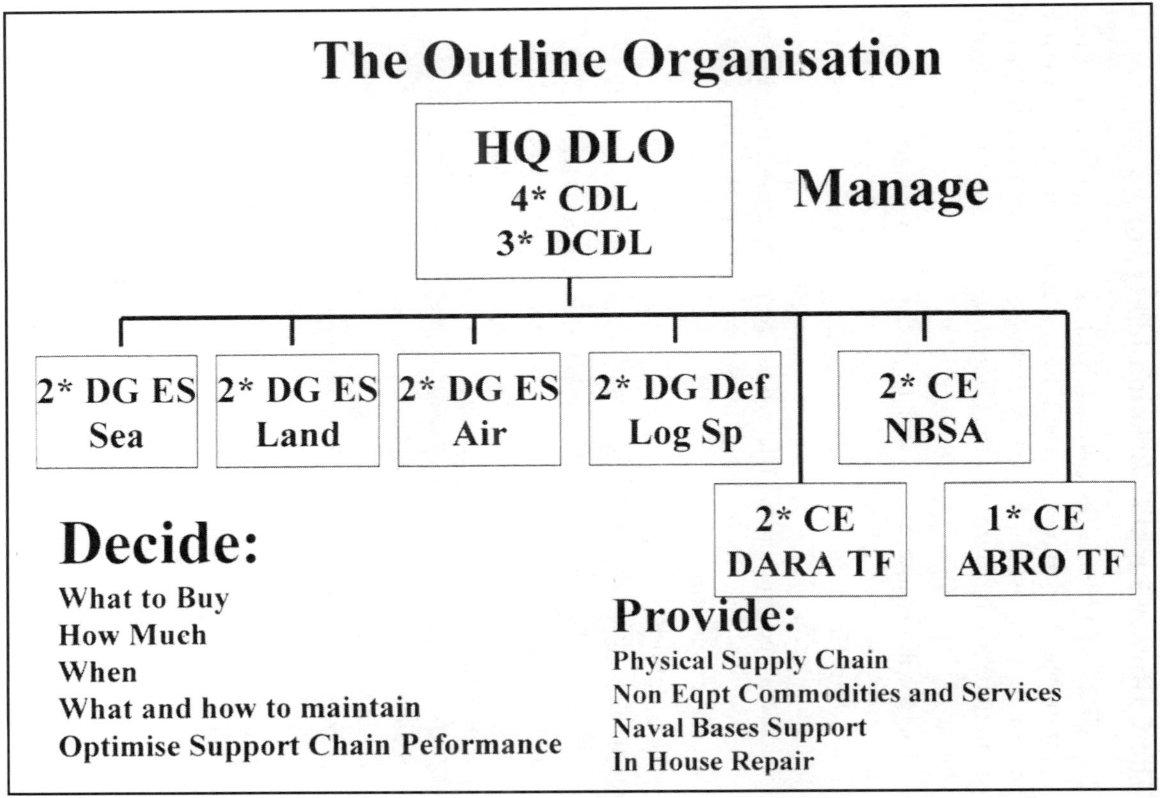

Figure 8. The Outline Organisation of DLO.

The Customer-Supplier Relationship (Two)

The Chief of Defence Logistics (CDL) will therefore have three separate MOD customers and will be accountable to them, in much the same way as the Chief of Defence Procurement (CDP) is accountable for his output to the Central MOD Customer (Customer One).

The frontline commands will be required to act as intelligent customers, saying what is needed, specifying support outputs, concluding Customer-Supplier Agreements (CSA) with CDL and then monitoring CDL's performance against these CSAs. Within the customers' requirements, CDL will define how support outputs are to be met, will specify a whole life support policy, and drive down the costs of support.

This sounds clear enough, but in practice it is rather more complicated than that, as CDL himself has pointed out:

> *'My future link with them [the single-Service Commanders-in-Chief] is crucial. Their control of their own integral logistic capability is not an issue, nor will their responsibility change for the logistic support of their deployed elements..... Clearly I must inherit the current PAOs' [Principal Administrative Officers'] responsibility to the three single-Service supporting commands for the provision of the logistic capability they require..... Clearly a new relationship with PJHQ [Permanent Joint Headquarters] will be required to enact the CJO's [Chief of Joint Operations] operational priorities.'*[39]

This hardly sounds like the taut customer-supplier relationship that Smart Procurement is seeking. There is much work to be done here, but little is in evidence as yet.

> *This hardly sounds like a taut customer-supplier relationship.*

[39] General Sir Sam Cowan: *My Job*, RUSI Journal, Vol 143, No.6, December 1998

The 'Throw-it-Over-the-Wall' Approach

During procurement, the Central MOD Customer (Customer One) and the Defence Procurement Agency will act as the MOD customer and the MOD supplier under a Customer Supplier Agreement (CSA). At around the in-service date, the project and the Integrated Project Team (IPT) managing it, will transfer to the in-service supplier, the Defence Logistics Organisation (DLO), and they will then become accountable to the Service Customer (Customer Two), the three front line Commanders-in-Chief. This project conveyor belt system from DPA to DLO is shown at Figure 9.

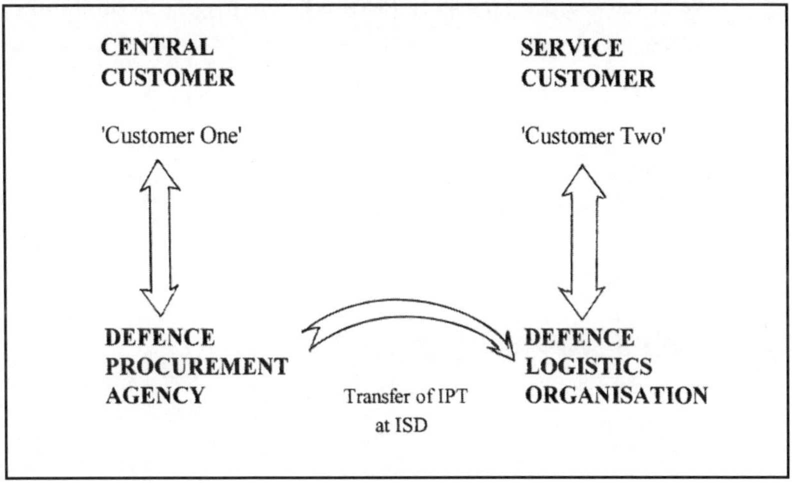

Figure 9: Accountability and the Conveyor Belt

While this is simple and gives clear customer-supplier relationships, albeit somewhat clouded by the multiple Customer Twos, there are concerns with this 'Throw-it-over-the-Wall' approach:

- Can Customer Two ensure that in-service support issues have been given enough priority and sufficient funding during the procurement phases, particularly when trade-offs become essential, to remain within cost and time parameters?

- Will Supplier One (DPA) ensure all the development and production loose ends are tidied away before 'throwing the IPT over the wall'?
- How will Incremental Acquisition, or major upgrades, be managed without clouding the clarity of the accountability shown in Figure 5? (Discussed in more detail in Chapter 4)
- How does the accountability chain apply to Cluster IPTs with their multiple projects at different stages of the acquisition cycle? (Discussed in more detail in Chapters 4 and 5)
- Given the sometimes long fielding period (e.g. BOWMAN will take some eight years to field fully), when will accountability change?

There are no clear answers to these questions.

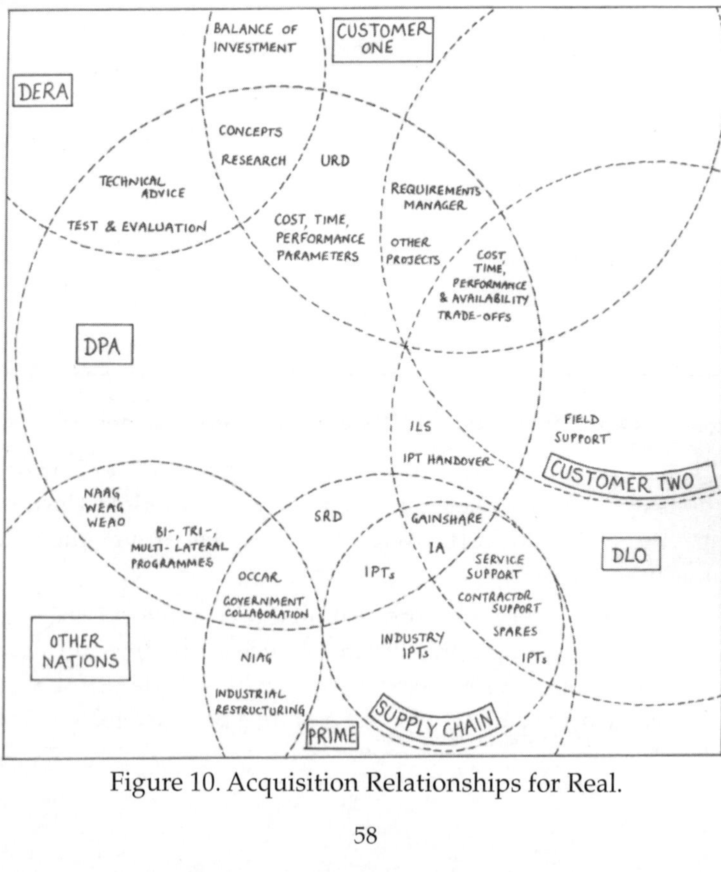

Figure 10. Acquisition Relationships for Real.

In fact, the relationships are far more complicated than this very simplistic model, and far more complicated than I am prepared to draw here. But the much simplified diagram at Figure 10 makes clear that many of the crucial equipment parameters and procurement processes are inextricably the responsibility of more than one customer and supplier. And when you add in industry and the Defence Evaluation and Research Establishment (DERA), the internal MOD customer-supplier relationship gets really blurred.

To ensure that accountability is clear, there must be a system for identifying who has primacy at each stage and at every interface. It is not enough to say that Customer One is in charge before the Initial Gate, DPA from there to the in service date, and the DLO thereafter, even if this is the desire. The reality has to be more complex.

The 'Four-Horned Monster'

Hence the MOD is looking at a less straightforward model, nicknamed the 'Four-Horned Monster' (no, not a dinosaur, but something further down the evolutionary path). This places the Integrated Project Team (IPT) permanently answerable to both MOD Customers and accountable to both MOD suppliers, as shown in Figure 11.

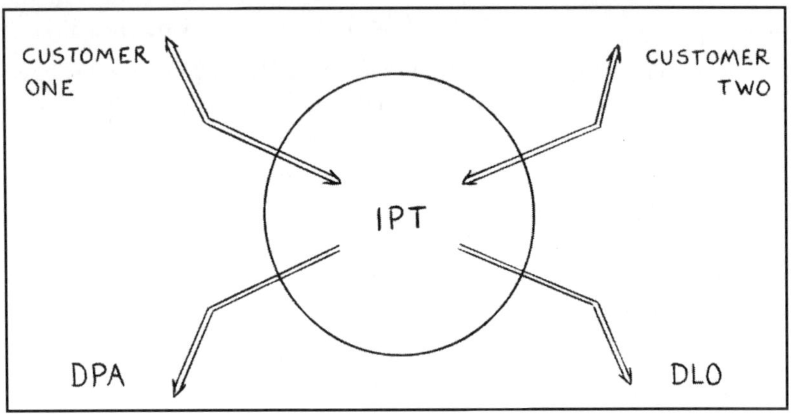

Figure 11: The Four-Horned Monster

While this approach is less simple and the basic customer-supplier relationship less taut, it will answer satisfactorily the five key questions above. It appears a better bet than the original 'Throw-it-over-the-wall' idea, even though many details will still have to be worked through, such as apportionment of operating costs. But it still requires a very clear plan for identifying accountability throughout the whole life of the equipment.

Future of CDP and CDL

A third approach, which has been officially ruled out, is a merger between the Defence Procurement Agency (DPA) and the Defence Logistics Organisation (DLO).

> *'A merger of the DPA and DLO looks to be necessary at the moment – even if it is politically unacceptable to consider it at this stage.'*[40]

Within the Ministry of Defence, there is no shortage of opinion that the posts of CDP and CDL will eventually merge. If that happens, a monster post will be created with an annual budget of around £10 billion and assets of some £40 billion. It would have to remain a four-star post. He would then have to deal with both the Central MOD Customer (Customer One) and with the three-plus Service Customers (Customer Two). Not a problem? Perhaps not, but the lack of clarity in the Customer Two-Supplier relationship remains.

The logical progression, after merging CDP and CDL, would be to return to a single MOD Customer making Customer One, the Deputy Chief of the Defence Staff (Equipment Capability), a four-star post reporting directly to the Chief of the Defence Staff, and therefore directly accountable for the performance of in-service equipment.

> *The posts of CDP and CDL will eventually merge.*

But that is probably unacceptable, at least in the foreseeable future, because of the sheer size of the organisation that would be created.

---

40 Professor Trevor Taylor: *A Sprinting Start*, RUSI Journal, Vol 144, No 3, June 1999

The Equipment Approvals Committee (EAC)

The top equipment committee is the Equipment Approvals Committee. The Chief Scientific Adviser chairs it and its members are the Second Permanent Under Secretary (2nd PUS), the Vice-Chief of the Defence Staff (VCDS), the Chief of Defence Procurement (CDP) and, since April 1999, the Chief of Defence Logistics (CDL). It is this committee which approves, or otherwise, all project spending after the Concept Stage.

There is one curious, and serious, anomaly. Both MOD supplier chiefs (CDP and CDL) sit on the committee, but neither Customer does, although the interests of both Customer One and Customer Two are represented by VCDS. This is hardly satisfactory. If DCDS(EC) is to become accountable for delivery of a capability, he must sit on the committee which tasks and reviews formally the output of the MOD suppliers. Neither should either CDP or CDL remain as full members, although they clearly need to be in attendance.

Military and Civilian Expertise

The Ministry of Defence claims it is now dispensing with parallel military and civilian structures to form joint military/civilian organisations, within which the civil servants will be responsible for 'delivering Government policy' and scrutinising expenditure, and the military for provision of front line experience and for running operations. There is said to be 'creative tension', and that separate lines of advice will be preserved.

This sounds like business as before.

What is new is the determined effort to purple-ise to lower levels than before. This is happening now in the new Customer One structure, but is perhaps best illustrated by the choice of an Army officer to lead the Type 45 Destroyer IPT. In procurement jobs, detailed background operational expertise in that particular capability area is clearly not essential, but in requirements and logistics posts, that is not so. We should beware, for as soon as it is accepted that a major can write a user requirement for, or sit as the

> *Expertise is the only basis for professionalism.*

requirements manager on an IPT of, an aircraft or a ship, there will be no good argument to oppose a move to a civilian doing the job. Expertise in these posts is essential: it is the only basis for professionalism.

Funding and Profiling

The Long Term Costings process is dead. In its place sit the 10 year Equipment Plan and the 4 year Short Term Plan and, although the Treasury has set the Defence Budget for 4 years, there will have to be some annuality to the construction of these Plans as project costs are reassessed and project schedules redrawn. Just how similar the new process will be to the old system will only become clear as it develops, but there is bound to be more similarity than the enthusiastic proponents of the change are claiming. Annuality, with all its unwelcome disturbance to commitment, is not dead.

However, it is to be hoped that, with the new authority of the Central MOD Customer, it will be a less painful process. But do not bet on this for, while there are still cost overruns and delays, there must be compensating cuts and reprofiling elsewhere. Firmer and longer-term commitment by MOD will not come easily, if at all.

One intriguing question is: how will we afford to reduce procurement cycle time in the short term? Bringing equipment in earlier means earlier spend, yet the Defence Budget will remain constant at best. Put simply:

> *'If the overall picture over a ten-year period is that projects come in 10 per cent early and five per cent under budget, more money will be needed in the first nine years than would have been the case had projects stayed on time and on budget.'*[41]

It could be argued that this is a short term problem and that once better forecasting, and better performance against that forecast, is achieved, a steady state will be produced. But we still have to cater

---

[41] Professor Trevor Taylor: *A Sprinting Start*, RUSI Journal, Vol. 144, No.3, June 1999

for the next ten years or more. Clearly some projects are going to be stalled, some reduced in scope, while the temptation, for profiling reasons, to ensure failures at the tougher Main Gate might become irresistible.

> Temptation to ensure failure at Main Gate might become irresistible.

The damage that could be done to the programme as a whole by the success of a high-grade IPT leader bringing in his multi-billion pound programme five years early, could be immense. The large programmes will be high profile and could hardly be deliberately stalled while proclaiming a Smart Procurement success:

> *'Most tiresome of all is the recognition that if it is the intention that smart procurement will prevent slippage, then the corollary will be that project deferment will become much less readily available and will change from a convenient device employed behind the scenes to a subject for critical scrutiny.'*[42]

And scrutiny delays. So it is a vicious circle. How do we break out of it? The temptation might be to delay lower-profile projects to allow the high-profile projects to come in early, but stalling dozens of smaller projects would be damaging to the whole programme balance.

If procurement time is to be shortened, without delaying or failing some projects, then costs must come down by more than the time reduction equivalence. That is the challenge and can only be met by implementing the whole Smart Procurement Initiative effectively.

Unfortunately, large reduction in cost in the early years can only come about through major reduction in procurement timescales. Unless performance is to be seriously degraded.

How Taut the New Customer-Supplier Relationship?

Profiling difficulties, together with the inevitable accompanying cuts within programmes (which could easily translate into cheaper design with larger downstream support costs) could create tensions between

---

[42] Humphrey Crum Ewing, *Slogan or Solution?* Global Defence Review, 1999

Customer One and Customer Two on levels of funding, priorities and responsibilities. This would show quite clearly that a taut customer-supplier relationship within the MOD had not been achieved.

> *'The worst thing a corporation can do is reorganise. Every time it reorganises it faces tremendous challenges from within the organisation as well as from every other affected stakeholder. Yet corporations insist on reorganising.'*[43]

Nevertheless, there is no doubt that the proposals that are now being carried out are a major improvement over the murky customer and supplier set-up that existed prior to Smart Procurement. However, the sought-after clarity in the internal MOD customer-supplier relationships has not yet been achieved, nor has a realistic plan to achieve it been produced:

- Two customers, one split into several components, two suppliers and no clear overall relationship.
- No customer sits on the top equipment committee, EAC, while both Suppliers do.

To claim that the Vice Chief of the Defence Staff represents both customers on EAC is evading the issue. He is jointly responsible, with the Second Permanent Under Secretary of State (2nd PUS), for the management of MOD Centre, but it is DCDS(EC) who is accountable for delivery of equipment capability into the field, and the Commanders-in-Chief who are responsible for the operation and maintenance of that equipment in the field.

More work needed.

---

[43] Lieutenant General William Pagonis: *Good Logistics is Combat Power,* The McKinsey Quarterly

CHAPTER FOUR

STREAMLINED PROCEDURES

Any procurement is complex. Procurement of equipment which cannot be bought 'off-the-shelf' is more complex. Procurement of such equipment using public funds is the most complex of all. There are two fundamentals which pull in opposite directions:

- Complex procedures cost huge sums of money.
- Public funds must not be wasted.

No practical procurement system can entirely eliminate waste, poor decision-making or even fraud. What it can do is reduce such instances. The more you wish to reduce waste, the more complex the minimum procedures you must put in place. So the trick is to balance procedural complexity with the cost of such complexity. In the past, this has not been done very cleverly with the result that the amount spent on the routine operation of the complex procedures that have been put in place is very high. Worse than that, the cost is unknown, so that no balance has been possible to achieve.

The trick is to balance procedural complexity with its inherent cost.

The present procedures for procuring equipment are complex indeed. A simplified diagram, constructed in 1994, is shown at Figure 12. It is not a joke.

Time and again the need for streamlining procedures has been recognised: during the Prospect Headquarters Review, during the Options for Change exercise and during the Defence Costs Study:

> *'The Defence Costs Study found that we are still too bureaucratic, paper dominated, hierarchical and over-inclined to seek to make decisions by concensus..... Similar recommendations were made*

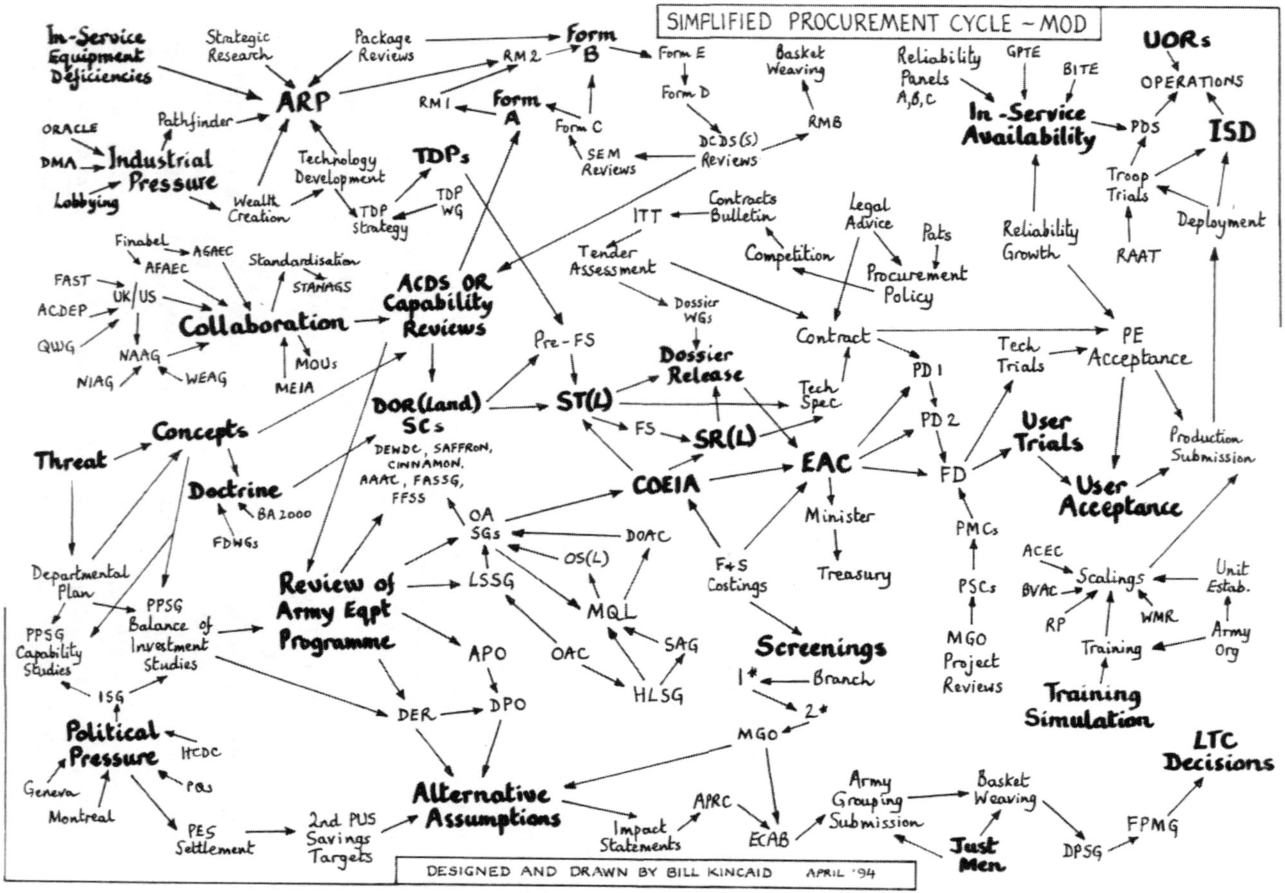

Figure 12: Simplified Procurement Diagram 1994

following the Prospect Headquarters review but..... the same old way of doing things continued.'[44]

This time, it seems that Ministers are determined to make changes. We shall see if the changes work this time.

The New Acquisition Cycle

The first major change to procedures is the establishment of a new acquisition cycle (Figure 13) to replace the thirty-year-old Downey Cycle.

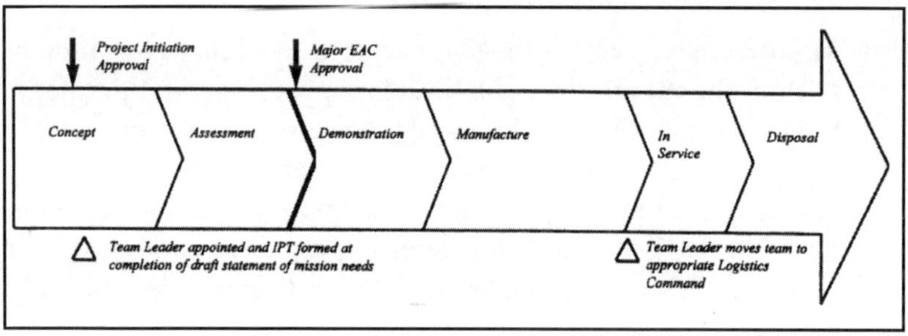

Figure 13: The New Acquisition Cycle

The basic content of each stage is as follows:[45]

- **Concept.** Produce and baseline a statement of required capability, framed as a URD [User Requirement Document]. Identify technology and procurement options for meeting the need that merits further investigation, and set outline performance, cost and time boundaries. Form Embryonic IPT [Integrated Project Team]. Obtain funding and agree plan for Assessment Phase. Pass Initial Gate, with approved broad time, cost and performance parameters.
- **Assessment.** Produce and baseline SRD [System Requirements Document]. Identify the most cost-effective technical and procurement solution. Develop SRD. Reduce risk to a level consistent with delivering an acceptable level of system

[44] *Focus*, House Journal of the MOD

[45] MOD's Acquisition Handbook, *A Guide to Smart Procurement,* April 1999

performance to tightly controlled time and cost parameters. Agree funding and plan for subsequent phases. Pass Main Gate with approved time, cost and performance parameters.

- **Demonstration.** Progressively eliminate development risk in order to fix performance targets for manufacture. Place contract(s) to meet the SRD. Demonstrate ability to produce integrated capability. In many cases, demonstration is the stage where a single contractor is selected. However, this could be done at a stage appropriate to the project, which could either be earlier or later in the project life-cycle.
- **Manufacture.** Deliver the solution to the military requirement within the time and cost limits appropriate at this stage. Complete system development and production, and accept equipment into service which meets user requirements, being effective, available and sustainable. Transfer line management of IPT to DLO [Defence Logistics Organisation] and customer function to second customer [appropriate Commander-in-Chief].
- **In-Service.** Provide effective support to the front line. Maintain levels of performance within agreed parameters. Carry out any agreed upgrades or improvements, refits or acquisition increments.
- **Disposal.** Carry out plans for efficient, effective and safe disposal of the equipment.

Differences from Downey

At first sight, there seems little to shout about as the Cycle seems very similar to Downey with different stage names.

There are, however, several differences which may, or may not, prove to be significant:

- There are only two formal approvals (Initial Gate, Main Gate) rather than the three in Downey. However, we all know that previously projects often returned to EAC four, five, six or even more times. Where is the proof that this will not happen in the future?

- Projects are initiated early in the Concept stage, thus eliminating the awkward 'pre-feasibility funding gap' where project funding for concept studies was not available. However, it may prove tricky to gain project initiation without carrying out concept studies beforehand, thus shifting the 'pre-feasibility funding gap' forward but not eliminating it.
- Main Gate approval is to be a more difficult hurdle than any Downey Cycle approval. Main Gate approval will set clear time, cost and performance parameters. However, these will only be realistic (and therefore practical for operating within during Demonstration and Manufacture) if risk has been properly identified, reduced and managed. This is only possible if Concept and Assessment stages are fully funded: to the 15% of costs that has been recommended.[46]
- The Assessment stage is likely to include some elements of the old Project Definition Stage: it will be less a paper Feasibility Study, more a hardware Demonstration. But this will only happen if enough funding is provided.

The new acquisition cycle, on its own, therefore, is likely to have little impact on reducing procurement cycle time, cost overruns and missed performance targets, and none at all if early stage funding does not materialise. It does, however, provide a slightly better process within which the major Smart Procurement innovations can work.

The MOD Central Customer

The Central Customer will discharge his capability and his IPT oversight responsibilities through four Capability Managers. Each Capability Manager:

> *'will look across a broad range of capabilities and develop specific equipment concepts to meet capability gaps, guided by the Departmental Strategic and the Equipment plans.'*[47]

---

[46] Strategic Defence Review, *Supporting Essay Ten*, Paragraph 15, July 1998

[47] MOD's Acquisition Handbook, *A Guide to Smart Procurement,* April 1999, page 7.

One two-star Capability Manager will head each of the following four areas: Strategic, Manoeuvre, Strike and C41/ISTAR, as described in Chapter 3. Each will form a number of Capability Working Groups (CWG) within his own area (a total of around19).

The Capability Working Group

A Capability Working Group (CWG), chaired by the Capability Manager, will have three roles:

- To manage a capability – taking a whole-life view.
- To undertake the work leading to the production of a User Requirement Document and to the submission to pass the Initial Gate.
- To review the work of the IPT during all development stages and to accept the equipment into service if it meets agreed Acceptance and Verification Criteria.

The CWGs will be chaired at colonel-equivalent rank, but he may have to let it do most of the more mundane work at a lower level, taking charge himself of the major decision-making meetings. But it will depend on how they will work and on how industrial input will be managed.

Membership of the CWG is as follows:

Capability Manager	Central scientific staff	DFD
Related Capability Managers	Technical scrutineers	Industry
Customer Two	Programmers	DLO
Doctrine staff	DPA	DERA

This already looks too large, given the tendency to expand: compare the original five or six members of the former Dossier Working Group with the roomful that developed over time. It is difficult to see where cuts could be made but, although many will not be resourced to attend on a regular basis, the potential for growth and stagnation is painfully obvious.

There are two innovative aspects to the work of the Capability Working Groups:

- Input from industry on such things as exportability, produceability and practical concepts.
- The emphasis on the whole life concept.

How the former will work, or not work, will be explored in Chapters Five and Twelve when discussing partnering arrangements with industry. The latter is to be taken care of by the introduction of Smart Requirements,

> *'a new method of capturing, engineering and managing requirements based on the principles of System Engineering..... to introduce a whole-life, evolutionary requirements process which will involve all stakeholders and deliver effective and sustainable defence systems to the front line..... it will focus on user needs rather than equipment characteristics, and be concerned as much with equipment in-service as with the shorter period of procurement.'*[48]

A rather grand way of saying Smart Requirements will do only what we should have been doing all along, which we sometimes have done, but more often have not. Whether the whole life concept will be taken care of any better than before under the Central MOD Customer remains to be seen. Words in a handbook are unlikely to be the answer.

> Smart Requirements are only what we should have been doing all along.

Smart Requirements replaces the former Staff Targets and Staff Requirements with:

- The User Requirements Document (URD), produced during the Concept Stage, approved at Initial Gate by the Capability Working Group and 'owned' by the Capability Manager.
- The Systems Requirements Document (SRD) which will be produced by the IPT during the Assessment stage, approved at Main Gate and 'owned' by the IPT.

---

[48] Ibid, page 16

Old wine in new bottles?

Well, nearly: there are still two documents, each formally approved, and each defining user requirements. So, not much change there.

The one significant difference is that the second requirements document is prepared not by the Capability Manager's (Operational Requirements in old-speak) staff, but by the IPT in the Defence Procurement Agency, albeit with the aid and concurrence of the Capability Manager's man (the requirements manager) in the IPT. While the URD may well be much the same as the old Staff Target (where the temptation to solutionise had been resisted), the SRD will not replace it, as the Staff Requirement did the Staff Target, but exist alongside it. It is likely to be more procurement oriented as it will be IPT (i.e. procurement) 'owned'.

Initial Gate

The first formal approval is at the 'Initial Gate' at the end of the Concept Stage. The basis for the approval will be the User Requirement Document (URD) which will define the outputs or results that users require from the capability or system. The Initial Gate submission will recommend the technology and procurement options for meeting the URD that merit further investigation, and also recommend outline time, cost and performance parameters.

The Initial Gate has been described as 'softer' than the Downey Cycle's first approval stage. Nevertheless, it will only be meaningful if enough funding has been made available for the Concept Phase; if not then the very much harder hurdle, the Main Gate at the end of the Assessment Stage, will be very hard to clear. The questions are:

- Will significant sums of money be available for early spend before the Initial Gate?
- Who will approve the spend?
- Is it too much to hope that such spend will be in the gift of a single three-star military officer?

One thing is for sure: if early spend is delayed or squeezed or unapproved, the Initial Gate (however soft) will be impossible to get through without a fudge.

The answer that has been provided so far is that up to £5M can be spent on the Concept Stage without formal central approval, presumably on the agreement of the Capability Manager. This sounds fine. But is £5M enough for the Concept Phase of a major, multi-billion pound, complex platform and weapon system? And why should it be acceptable to spend up to £5M on the Concept Stage of, say, a new small arm and the same sum, and no more, on the Concept Stage of a new aircraft, ship or missile system? Expenditure in excess of £5M 'can be agreed by the approving authorities following submission of a three page note'.[49] But why is this to be necessary? After all, a group of one-stars can approve procurement spends of up to £100M, so why cannot a three-star, provided both the Equipment Plan and the Short Term Plan have the relevant funds earmarked (and therefore agreed by the Principal Finance Officer), approve more than £5M?

> *Why cannot a three-star officer approve more than £5 million?*

This is illogical and needs re-visiting.

The Integrated Project Team (IPT)

Once through the Initial Gate, the project becomes the responsibility of the Integrated Project Team, which will have been formed and run in parallel with the Capability Working Group (CWG) during the latter part of the Concept Stage. The IPT will be headed by an empowered leader, who might be from a procurement, a capability management, a financial or other MOD background, or from outside the MOD from industry. The intention is that the best man for the job will be the criterion for leadership of an IPT, although we will see later that there are serious constraints in achieving this.

The IPT is responsible for: [50]

- Translating the Central Customer's URD into the SRD

---

[49] MOD website www.mod.uk/policy/spi, *Smart Procurement: A Simplified Approvals Process*, page 5

[50] *Ibid*, page 8

- Devising and costing equipment solutions to meet the SRD
- Providing the input into the Central Customer's submission at the Main Gate
- Managing the development, manufacture, in-service support and eventual disposal of the equipment.

The IPT will include representatives of all stakeholders – capability manager, procurement, financial, contracts, technical advice, scientific, logistics and, **when competition permits,** industry (what this means will be explored in Chapter Five). There will also be associate members from front-line commands (Customer Two), the training organisations, DESO, DTI and, of course, financial and scientific scrutineers.

The first question many people ask is: so what's new? The old project management system was run by a Project Manager (Team Leader), who had procurement management, contracts, finance, scientific, logistic and requirements experts as part of his 'team' and held regular meetings with industry at all levels. Under the old system, a good Project Manager produced good results. So what is new?

The first difference is that he will have 'line management' of all members of his IPT (except, presumably, the industrial representatives), so that his team will be more tightly knit and should all pull in the same direction more strongly than before. But the requirements and logistics people (and probably also contracts and finance), because of lack of numbers, may be members of several IPTs and cannot therefore be under the 'line management' of all the IPT Leaders they will serve. Moreover, they will retain functional links, or dotted lines to their own senior specialist.

If there is conflict, which is bound to occur from time to time, it will be interesting to see whether solid or dotted lines will win. If the solid lines of line management under the IPT Leader prove stronger, this could be a victory for Smart Procurement; if the dotted lines to functional superiors win, Smart Procurement could notch up a loss.

But every source of conflict is different. Whatever it is, it must be hoped that the IPT system will not allow a stand-off to develop.

By way of example, the URD and the SRD must remain in synchronisation throughout procurement and even beyond. If not, there is the distinct chance that the DPA and industry will together produce something perfectly made, but not required. This has happened in the past, but could happen again if the SRD departs from the URD. Presumably, it will be the requirements manager in the IPT who will ensure they are synchronised. But will the URD be altered to fit the SRD or vice-versa. And how will the requirements manager decide when his line manager's (the IPT leader's) head is on the block to make his targets, and his 'dotted line' superior opposes a change because of possible knock-on effects on other projects in his capability area? Who will resolve the dispute if there is one, and how? Dotted lines versus solid lines, again.

This may seem an unlikely case, but it is a perfectly possible occurrence. What is worrying is that there is clear evidence that many in the DPA see this as the licence to have the final word. They see it as 'the power to boss the Capability Managers', not as the basis for resolution with all parties pulling in the same direction. Hardly Smart.

The next difference, the new relationship with industry, is supposed to replace the current adversarial relationship with partnering arrangements and is envisaged as a profound change. The retention of competition, while essential, does pose many problems to a genuine partnership with industry and, as yet, many of the likely arrangements are still vague despite the mountain of paper which has been created. Clearly there will be a difference, but exactly how much difference is for debate and will be looked at in detail in Chapter Five.

The third, and most crucial, difference is 'empowerment' or clear accountability. Ministers, and senior officials in the Ministry, have made much of 'empowerment', particularly of IPT Leaders. There is no doubt of their firm intention and this has been in evidence with the Pilot IPTs over the last nine months or so. But there are questions lurking in the undergrowth:

- The Pilot IPT Leaders have reported directly, and frequently, to the Chief of Defence Procurement himself. This has been most successful. But is this true 'empowerment'? Or is it a special case of hierarchical decision-making?
- Leaders of 90-plus IPTs cannot report directly, and frequently, to one man. Neither the one-star, nor the two-star, directors in the Defence Procurement Agency have been given the role of 'managing' IPTs or 'vetting' their decisions. Will there not be a tendency to hedge IPT Leaders in with increasing numbers of rules and regulations?
- Historically, whenever mistakes are made, more rules and regulations are brought in to limit the scope for errors, usually by limiting an individual's authority. If mistakes are made by IPT Leaders, will public accountability demand such action?

Ministers have said that empowered individuals must be allowed to make mistakes and learn from them. Will they be quite so keen when giving evidence to the Public Accounts Committee, or will they then wish to point to action to ensure it does not happen again? I believe they will retain the courage of their convictions. But will their successors be motivated by their predecessors' convictions? Indeed, is the whole current concept of public accountability at odds with individual empowerment propounded by the Smart Procurement Initiative? If it is, which will falter?

> *Is the concept of public accountability at odds with individual empowerment?*

The IPT and Competition

Competition is to remain the primary tool of MOD procurement, because the belief is that it is the best way to reduce costs. Competition is likely to be run throughout both the Assessment and the Demonstration Phases, with at least three competitors in the former and a minimum of two in the latter, although this may well vary from project to project. There will be occasions when competition is dispensed with after the Main Gate or, indeed, altogether, but this is expected to be the exception rather than the rule.

Industry's involvement in IPTs during competitive phases is not at all clear. It has been described as 'except during periods of competitive tender',[51] 'except during competitive phases',[52], 'except during the assessment of competitive bids',[53] and 'where competition is no longer viable.'[54] The MOD's Acquisition Handbook is surprisingly reticent on this subject, but the Defence Procurement Agency (DPA) states clearly that industry will be core members of the IPT during competitive phases, except during bidding stages.

Competition and partnering with industry will be further discussed in Chapter Five.

Scrutiny and Audit

A (perhaps the) major cause of delay in the procurement cycle is the hiatus around the various decision points, both the formal, high level ones and the less formal, lower level ones. A medium to large project can cost £1M per month while these hiatuses suspend work: £1M per month for doing nothing very useful in output terms. These decision making delays are far longer than they should be. For example:

- In its first 6 years, the TRACER project achieved one year of envisaged industrial work: the feasibility study.
- ASTOR lost perhaps ten years through lack of clear programme decisions.
- Phoenix was nine years late into service, the majority of the delay being due to difficulties in decision making in MOD and industry.

---

[51] Presentation by Simon Webb to MOD/DMA Seminar on Smart Procurement at Didcot on 24 June 1999

[52] Presentation by Simon Webb to MOD/DMA Seminar on Smart Procurement at Swindon on 2 February 1999

[53] MOD's Acquisition Handbook, *A Guide to Smart Procurement*, Edition 1, April 1999, page 6

[54] Strategic Defence Review, *Supporting Essay Ten,* Paragraph 8, July 1998

A delay of at least six years in the procurement of a major project is by no means unusual and is certainly not the maximum. But a delay of six years could easily cost £72 million, or a cost overrun of around 10% of the whole project.

There must, of course, be some pauses while decisions are made, and 'scrutiny' is carried out, but I have argued before[55] that MOD scrutiny of projects is time-wasting and ineffective: it is a symptom of a 'tick-in-the-box' mentality. This apears to have been recognised within the Smart Procurement Initiative and that mentality, we hope, will be ousted by empowerment. Surely, by giving individuals more authority, there will be less need of repeated scrutiny, won't there?

But I have yet to see any credible statements on scrutiny. I would like to think they are not necessary. Will they remain unecessary when mistakes are made, and the Public Accounts Committee is on the warpath? Or will there be an irresistible urge to be seen to be 'putting things right'?

Scrutiny by the Equipment Approvals Committee (EAC) has been taken to extreme lengths over the last decade or so, with projects returning to EAC year after year to report progress. The new Acquisition Cycle is designed to avoid this with only two appearances in front of EAC in the whole procurement period. But will they not want to recall projects again and again if things are not all rosy? And what project is ever rosy all the time?

Repeated returns to EAC suggest either a lack of confidence in the IPT leader or poor performance by them. Repeated returns to EAC, therefore, will treat only the symptoms of the disease, not the cause. The need to return to EAC outside the two Gates should flag up that something is wrong and should trigger an in-depth audit. If there is obviously nothing significantly wrong, EAC should keep out of it and leave it to the capable IPT leader to get on with it.

> *Repeated returns to EAC will treat the symptoms, not the cause.*

---

[55] *A Dinosaur in Whitehall*, Bill Kincaid, Brassey's, September 1997, page 50

The COEIA

The Combined Operational Effectiveness and Investment Appraisal (COEIA) is:

> *'a formal comparison, on a cost-effectiveness basis, of particular equipment options (or combination of options) for satisfying an operational requirement.......Its purpose is to inform the decision to select one of the procurement options, and to reject the others, before proceeding further with the project, and to confirm the validity of this choice at all subsequent approval stages.'*[56]

Under the Downey Cycle, the first presentation of the full COEIA was required by EAC when they were considering the request for entry into Project Definition, which is roughly equivalent to the Main Gate of the new Acquisition Cycle. However, there was also the requirement to produce a concept of analysis for the COEIA with the request for approval of a Feasibility Study, roughly equivalent to the new Initial Gate. It is assumed that the COEIA requirements will remain the same.

The COEIA will consider the following options:

Do Nothing: Allow existing equipment to go out of service without replacement.

Do Minimum: Run on existing equipment or refurbish it with no change in performance.

Replace with the Same: Procure new or second-hand equipment with broadly the same capability.

Refurbish: Refurbish existing equipment to improve its capability.

Buy Follow-on: Procure an improved version of the same equipment.

Buy off the Shelf: Buy new equipment with improved equipment 'off the shelf'.

Develop and Procure New: develop and procure new equipment from scratch.

---

[56] MOD DCS(S&A), *Guidelines for the Conduct of COEIAs,* April 1996

The COEIA is just one of a number of decision making aids.

'COEIA inputs are derived from and dependent on expert military and technical judgements, and COEIA outputs must be qualified by military factors and procurement uncertainties......The outstanding virtue of the COEIA process is that it provides a rational, structured and traceable framework for reviewing the cost and effectiveness of alternative equipment options.....'[57]

The COEIA will be a major input to the Main Gate approval submission. There is much unease in industry over the conduct of the COEIA within MOD and the Defence Evaluation and Research Agency (DERA), but it is unlikely to become a much more open process. Industry may be given outline information, general approach and concept of analysis, but will not be given the models or the detailed data, because as one MOD scientist said:

'It is analysis, not modelling, that has to be done.'

This, however, is unlikely to satisfy industry, which still regards the COEIA as a major sticking point in its relations with MOD, a view that is likely to get firmer still with any further move by DERA towards commercialism.

The Main Gate

The second formal approval of the project, the Main Gate, occurs after the Assessment Phase. It is meant to be a tougher hurdle than any of the former approval points in the Downey Cycle and it is expected that a proportion of projects will fail at this stage, despite the higher level of funding that is to be spent by this point. This higher level of funding is essential for success (and that includes failure for good reasons rather than lack of evidence) at Main Gate, for:

- Without adequate funding (c.15% of procurement costs), the Assessment Phase cannot be technology-based and will revert to

---

[57] *Choose Your Weapon,* by David Kirkpatrick, RUSI Whitehall Paper Series 1996

a paper Feasibility Study, thus not providing the basis for a case to clear the tougher Main Gate hurdle.

A full business case (discussed further in Chapter 22) will be required for the Main Gate submission. There seem to be two schools of thought about this business case. One has it that the submission must provide the minimum constraint, consistent with accountability of public funds, by minimising the essential parameters in the URD so that the IPT Leader has the greatest freedom to trade-off between time, cost and performance. The other says that the case must be as full as possible to ensure that the Capability Manager gets what he wants at the end of the process.

It seems to me that the second school of thought is not on the Smart Procurement wavelength, any more than are those who see any freedom for the IPT leader as a chance 'to boss the Capability Manager'. The IPT Leader must have certain freedoms to exercise his delegated authority, but he must realise that, at the end of the process, he must present what the MOD Central Customer wants if it is to be accepted into service.

The one great weakness of the new Acquisition Cycle would appear to be the positioning of the Main Gate. It is the final formal approval hurdle, yet it comes earlier than the final Downey approval and seeks to be a stiffer examination. In addition, not only will it set clear parameters for cost, time and performance in Demonstration (Downey Project Definition 2), and Manufacture (Downey Full Development and Production), but will examine in-service costs and performance as well under the whole life approach. But the earlier you attempt to do this in the procurement cycle, the less accurate you will be. By setting the parameters to be achieved in the remainder of the cycle before competition in the Demonstration Phase has taken place, and before the final prime contractor's contract has been negotiated, will lead to one or more of the following penalties:

One great weakness is the early positioning of the Main Gate.

- One or more returns to the Equipment Approvals Committee for permission to update or breach the parameter 'box'.
- More certain cost overruns due to immature costings at Main Gate.
- Increased delay in awaiting further approvals.
- Need for more trade-offs in performance to cater for increased time and cost.

When taken with the fact that there will almost certainly have to be some sort of approval at the end of the Demonstration Phase to confirm the final winning prime contractor, it seems as if the Main Gate needs to be later than it is, or split into two parts. Either way there are disadvantages: by placing Main Gate at the end of Demonstration, the Initial Gate will need to be tougher to ensure that the greater spend between the more separated gates can be properly approved; by splitting Main Gate into two, you revert to the Downey Cycle. Perhaps Downey was not so bad after all!

The move towards the new two gate structure is driven by the wish to reduce the number of formal approvals from three to two. Very welcome. But if their placement leads to further quasi-formal approvals, then nothing has been gained. If it does not, there will be pressure from the public accountability freaks to limit risk by further informal scrutiny.

A final question: is there any recognised method of balancing the costs and benefits of delay with those of performance and cost? Yet this is what the IPT leader may have to do, and perhaps to convince EAC of the trade-off.

Scientific Scrutiny

The scientific scrutiny staff is small and cannot involve themselves in the detail of all projects or attend all Capability Working Groups (CWG) and Integrated Project Teams (IPT). They are 'associate members' and aim at being proactive on projects which are either large, or high risk, or in trouble. They do not see themselves as there to 'stop' projects, but rather to facilitate passage of projects through the formal approval stages, by asking the awkward questions early and insisting on acceptable answers.

They will probably be most active between the Initial Gate and the Main Gate and will play a key role in establishing performance criteria at the latter point. However, they will still have a key role after Main Gate, particularly when trade-offs between cost and performance criteria are being made. While the IPT Leader can do this without approval while cost, performance and time remain within the criteria box laid down at the Main Gate, it is the scrutiny staff, together with the Capability Manager's staff, who must ensure that such trade-offs do not have an overall impact that may be unforeseen, particularly on other projects in other IPTs.

This will be difficult and could lead to the demand for more modelling and, consequently, to more delay.

Selection of the Prime Contractor

At some stage after the Main Gate, probably at the end of the Demonstration Phase, the final prime contractor will be selected, apparently without formal approval. However, it is unlikely that the IPT Leader will select the winner without gaining approval from Ministers, except for the smallest and most obvious outcomes: the recent Ministerial gnashing of teeth over the ASTOR competition outcome is a case in point. It is sincerely to be hoped that Ministers will not allow a major hiatus to develop around this 'no approval' point.

Once the prime contractor has been selected and contracted, MOD can get down to serious partnering (see Chapter Five), sharing the risks but also the benefits. The prime, plus possibly representatives of sub-contractors, become core members of the IPT and must contribute to bringing the project into service on time, within budget and meeting the URD – or better.

ISD and Transition to DLO

Once the project has arrived in service, the IPT (including industry) will transfer to the Defence Logistics Organisation, under current thinking, although the 'Four Horned Monster' approach would change that, if adopted (see Chapter Three). At this point, the IPT may physically move to the relevant logistics base, will see a change of personnel to reflect the change of responsibility and business to be transacted (e.g. replacement of some procurement experts with in-service support specialists), and may change its leader. It has also been said that:

'The IPT after ISD [in-service date] may be smaller and staffed with more junior personnel.'[58]

However, the IPTs being planned in the DLO are very large in scope, as they have to be given that all in-service equipment will be the responsibility of only around 40 IPTs. It is expected that Army equipment will be managed by just 15 IPTs:

Tank systems	IS and communications	Bates
Light armoured systems	Guided Weapons	Workshop support
CVR(T)	Surveillance & target acquisition	Combat support equipment
Challenger 2	Engineer Systems	Combat support vehicles
Field artillery systems	Special projects	Phoenix

More interestingly, each IPT will apparently report to a senior level of equipment management, the level being as yet unspecified, but likely to be one-star. This raises the same questions as apply to IPTs in the Defence Procurement Agency (DPA): to what level will the IPT Leader report and what delegated powers will he have?

The transfer from DPA to DLO may not be a quick one. The leader of the Challenger 2 IPT has investigated such a transfer for his team and:

'The transfer will be handled by a phased approach over the next two years, with the aim of minimising disruption..... The IPT has..... staff at the Agency's Abbey Wood headquarters and at Andover..... The close relationship already forged between the Abbey Wood and Andover teams will ensure that working with a team split between two sites will be a success..... Later this year [the IPT] will be transferred

[58] *A Guide to Smart Procurement,* MOD Video D03/99

from the DPA to the DLO, but the project staff will continue to be based at Abbey Wood and Andover.'[59]

The IPT is to remain in being until the final disposal of all equipments. The resource implications of this are enormous, if it is to be pursued effectively for, at least in the shorter term, more IPTs will be created at the start of the cycle than will disband after disposal for two reasons:

- If some projects are to fail (as expected) at the tougher Main Gate, more IPTs will be created than eventually get through to the end of the cycle.
- There are too few IPTs in the Defence Logistics Organisation to cover all current in-service equipment effectively.

A steady state should eventually be reached, but this will involve more (perhaps many more) IPTs than will have been created by the end of Wave 3 (the final group of IPTs to be created next year). If this increase can be resourced, no problem. If it cannot, then something will have to give. The obvious outcome would be the creation of many more Cluster IPTs with all their difficulties.

Cluster IPTs

The IPT for a single large project is a relatively straightforward concept, but there are around 1500 projects and the MOD could not possibly resource 1500 IPTs. In any case, an IPT for a small project is hardly likely to keep all employed full time. So small projects will be grouped in 'Cluster IPTs', with anything up to 50 to 60 projects in each. The theory so far is fine, but there are questions to which there are no answers, as yet:

- What happens when one project is ready to transfer from the Cluster IPT in the Defence Procurement Agency (DPA) to the Defence Logistics Organisation (DLO) at its In Service Date?

It may be that few, if any, of the other projects in the Cluster are at, or near, ISD and in such a case, the official answer is that: 'in some

[59] *Preview,* the Journal of the Defence Procurement Agency, No.59, 1 April 1999, page 25

cases it will be more sensible for individual projects to transfer from a Cluster IPT in the DPA to an appropriate Cluster IPT in the DLO.'[60]

The team leader of the Air Armaments and Equipment IPT has the job of transferring many of his cluster projects to the DPA:

> *'Special care is needed to ensure that these are handed over to the DLO in the most professional and efficient manner.'*[61]

He apparently sees little problem, but this is because a number of them will be going across together to join other related projects. This will not always be the case. A better answer would be to adopt the 'Four Horned Monster' approach, explained in Chapter 3, so that an individual small project does not have to be extracted from its IPT and 'thrown-over-the-wall' to a possibly inappropriate IPT.

The IPT, in any case should have logistic membership, either as part of the core, or as associates, so this should ensure that this approach has the relevant expertise as the equipment comes into service, but without the possible hiatus of transferring.

- How will the Cluster IPT be resourced? With so many projects, there are likely to be several representatives from the Capability Manager, logistics, DERA and others. The IPT could be enormous.

The cluster could be broken down into mini-clusters, but this hardly reduces the overall resource problem. All it does, in effect, is to create several IPTs with a single leader trying to run them all. However, given the right quality of person, mini-clusters run by capable subordinates with suitable delegation should work perfectly well.

- How will industry be involved, when most of the Cluster IPT projects are in competitive stages?
- How will incremental acquisition be managed for Cluster projects whether each is thrown-over-the-wall or not?

---

60 MOD's Acquisition Handbook, *A Guide to Smart Procurement,* Edition 1, April 1999, page 8

61 *Preview,* the Journal of the Defence Procurement Agency, No.59, April 1999, page 38

These are difficult questions and will be examined below and in Chapter Twelve.

Upgrades and Incremental Acquisition

The desire to get leading edge technology into the field more quickly is an aim of Smart Procurement and one key feature to achieve this aim is incremental acquisition:

> *'Incremental Acquisition provides for equipment capability to be upgraded in a planned way, from the initial delivery of a specified baseline capability to eventual achievement of a higher full capability.'*[62]

The MOD diagram for such incremental acquisition is shown at Figure 14.

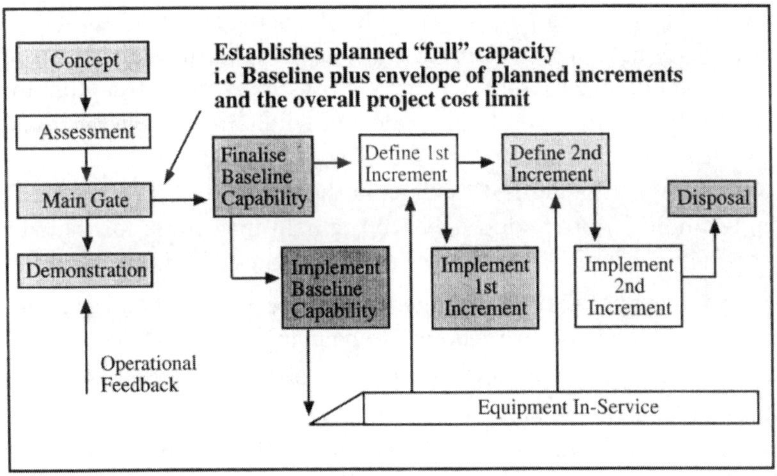

Figure 14: Incremental Acquisition

Incremental acquisition is an excellent idea, but with the following important caveats:

- The original less capable equipment must be brought into the field much more quickly than hitherto, or even than envisaged

[62] MOD's Acquisition Handbook, *A Guide to Smart Procurement,* Edition 1, April 1999

under Smart Procurement procedures, otherwise we lose performance without earlier deployment to offset that disadvantage.

- Incremental enhancements must not impose significant non-availability of equipment during incorporation of the enhancements (ideally they should involve minimal activity within regimental lines).
- Incremental enhancement must not impose any significant training burden (ideally they should be totally transparent to the operator and maintainer).
- Funding must be in place for each increment and must not be used as a funding regulator.

There will be difficulties with achieving all this. The first is the difficulty with technology forecasting, which currently is not good and is far from impartial. It is least accurate when immature technology is being considered, and this is the norm with such long procurement cycles that we have now. Incremental acquisition should shorten the overall timescale, but will it do so enough to make use of mature technology only? This is questionable in areas where technology is moving fast, such as in the whole digitization field. If so, technology forecasting may well remain inaccurate for the later incremental stages when the basic stage reaches the Main Gate.

And if technology forecasting is inaccurate, then cost and schedule forecasts of later stages are bound to be inaccurate, too.

Here we come to the knotty question of Main Gate approval for successive incremental improvements, where technology may still be immature and where cost-effectiveness is still difficult to determine. The MOD model recognises this problem:

'Incremental Acquisition raises a particular challenge for the Approvals process because, unlike non-IA projects, the cost, time <u>and</u> performance envelope established at Main Gate will have to bound a succession of incremental activities subsequent to Main Gate.'

The MOD answer is to impose an overall cost limit for the project as a whole with target cost and performance envelopes for each planned incremental step, re-setting the envelopes for the remaining increments as each is attained. It has been represented as in Figure 15.

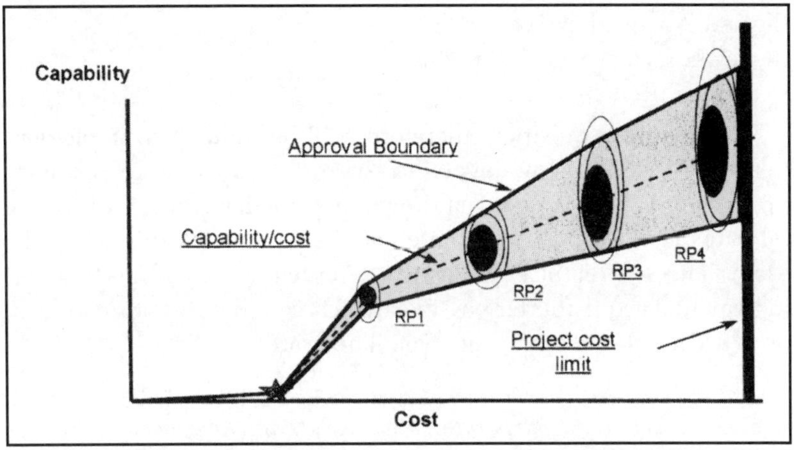

Figure 15. Capability-Cost Envelopes for an Incremental Acquisition Project.

However, if significant sums of money for increments (each increment could perhaps cost a sizeable fraction of the original and all increments together could cost more than the original procurement bill) are to be approved at Main Gate, the Equipment Approvals Committee (EAC) will be taking much greater risk than hitherto.

This risk could be extreme in the case of a system (say, a major IT system), where Stage One can be defined pretty well, but where the later phases cannot be defined even in outline until Stage One is in the field, allowing users to play with it. Any attempt to define the later stages prior to fielding of a prototype of the first stage risks unstitching things later, possibly at significant cost. The risk is large.

What are the options for EAC? They could insist that the project be broken into its component stages, each one becoming a separate project to be presented separately to EAC when it is defined. But it then ceases to be an incremental acquisition procurement. Alternatively, they could accept the increased risk but if they do, they will only be human if they demand that the project be returned to

EAC for approval of each incremental improvement, thus negating the main rationale for the new Acquisition Cycle; that is the fewer formal approval points in the procurement cycle.

The tendency will be to avoid incremental acquisition if possible.

Incremental acquisition, therefore, will be difficult to implement (except for small, low-level increments more akin to ordinary upgrades). Where it is, it may involve a greater amount of formal bureaucracy; if it does not, there may be higher risk to passing the Main Gate successfully. Either way, the tendency will be to avoid incremental acquisition if possible, which would be a failure indeed, or to use it only for sufficiently small upgrades.

> *'The cost effectiveness of Incremental Acquisition over a project's life cycle has yet to be demonstrated. In past years, upgrades of UK defence equipment often encountered unexpected technical difficulties and consequent delays and cost growth. The cost of upgrades varies with their scale and complexity, but a major upgrade (such as the Mid-Life Update of Tornado to GR4 standard) can cost a substantial fraction of the procurement cost. Incremental Acquisition will only be viable if time and cost of each technology insertion are sufficiently small that their total effects do not seriously reduce equipment availability or offset the savings achieved in the initial procurement.'* [63]

Dr David Kirkpatrick may be correct in this assertion but, if so, the whole ethos of incremental acquisition may be at risk.

Digitization will be the test case for incremental acquisition.

It is generally asserted that incremental acquisition is of most benefit in CIS projects, but it could have tremendous advantages for all projects, CIS or non-CIS. The Army's Digitization programme is an example where Incremental Acquisition must be firmly

[63] *Partnering-not Partnership* by Dr David Kirkpatrick, RUSI Journal, Vol.144, No.3, June 1999, page 80

embedded. This is, without doubt, Smart Procurement's test case for incremental acquisition that works.

Segmented Acquisition

The Smart Procurement Initiative included what was originally thought to be a major improvement in the procurement process: segmented acquisition. Strangely, progressively less has been made of it over the last year or so, and it is not at all clear whether or not it has been introduced and, if it has, whether it is contributing to improved output.

Future procurement was to be divided into three tiers, according to the unit price and the technical risk:

- **Tier One.** Low cost, low risk: Items available in the market, often for non-defence application, such as standard vehicles and commodity items.
- **Tier Two.** Medium cost, medium risk: Defence specific items for which MOD needs to be an intelligent customer (a stand alone weapon or an upgrade to an existing system.
- **Tier Three.** High cost, high risk: The most complex systems.

Procurement under each tier would be carried out under different rules. Tier One items would be a purchasing process using credit cards or electronic billing; Tier Two would be subject to 'low level oversight' and 'streamlined risk reduction' (whatever those terms mean); and Tier Three would continue to go to the Equipment Approvals Committee (EAC).

While superficially this is attractive, there are three major weaknesses. The first is that it divides projects into three types when, in reality, every project is different and attempting to strait-jacket them in this way will only impose a new dogma for the old, which in any case usually had to be circumvented.

The second weakness is the categorisation by cost as well as risk. The key must be risk (technical, programme, cost, schedule, performance et al), not cost. A major system bought off the shelf might well have much less risk, and therefore require less exalted oversight, than a stand-alone weapon of 'intermediate scale' being developed from scratch. Under the announced segmented process, cruise missiles and the AS 90 howitzer would have been in Tier Three, with Phoenix and Vixen in Tier Two. That would clearly have been an inversion of what is really required. The real discriminator should be risk.

The third weakness is that it ties the Integrated Project Team (IPT) leader's hands. If we are serious about empowering him, we should leave it to him to select the segmented process that best fits the project. He will have to get it approved at the Initial Gate in any case.

New Wine?

The new Acquisition Cycle is very similar to the old Downey Cycle and much of the latter has been given new labels without changing the content. There are, however, some differences which should genuinely make an improvement.

- Proper funding of the Concept Phase (but why limit it to £5M for all projects, small or huge?)
- Fewer approvals (but will Ministers and senior officials seek to restore the status quo for competitive projects and incremental acquisition?)
- 'Empowerment' or personal accountability with matched responsibility and authority, particularly for IPT leaders (but will fears of public accountability progressively erode the good start that has been made?)

..... Or Just New Labels?

The above differences if allowed to bloom will lead to improvement. Other differences by themselves may not, however hard they are trumpeted:

- The Integrated Project Team (IPT) is only a more formal grouping of procurement committees of the past. On their own, they may achieve little. Cluster IPTs face grave difficulties.
- The problems associated with incremental acquisition may well sink the Smart Procurement Initiative.

- Main Gate may prove to be too early to set sensible cost, time and performance parameters with the need for subsequent resubmissions thus negating one of the few improvements noted above.
- The whole life approach, which has been followed to some extent for some years now, is dependent on good initial in-service cost and performance estimates that are extremely hard to make accurately early in the cycle.

A Reduction in Cycle Time?

The aim of the new Acquisition Cycle and its associated procedures is not, apparently, to reduce procurement cycle time from the twelve, fifteen or twenty years of the recent past (a pity), but to reduce or eliminate time and cost overruns by reducing risk earlier in the Cycle. So any reduction in actual cycle time will be limited to around 3 years – welcome but hardly what is needed.

One ex-Procurement Executive director believes the cycle may actually slow down. If coming in on time and within budget is so important, he argues, then IPT Leaders will set 'more realistic' ISDs that they know they can meet so that schedule risk is eliminated or at least minimised. Because work expands to fill the room allotted, cycle time under his argument would not decrease and could actually increase. It depends on the targets given to IPT leaders in the first place, a subject covered in Chapter Ten.

So overall, given the recent hiatuses at decision-points on medium-range TRIGAT, ASTOR, CASOM and BRIMSTONE, it is difficult to see that procurement cycle times will markedly decrease, although the proper evaluation of risk early in the cycle and its management throughout do at least give promise that delays might decrease.

Not exactly a revolutionary improvement.

CHAPTER FIVE

A NEW RELATIONSHIP WITH INDUSTRY

The Strategic Defence Review called for:

> *'a new relationship between the Ministry of Defence and its suppliers in which both sides can operate to their strengths, under formal partnering arrangements where appropriate, and which provides industry with the greatest incentive to perform.'*[64]

But this relationship was not to be a return to the 'bad, old days of cosy cost-plus contracting.' The primary tool of procurement is to remain competition to obtain:

> *'the greatest advantage from competitive leverage, at prime and sub-contract level..... there is no conflict between robust contracting and mutually beneficial team working.'*[65]

This may be true, but the adoption of both competition and long-term partnering arrangements raises many problems. The whole concept of competition and partnering needs to be very carefully thought through.

Competition and Partnering

> No-one seriously opposes the retention of competition.

No-one seriously opposes the retention of competition. The National Defence Industries Council recommended[66] that

[64] Strategic Defence Review (Cmnd 3999), *Supporting Essay Ten*, Page 10-3, July 1998

[65] MOD's Acquisition Handbook, *A Guide to Smart Procurement,* Edition 1, April 1999, page 23

[66] *Strength Through Partnerships,* NDIC, October 1997

competition should remain a cornerstone of MOD procurement policy, the policy of competition being widely viewed as a (perhaps the) major factor in the increased competitiveness of British defence companies and to have saved the Ministry of Defence large sums of money.

But the retention of competition 'as the cornerstone of our procurement policy' sits uneasily with the move to long-term partnering arrangements, or even with larger incentivised contracts. It has been suggested that competition will be invariably employed with very few exceptions. This sounds like inflexible dogma, and dogma is never very 'Smart'. In fact, the instances of competition have remained remarkably steady over the years: in 1981/2, before the Levene 'competition revolution', 40% of all procurement contracts (by value) were let after competition, while in 1992/3 when competition policy was in full flood, only around 55% went to competition.[67]

This suggests that a substantial proportion of contracts will never go to competition, probably in the same particular areas, whereas elsewhere they will always go to competition so long as competition remains the cornerstone of procurement policy.

If competition and partnering are to cohabit the procurement boudoir, the simplest answer is for MOD to hold one or more competitions before selecting a prime contractor with whom to enter into a partnering arrangement. But selection of the prime contractor too early will lose the full benefits of competition; on the other hand, selection too late will limit the benefits that partnering can bring to both MOD and prime. MOD Guidelines state:[68]

> *'Consultation with the private sector on potential partnering opportunities should begin at the earliest possible stage of a project.'*

and:

---

[67] NAO Report: *MOD Defence Procurement in the 1990s,* 30 May 1994.

[68] MOD Guidelines for Industry, *Partnering between MOD and its Suppliers,* a joint guidance note issued by MOD and CBI in September 1996

'Partnering arrangements will be a long (7/10 years) relationship since it is unlikely the full benefits of partnering can be realised in the short term.'

In a major equipment project, the full benefits of partnering can only be realised if a partnering arrangement, or something similar, is in place when major design decisions are being made. That is, during the Demonstration Phase, as well as during Manufacture. This all points to getting competition out of the way early, perhaps by the Main Gate approval point which would certainly help to negate the need for a return for approval of later competition outcome, as discussed in Chapter 4. Indeed, the MOD/DMA Panel on Partnering and Competition recommended early down-selection to be highly desirable,[69] while the joint MOD/CBI view is that:[70]

'consultations with the private sector on potential partnering should begin at the earliest possible stage of a project.'

This suggests to me that potential partnership discussions should be under way in the Concept Phase. This official MOD view seems to be at odds with the fact that MOD seems set on maintaining competition through the Assessment and Demonstration Phases. In theory, an aggressive approach to reducing costs and increasing performance by MOD with each competing prime separately could be pursued and the benefits reaped later, but the difficulty of doing so without the resources to staff two, three or more completely separate MOD teams is overriding; without separate MOD teams, there will not be the time, or the commitment, or the credible 'Chinese Walls' to draw out the full benefits.

The Cost of Competition

Competition has apparently saved an estimated £1 billion a year on equipment projects and spares, but the cost of bidding for a large competitive project is high, put at £50M or more by some companies, just for the unpaid bidding phase. National Audit figures show:

---

[69] MOD/DMA Seminar on Smart Procurement, Swindon, 2 February 1999

[70] MOD Guidelines for Industry No 4, *Partnering Between MOD and its Suppliers,* May 1997.

- Estimated industrial bidding costs for 24 different competitions varied between 0.04 and 5.8 per cent of the contract value.
- MOD Contracts Branch input was estimated at 0.5 per cent of the contract value.
- Annual cost of competition to industry, excluding costs incurred by companies who decide not to tender, is put at £400 million, (some of which might be recovered from MOD later on other contracts).
- The average number of tenders invited, across 13,000 competitions, was 6.4.

This is a lot of money for industry to find. It is also a lot of money for MOD to find as losses will of course eventually be paid for by the customer, either in the tender price, or downstream or in other projects: the money does not come out of the shareholders' pockets. To the MOD, that cost (approximately about 8% of the MOD's total equipment budget) is apparently off-set by the reduced price that competition has won. Or is it? Do we really know?

This competition cost may be a satisfactory premium for the winner, but not for the loser and the cost to some defence companies is too high. One industrialist asserts that,

'the cost of competition is driving some traditional defence companies out of the UK MOD arena.'

This will inevitably reduce the number of UK competitors, thus reducing the standard of competitions and hence their value to MOD. Competition for competition's sake must be avoided. But just as important is the longer time that competitive phases necessarily take. Not the industrial work, which often has to be done faster, but the MOD decision-making periods. ASTOR started Project Definition in early 1995 and, after an extension caused by the addition of a third bidder, finished in September 1996. Yet it was not until May 1999 that the winner was announced. This period of almost three years was partially explained by:

'Extensive lobbying and media interest in the competition [which] led to a diversion of effort by the team..... we had to spend time developing

briefing material so that Ministers could be kept advised and could respond if necessary to some of the claims being made in newspapers and defence journals. That took time that we would rather have spent on the project. [71]

The earlier the competition is held, the less is spent by the competing primes and the less the media interest.

Competition and Risk

One senior executive in a large prime contractor company believes that competition increases risk. To ensure success, bidders reduce the price as far as possible. This can only be done by cutting out work which inevitably increases risk. It is primarily the remaining risks in the later stages of a project that lead to cost and time overruns, so if competition is held in the later stages, extra risk is imported and time/cost overruns increase. Conversely, completing competition early in the cycle will reduce risk and, consequently, reduce time/cost overruns.

> *Retaining competition into the later stages imports risk.*

Thus, the aim should be to conclude competition by the Main Gate approval point. Regrettably, this is not current MOD policy.

Reduction in Competitive Teams

If MOD holds dogmatically to competition for most projects, with competition retained to the latest possible point in the cycle, the costs may drive many companies out of the market. In time this will reduce the number and enthusiasm of potential bidders. At some stage, an increasing number of projects will be left with single bidders: the benefits of competition will not have been gained and the benefits of partnership will not be maximised.

Although MOD will think it has lost if there is only one team bidding, there are major benefits to be had. Earlier partnering,

[71] Chris Trout on the ASTOR competition, Preview No.63, July 1999, page 12

perhaps right from the Concept Phase (or even in research) could lead to spectacularly reduced risk, and consequently to shorter timescales, and reduced costs.

Smart Procurement, in other words. After all, we already do it in some areas, such as tanks and nuclear submarines, where the size of orders, the lack of export potential and the large gaps between orders make industrial survivability questionable without some sort of partnering between MOD and the primes concerned.

Partnering: What is it?

Partnering is not 'Partnership' which is a legal term defined in the Partnership Act of 1890 (neither MOD nor individual companies will want, I imagine, to sign up to responsibility for the other's debts). According to the Confederation of British Industry (CBI) and the Department of Trade and Industry (DTI), partnering is:

> *'A commitment by both customers and suppliers, regardless of size, to a long term relationship based on clear, mutually agreed objectives to strive for world-class capability and competitiveness.'*[72]

Partnering between MOD and its suppliers is therefore:[73]

- A commitment to achieve excellence in the timely supply of high quality products and services and excellence in relationships for all those involved.
- An attitude of mind that builds on MOD's current procurement policies.
- About securing best long-term value for money.
- A culture of trust and openness.

Two phrases are particularly important: 'long term' and 'trust and openness'. We will come back to these.

Although MOD and its industrial partner may have different overall goals (MOD to get equipment into the field faster, cheaper,

---

[72] MOD Guidelines for Industry No.4, *Partnering between MOD and its Suppliers,* MOD/CBI, September 1996

[73] MOD/CBI Partnering, MOD website www. mod.uk/policy/spi, 26 November 1998

better; the company to make a profit), partnering can be successful if there are some common objectives on the way to the different goals. Even then partnering will only be successful if both risks and benefits are shared. It is therefore very different to the adversarial, risk-aversive, benefit-grabbing culture which preceded it.

What Does MOD Want?

This is simple: MOD wants equipment brought into the field and supported there 'faster, cheaper, better'. MOD wants Value-for-Money although measuring that is difficult and often open to different interpretations.

It is not clear how much 'faster, cheaper, better' (this will be discussed further in Chapter Ten), and currently the emphasis is on reducing cost and time overruns in development and production. Anything more than this appears to be no more than a welcome bonus, which is a major weakness in MOD's approach. But the National Audit Office (NAO) Major Projects Reviews primarily report time and cost overruns and these seem to be the most persistent and the closest of the alligators to the MOD's canoe.

Not surprisingly, but a little short-sightedly, MOD has focused on this.

What Does Industry Want?

This is less easy to identify clearly. At the top level is the need to make profits for shareholders. With cut throat competition in most areas, the early stages of procurement make no profit and often incur a loss, particularly to the losers. Even the winning prime contractor is unlikely to have made a profit and is then stuck with a price for full development, production and initial in-service support. If he has cut his 'competitive price' too much into the bone, he may well fail to make a profit in these stages, too. Where he will make his major profits is in follow-on production, in in-service support over a long period and, perhaps most of all, in the export market.

Industry, therefore, wants:

- Longer and firmer commitment by MOD to projects, project timescales, project funding and project numbers.
- Longer contracts to include a good slice of in-service support.
- Greater priority given to exportability considerations in the early (Concept and Assessment) phases of a project.
- More continuity in the procurement cycle and fewer/shorter hiatuses.
- Better understanding of the MOD Customer's requirements, particularly in the long term.

The Timescale of Partnering

Smart Procurement envisages a new relationship with industry right through the acquisition cycle. However, it is clear that, in many minds, partnering as such does not start until competition is concluded and the final prime contractor selected.

> *'Partnering does not exist until a contract is placed.' A senior industrialist.*

> *'Once a contract is placed, the nature of the relationship between the parties changes and..... common goals can be identified.' MOD website.*

In a joint MOD/Industry panel discussion on partnering[74] there was some confusion but most believed that partnering could only take place after the final prime contractor had been selected.

This is not to say that closer relations between MOD and industry cannot exist earlier than this and it is clearly in the interests, and is the intention, of both MOD and industry, to forge these closer links. For the sake of clarity, I shall use 'partnering' for the relationship between MOD and the winning industrial team, and 'smart relations' for all relationships between MOD and competing, or potentially competing, companies.

---

[74] DMA/MOD Seminar on Smart Procurement, Didcot, 24 June 1999

Partnering without Cosiness

Ministers have repeatedly made clear that there will be 'partnering without cosiness'. There is an understandable, although misplaced, worry that any move to a closer relationship will be a return to the 'bad old days of cost-plus' and even greater cost-overruns, but this is a concern that can only be realistically held by those who think the procurement clock can only operate if the pendulum is stuck either hard left (cosy cost-plus) or hard right (adversarial competitive fixed-price). Smart Procurement quite rightly seeks to return the pendulum to the vertical with regular left and right oscillations to give flexibility in application.

This feeling that a closer relationship cannot exist without cosiness undermining value-for-money is engendered by the culture of suspicion that exists between MOD and industry. To many in MOD, profit is a dirty word and industry's only motive is to rip-off its customer; to many in industry, MOD is interested only in screwing the lowest price out of its supplier. Not so in the US.

> To many in MOD, profit is a dirty word.

'In the US, the Department of Defense – industry link is much warmer and each takes the views of the other much more into account than here.' A senior ex-military industrialist.

'There is more sharing of ideas and concepts with the Department of Defense and the culture is more honest, more forthright.' A senior executive in a UK-based, US-owned company.

It can be done. Ministers are determined that it shall be done. They have not won their battle yet.

Smart Relations in the Concept Phase

Leaving aside collaboration in research which we shall look at in Chapter 7, the Concept Phase is the start point for the new relationship with industry. The Capability Working Groups (CWG), headed by the Central MOD Customer (Customer One), will include industry. This gives, in theory, advantages to each: to MOD, which will welcome input, inter alia, on possible concepts from a practical industrial viewpoint, on trade-offs in likely cost/performance of such concepts, and on their likely exportability; to industry, which will gain a clearer and earlier insight into MOD future plans, its priorities of investment, its requirements thinking and scheduling.

I say in theory because there is one problem. Many people in industry have said that their contribution to a group, where their competitors of the future are sitting with them round a table, will be limited: they will not be compromising their Intellectual Property Rights (IPR). This is a pity because the best discussions take place when many experts sit down together. If this is not going to be possible, full industrial input to the User Requirement Document (URD) through the CWG is doomed. Such input will then have to be made in the same way as in the past – by one-to-one discussions between MOD and a particular company. This is inefficient and is likely to become more and more difficult for MOD to resource.

I sympathise with industry but would caution them that they may lose more by staying away or staying silent. They must balance their risk. They should place against the possible loss of IPR, the following potential gains:

- Much clearer understanding of MOD thinking.
- Some understanding of potential competitors' problems and weaknesses.
- Insight into teaming possibilities.
- Some ideas of merit from potential competitors.

Above all, the lack of input from a company to the CWG may well signal to MOD a lack of interest in the project and exclusion from the early stages of a competition. It is to be hoped that MOD will reward those who make significant contribution to the CWG, and those only, with the invitation to compete. This seems to me to be an ideal compromise between the attractions of the widest possible competition spectrum and a smart relations ethos.

MOD must reward those who make significant contribution to the CWG.

By doing this, MOD will be signalling that industrial input to the CWG is a passport to competition. Conversely, if MOD takes the input and then opens up the competition to include those companies that have chosen not to contribute, or have been incapable of contributing, it will be signalling that hard-nosed competition is all it cares about. Then smart relations in the Concept Phase will really be shot down. Sadly, this seems to be the most likely outcome, as reward downstream for input at the CWG lies not in DCDS(EC)'s gift but in CDP's, and he will be more interested in what potential competitors can offer in competitive terms, not on what has happened earlier.

But it could work. In some CWG-equivalents (FIST, Digitization) potential competitors have been suspicious and very wary about commercial confidentiality, but have slowly loosened up and input ideas increasingly frequently. If the eventual prize at stake is big, it is impossible to see how a company can gain by holding back.

But MOD must do their bit to maximise industrial input.

Smart Relations in Competitive Phases

In the latter stages of the Concept Phase, industry may well be invited to join the embryonic Integrated Project Team (IPT) in addition to its membership of the CWG. Whether membership of the CWG will continue after the User Requirement Document (URD) is complete is not yet clear, but membership of the IPT will continue (where competition allows) throughout the acquisition cycle. Who the industrial members will be, and how they will be resourced, will be looked at in Chapter 13.

During competitive phases, it will not be practical to do all business in one IPT with the competing industrial members sitting round the same table. While some of the business can be done this way, some of it will have to be conducted one-to-one between MOD and each potential supplier. Thus either:

- Separate IPTs will have to be created, one for each industrial team. This is done in many projects in US, but is a major resource burden.

Or:

- One MOD team will have to conduct IPT business with each industrial team in turn. This can only work if both sides have confidence in MOD 'Chinese Walls'.

The first will be the exception rather than the rule: it is conceded that, in exceptional circumstances (e.g. very large, complex projects), MOD might run two separate IPTs. Normally, MOD will 'timeshare' its own staff with each competitor.

Competitive Confidentiality and IPR

One of the causes of friction between MOD and industry during competitive phases is to be removed, for MOD has said that the automatic copying of answers to questions from one competitor, to all other competitors will cease. Where such copying of answers is considered necessary, to keep the playing field level, the originator of the question will be asked if he objects to others having the answer; if he does, the question will not be answered. But this is intended to be the exception rather than the rule.

MOD is to make greater recognition of the importance of competitive confidentiality to industry. Intellectual Property Rights (IPR) provides one of the main bases for competitive edge and, therefore, profitability. However, the recent changes in intellectual property DEFCONs[75] have been made in conjunction with CBI and, while there are some areas which industry has not persuaded MOD to change, most of the major issues have been satisfactorily renegotiated.

IPR may refer to the concept, design, methods of fabrication or the management plans, and these may be at system, sub-system or component level.

'Much ado is made about IPR, yet the majority of those interviewed for this study believed that IPR was not a major difficulty, except in cases of 'gold nuggets' particularly for small firms. The rate of technology change is increasing so that critical IPR has a shorter lifespan. It was

[75] MOD Guidelines for Industry No.10, *The Application of Intellectual Property (IP) DEFCONs*, 16 February 1998

suggested that larger companies gained more value from concentrating on excellence and timeliness of deliverables than on protecting IPR..... However, all recognised that occasionally IPR would be a major issue and that this must be clearly identified at the start of a project.[76]

It is this failure to clarify IPR at the start which causes the greatest difficulty. Because it can be difficult, clarification of what IPR is whose is left until too late in the day, at which point it is even more difficult to unravel, and the legal arguments start. It is imperative that IPR is identified from Day One.

It is imperative that IPR is identified from Day One.

MOD must recognise, and be seen to give it the importance it deserves, that some IPR is the lifeblood of the company, and must be properly protected. Avoidance of conflict here will do much to generate trust between MOD and industry. And it is trust which is at the heart of any workable partnering arrangement between MOD and the selected prime contractor.

Selection of the Winning Prime Contractor

Selection of the final prime contractor will no longer be made solely on price for achieving a set level of performance, as has been done at times in the past. While both these things are important, and may still determine some (or even the majority) of competitions, MOD will take into account such aspects as:

- Track record of the company
- Ability to deliver to cost and time
- Capability in the particular technological fields
- Contribution in earlier phases and to trade-off debates

Some of these pose problems. For example, it is not always clear, in these days of rapidly changing company organisations, mergers and joint ventures, what the actual track record of a particular company

[76] Smart Procurement, *The Mysteries of Implementation Unravelled* by Bill Kincaid and David Arthur, DMA, December 1998

is, and what relevance it has for a specific project. The same is true of assessments of ability to deliver and of technological capability.

In the Civil Sector, when alliances and partnerships are being forged, price may not be a determining factor whereas behaviour, attitude, track record, systems engineering and team expertise may all carry greater weight. This is partially re-inforced by the MOD/ CBI view of the aspects that should be considered when a partner is being chosen:[77]

- Compatibility of management processes and culture.
- Common and non-conflicting short and long term business objectives.
- Understanding of MOD's needs and willingness and ability to work within MOD procurement policy.
- Financial strength.
- Willingness and ability to share risk.
- Presence in and ability to develop the market.
- A proven ability to integrate and motivate people.

Despite this, there is little as yet to suggest that MOD will actually change its way of assessing a competition, which is currently based on compliancy, management ability and price.

Partnering Arrangements

Once the winner has been selected, a clear partnering arrangement can be entered into and the single Integrated Project Team (IPT), whose core will now include representatives from the single industrial team, can get on with the job of getting the equipment into service:

- On time and within budget.
- Where practical, with increased performance and/or reduced cost and/or earlier.

MOD has said that:

---

[77] MOD Guidelines for Industry No.4, September 1996, page 5

'For low risk, well-defined requirements, the Department's practice of seeking firm prices remains the preferred approach. Other forms of incentive contracting exist..... one area for extending those incentives is through gainshare contacting. A greater willingness to consider pricing mechanisms incorporating the use of bonus payments to reward, for example, faster delivery or improved performance where it will yield benefit to the MOD, is another; but Parliament will expect to see comparable compensation for MOD extra costs arising from delays [presumably industrial-inspired delays].'[78]

This, like most of the statements on contracting, applies to the post-competition phase and here, perhaps, the major difficulty will be to incentivise contracts in the competitive stages. If this is not done, and competitors are held to fixed-price, insufficiently incentivised contracts in the Assessment and Demonstration Phases, the technological design may not be the ideal springboard for the target cost incentive fee (or other type of incentive) contract, thus reducing the gainshare that might otherwise have been possible.

Gainshare

Gainsharing is:

'A means of reducing costs to both MOD and its contractors. The basis of gainsharing is that MOD and industry, through the forum of the IPT, identify, agree and implement changes to parts of an existing contract without necessarily changing the whole contract. This allows a budget saving to be achieved whilst retaining the effectiveness of the product and contract.'[79]

The Brimstone Pilot IPT was chosen to help 'pipeclean' the IPT structure by applying the concept of gainsharing. There a list of 40 possibilities was filtered down to ten and these were then prioritised according to likely payback using the following criteria:[80]

---

[78] MOD Website www. mod.uk/policy/spi, *The Role of Industry*, page 9, 26 November 1998

[79] *Brimstone and Gainsharing, A Case Study,* Alenia Marconi Systems, June 1999, page 1

[80] *Ibid*, page 2

- **Criterion 1:** Re-scoping the project without significantly changing the performance of the Brimstone missile
- **Criterion 2:** Mitigation of cost problems and delays that would have adversely affected the Brimstone project and are not within [the contractor's] control
- **Criterion 3:** Improved performance that is achievable without increasing the total project cost
- **Criterion 4:** Re-scoping the project to allow reductions in costs to associated contracts (e.g. additional modelling work on the Brimstone contract that would reduce the number of aircraft integration trials).

Savings at that stage could not be fully quantified, so that they were estimated in three savings categories: greater than £10 million, between £1 million and £10 million, and less than £1 million. The key success factors for making gainsharing work are said to be:

- Clear definition at the outset of what constitutes gainshare and what is a normal contract action cost saving.
- Achievable timescales for delivering gainshare.
- Supply chain 'buy-in' to ensure savings are maximised and shared.
- Openness and lateral thinking.

Gainshare, Trade-offs and Competition

If MOD and industry are each to obtain the greatest benefit under partnering arrangements after the selection of the final prime contractor, then it is essential that MOD bureaucracy and overdue sensitivities are not allowed to limit its potential gains.

The first concern must be the Main Gate approved performance, time and cost parameters which by now may be thoroughly out of date after the competitive Demonstration Phase and subsequent trade-off discussions have taken place. These parameters may have been updated but it is inconceivable that they will be allowed to change greatly without a return to the Equipment Approvals Committee (EAC) and the spectre of increasingly frequent bureaucratic hiatus. Significant changes will, in any case, bring the financial and scientific scrutineers onto the playing field with calls for COEIA reruns and more modelling.

Inevitably the IPT Leader (to ensure delay is not imposed on him) is likely to ignore the more radical gainshare/trade-off proposals if they take one or more parameters 'out-of-the-box'. This must not be allowed to happen and MOD must ensure that further approval delays are not imposed and gains consequently lost.

The IPT leader will ignore the more radical gainshare proposals.

The second major concern is MOD fear of a cry of "foul" from the Demonstration Phase losers that the gainshare/trade-off changes invalidate the previous competition. MOD must stand firm. Major changes to one or more of the performance, cost or time parameters must be allowed under partnering arrangements with the selected prime. After all the selected prime has won a competition and has therefore gained the right to propose and, in conjunction with MOD, to agree changes that may well take the parameters well away from those in the original competitive ITT.

In-Service Support

Once the equipment enters service, there will be a twenty to thirty year support programme managed by the IPT which will transfer to the Defence Logistics Organisation (DLO). There are several potential changes:

- In order to secure the maximum benefits from the MOD-industrial partnership, the prime contractor may well be given a greater initial responsibility for in-service support (say, ten years rather than two) and for driving down support costs, and perhaps also driving up performance, year on year.
- If so, spares would be more often bought through the prime, thus adding a mark-up to the spares supplier's price. This will inevitably lead to a squeeze on the supplier/supply chain.

These could pose some difficulties. Conversely, upgrades and incremental acquisition would be managed more easily because the IPT will be responsible for these as well as for maintaining the equipment in service, and have requirements, procurement and scientific representatives on board when required. This will be easier if the 'Four Horned Monster' approach (see Chapter 3) is adopted. Moreover, the difficulties inherent in upgrades and incremental acquisition will be still further eased if the final procurement prime contractor has the in-service support contract.

In-service support aspects are further considered in Chapter 6.

Partnering and Procurement

As yet, there are few (if any) valid examples of partnering arrangements in procurement projects. Delegates at the MOD/DMA Partnering Panel[81] could not think of a single true partnering example, and, in answer, the Chief of Defence Procurement only cited partnering arrangements in the support arena.

Major projects will be the test. With the eyes of the Public Accounts Committee et al upon them, the Defence Procurement Agency (DPA) is bound to tread very carefully to avoid charges of 'cosiness' and to demonstrate value from long-term partnering arrangements. Will, for example, Digitization or the Future Offensive Aircraft System (FOAS) be the subjects of true partnering during full development, production and in-service support for perhaps ten years? We shall see.

Certainly, it will be a major defeat for Smart Procurement if partnering does not become the norm in procurement and is confined to small projects and in-service support.

Trust and Transparency

Trust is fundamental to partnering but cannot be achieved without openness, which means transparency.

> *'Trust and transparency..... among the keys to the future' – Chief of Defence Procurement.*[82]

---

[81] MOD/DMA Seminar on Smart Procurement, Didcot, 24 June 1999

Trust must be earned; it is not enough to say 'Trust Me'. Trust must be based on:

- A sound contract with gainsharing proposals.
- Common objectives.
- A two-way street of openness/transparency.
- Professionalism on both sides.
- Risk, benefit and disbenefit sharing.
- Knowledge of each other's constraints, organisation and aims.

Knowledge and Joint Training

Knowledge of industry in MOD, and of MOD within industry, is patchy and generally very poor.

> *'Neither side understands the other.' – An ex-military requirements officer, now working as a consultant in industry.*

> *'Understanding is poor, but industry is more sophisticated about MOD than vice-versa.' A senior executive in a large UK prime.*

The latter is only partially true. Industry generally has a reasonable knowledge of the Defence Procurement Agency (DPA) and a sketchy understanding of the requirements staff and the Defence Logistics Organisation (DLO), but have little or no knowledge of the complications of the Main Building, for example. In the DPA and in some parts of the DLO, there is some knowledge of industry organisation, but little of process or decision-making. Elsewhere in MOD, knowledge of industry is virtually non-existent.

If trust is fundamental to successful partnering, and if knowledge of the partner is a basic component of trust, then the lack of knowledge that exists now must be quickly and effectively eliminated. This can only be done by true joint training, not just by opening up some places on some MOD courses. This is discussed further in Chapter 9.

---

[82] *Preview*, The Journal of the Defence Procurement Agency, No.63, July 1999, page 18

Risk Sharing

Risk sharing is the opposite side of the coin from gainsharing, but, like gainsharing, risks must be carefully identified and these must then be apportioned to those (MOD, prime, sub-contractors, suppliers) who are best placed to manage them.

Risk analysis is not always (perhaps not often) done well:

'Historically, DERA risk assessment performance is not encouraging.'
– A senior executive in a large prime.

But here it must be added that the Defence Evaluation and Research Agency (DERA) is investing in risk analysis tools to provide a risk analysis service.[83]

In the past, MOD has often kept a separate risk register from the 'joint' MOD-industry risk register, but this is not a possibility in a new transparent partnering arrangement. More time and effort must be given to identifying risk jointly and to maintaining the truly joint risk register.

An Industrial Policy?

One academic asked me how the MOD could partner industry in the absence of a credible industrial defence policy. The government will claim that it has: competition and partnering. In its pre-election strategy,[84] the present Government wrote:

'A strong defence industrial base is therefore vital to our national interests, as well as being a high-technology preserve we cannot afford to lose..... Labour believes in a competitive and world class defence industry which offers the best quality equipment..... the proposals set out in this document will secure these requirements.'

The question at issue is not what the Government wants, but how it intends to get it. Partnering and competition has been thrown up in Smart Procurement, not as an industrial policy, but as one way

83 *DERA News*, July 1999, page 13

84 *Strategy for a Secure Future*, Labour's Approach to the Defence Industry, October 1995

(perhaps the best) of achieving more cost-efficient procurement. Thus a Government industrial policy still seems to be missing.

The adoption of both partnering and competition has to stand in for such a policy. The weakness is that there are many problems in implementing them effectively and, if implementation is not effective, it will be the defence industry, in the absence of any industrial policy, which suffers rather more than MOD and its procurement processes.

Partnering is a key element of the new relationship with industry. Unless it is implemented effectively, Ministers' vision of 'MOD and industry working together in mutual benefit'[85] will be no more than a mirage.

---

[85] John Spellar, Under Secretary of State for Defence, to the MOD/DMA Seminar, Didcot, 24 June 1999

CHAPTER SIX

THE DRIVE FOR EFFICIENCY

The drive for efficiency is not new, but the decline in the Defence Budget (more than 29% since the end of the Cold War) has made efficiency gains even more vital. The Secretary of State for Defence, soon after announcing the Strategic Defence Review, said:

'The Strategic Defence Review will be seeking to ensure that, as far as humanly practicable, every pound spent on defence will be spent both wisely and well.'[86]

This applied very much to procurement and, in particular, to defence support and infrastructure in the logistics area, where the annual spending approaches £5 billion. Efficiency savings here, through rationalisation and convergence, would yield a great deal.

'Careful consideration was given to our arrangements for the provision of logistics support to the front line. The current position, with three single-Service logistics organisations, ensures the necessary close relationship between the logistics area and the front line forces it supports, but is less well suited to maximising the scope for rationalisation and convergence on a functional, defence-wide basis.'[87]

As a result, it was decided that all three single-Service organisations would be brought together under a four-star, uniformed Chief of Defence Logistics (CDL), as described in Chapter 3.

The whole life concept should yield large savings in support costs as effort, under the Smart Procurement structure, should have been

---

[86] George Robertson, Secretary of State for Defence, to RUSI, 18 September 1997

[87] Strategic Defence Review, *Supporting Essay Eleven*, July 1998, Page 11-15

devoted to minimising these throughout the procurement cycle, particularly in the concept and design stages. Whether this effort will have both taken place and been effective remains to be seen, but it has a much better chance if the 'Four-horned Monster', rather than the 'Throw-it-over-the-Wall', approach is adopted (see Chapter 3).

Over and above these in-service equipment savings, a target of 3% per year has been set for improved efficiency in logistics. It is very doubtful whether this level of savings would or could have been achieved without logistic unification, but unity provides the opportunity to find savings (probably large) in areas which cross inter-Service boundaries.

> *'Current support chains are bureaucratic, fragmented and sub-optional. Operational capability was only maintained through high stock levels and excess costs. "We're trying to deal with too many suppliers, with too great an emphasis on unit cost. We're buying too much of the wrong stock; management information is poor and there is a lack of appropriate managerial and technical skills", he [CDL] said.'*[88]

So, much scope exists, it appears.

CDL has focused on 42 projects to realise the potential benefits, the first wave of which is made up of:

- Sale and leaseback of the landrover fleet.
- Non-project procurement organisation.
- Review of depot rotables.
- Performance indicators for rotables.
- In-repair performance measurement.
- Expert provisioning.
- VMI for vehicle spares.
- Supplier development.
- Electronic commerce.

---

[88] *Preview*, the Journal of the Defence Procurement Agency, No.63, July 1999, page 18

Past Failure of Attempts to Apply a Whole-Life Concept

The whole life concept for equipment is nothing new:

> *'This is by no means a new approach, and is universally applied by individuals and private companies which take account of expected in-service costs (as well as of the initial cost of procurement) when purchasing capital equipment. MOD guidelines[89] prescribed a through-life approach 25 years ago; it has since been supported by reports by both the House of Commons Defence Committee[90] and the National Audit Office[91] and it is a fundamental feature of the investment appraisal methodology[92] stipulated by HM Treasury for all public sector projects.'*[93]

So, we have tried to implement a whole life concept for a quarter of a century and failed. Why?

Although several cultural reasons exist (logisticians are treated as second class citizens, implications of procurement decisions on logistic costs are way downstream, spares are not exciting etc), there are two major process reasons.

The first is that it is very difficult to forecast costs and, the further into the future those forecast costs lie, the more inaccurate they are likely to be. Thus procurement costs forecasts will be unreliable because they are made a few years ahead, but support costs predictions will be far more inaccurate as they will need to be made (under a real whole-life concept) decades ahead. As whole-life support costs are

Support cost predictions will be far more inaccurate.

---

[89] *Defence Life Cycle Costing – Introduction and Guide,* MOD leaflet, April 1974

[90] HCDC 5th Report 1987/8, *The Procurement of Major Defence Equipment,* HC 431, June 1988

[91] NAO, *MOD: Planning for Life Cycle Costs,* 1991/2, HC 174, Jan 1992

[92] HM Treasury, *Economic Appraisal in Central Government,* 1991

[93] Dr David Kirkpatrick, *Partnering, not Partnership,* RUSI Journal, Vol.144, No.3, June 1999, page 79.

usually much larger than the procurement costs, overall whole-life costs may not even achieve ball-park accuracy.

This inaccuracy is not the fault of any individual or branch: it is a fact of life. Forecasting can be improved, but almost certainly not enough to change things significantly. Some of the factors that will see to this are:

- Changes to requirements.
- Changes to programme plans.
- Political and world order changes.
- Adverse outturn of programme risks.
- Basic assumptions proving unjustified.
- New and fast evolution of technology.
- Industrial restructuring.
- The lack of recognised methods for evaluating the cost of delay.
- The ratio of peace to operational usage.

Each of these factors can disrupt earlier forecasts; each of these factors is more likely to appear over a whole-life of 40 years, than over a procurement timescale of much less.

And Smart Procurement may have made the situation worse by demanding whole-life costs at the Main Gate, which is rather early in the Acquisition Cycle, and setting them firmly as a project cost parameter, which is then thrust upon the IPT leader to achieve. What odds on sensible trade-offs in design between procurement and support costs, when the latter are so inaccurate and largely outside the Equipment Plan timescale? Procurement costs are what will continue to take the eye.

The second major reason for failing to implement a whole-life approach before now is that we have had little idea of what everything costs.

> *'The current financial management system focuses on what we buy and who buys it. The Vote Structure identifies the first in great detail and the budget hierarchy identifies the second. It does not, however,*

collect and analyze financial information in such a way as to show clearly how costs relate to the activities and purposes of that budget.'[94]

CDL has stated[95] that his job would be just about impossible if MOD was still managing its business on a cash, input related basis.

However, in November 1993, the Chancellor of the Exchequer announced that resource accounting would be introduced in all government departments by 1 April 1998.

Resource Accounting and Budgeting

The move to resource accounting and budgeting (RAB) has been hailed as one of the biggest change management projects ever attempted in Europe and, according to the Public Accounts Committee, the challenge for the MOD is perhaps as great as for all the other government departments combined.

> *In itself, resource accounting will not ensure better decision making.*

The major value of RAB is that it provides managers with more accurate and relevant management information with which to cost the resources they use, and to match them with the outputs they deliver. It produces a basis for better informed decisions to be made, but in itself RAB will not, contrary to what so many people claim, ensure better decision making. Like so many other management tools, it provides information which then may or may not be used correctly.

There is, however, evidence already that resource accounting is having a dramatic effect in highlighting areas for improvement and, in turn, on short to medium term decision making. But one of the problems in the past has been that in-Service costs have often lain largely or wholly outside the ten-year long term costings (LTC) when procurement decisions that might effect those costs are taken, and consequently they have been largely ignored, except for a little lip-service. If you are trying to find ways of cutting ten-year expenditure,

---

[94] The Craine Study

[95] General Sir Sam Cowan, My Job, RUSI Journal, Vol143, No.6, December 1998

reducing or delaying procurement spend is the overriding consideration; not in-service costs which are hardly a consideration in that ten-year period, even though in-service equipment waiting to be replaced may be costing a bomb. The theory is that, under RAB, the size of that bomb will be clear and that will drive decisions.

That, however, may be optimistic. The long term costings (LTC) has now been replaced by a short term (4 year) plan and a long term (10 year) equipment plan. While RAB may exert pressure for rational whole life cost decisions, the detailed costed plans over 4 and 10 years may still prove to be the more powerful so that:

- Procurement may be delayed to keep procurement spend within budget if the in-service benefit lies outside the plan timescales.
- Procurement projects may be reduced in cost (perhaps trading off against performance or time) with adverse knock-on effects on in-service costs outside the timescales of the short- and long-term plans.

Once such decisions have been made during procurement phases on purely shorter term financial grounds, in-service costs may as a consequence be higher than necessary, either because increased run-on of old equipment becomes increasingly uneconomic, or because cheaper design decisions make the future equipment more costly to support when it eventually appears, or both.

It is difficult to see how practical realities will not be allowed to dominate whole-life theory unless either procurement timescales are hugely reduced, say to five years for a major system (although this looks increasingly unlikely under Smart Procurement as it is being implemented); or costed plans are extended to thirty or forty years which is probably impractical given current costing methodologies.

RAB may force the whole life concept more to the fore, but it might not be able to overcome the power of the short term financial imperatives. I hope I am wrong, but I am not betting on it.

Integrated Logistic Support

Integrated logistic support (ILS) has been a feature of MOD projects for a decade or more, with an ILS manager for each project and ILS representatives at procurement committees. Its aim is to achieve optimum equipment capability at minimum life cycle cost. ILS documentation is extensive and comprehensive. Despite this, ILS has not worked as well as it should have done, either in MOD or in industry. The reasons for poor industrial performance will be examined in Chapter 22, but the main reason for poor MOD performance, hinted at above, lies in the fact that in-service costs are locked in during early development. Typically 80% of life cycle costs are locked in by the start of full development which is where partnering arrangements with the final prime contractor are due to start under current Smart Procurement thinking. Thus partnering from this stage has severely limited potential for reducing costs. Commitment and spend are illustrated at Figure 16.

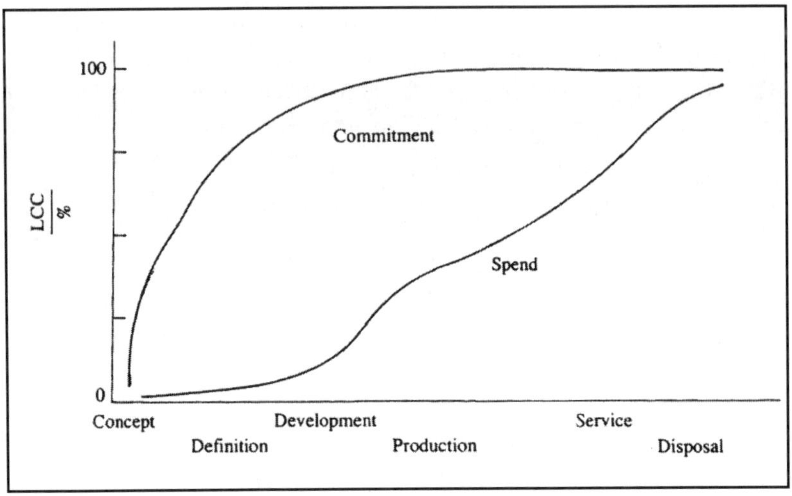

Figure 16: Life Cycle Costs – Commitment and Spend

MOD Agencies

The Efficiency Unit's report on *Improving Management in Government: The Next Steps* recommended the setting up of agencies to carry out certain functions, either as part of a government department, or wholly outside government. While most agencies were set up outside to provide a service to the public, MOD agencies were set up within the Department to provide a service to the MOD. A significant difference.

Most of these agencies were set up in the logistic organisations under a Chief Executive who was supposedly accountable. However, he was not often given the power to discharge his responsibility, the funds lying in the budget of the Principal Administrative Officer (Chief of Fleet Support, Quartermaster General or Air Member for Logistics) and, without a clear and enforceable contract (many operated only on a Service Level Agreement), his power was illusory.

To some extent the much larger Defence Research Agency (later the Defence Evaluation and Research Agency) had greater powers, but even these have proved insufficient if its Chief Executive's desire for a public-private partnership (PPP) future is any indication. So why has the Procurement Executive become the Defence Procurement Agency (DPA)? The reasons given are:

- It provides a clearer customer focus.
- It gives greater delegated powers to the Chief Executive.
- It allows freedom to shape policy to fit the business.
- A change of status facilitates change.[96]

Certainly, the change to agency status in the DPA has provided impetus to the changes in procurement processes and organisation that were called for. Change has taken place at breathtaking speed, and agency status has demonstrably caused

> *Agency status has caused more people to think more clearly.*

[96] John Howe, *Structure and Operation of the DPA,* MOD/DMA Seminar, Didcot, 24 June 1999

more people to think more clearly about how to do business. Good. In fact, by 1998, a number of other MOD agencies had achieved savings of over 20% in their first two or three years and have been principal contributors to the MOD's efficiency programme, achieving rates around double that of the rest of the Department.

Clearly agencies are here to stay.

Public Private Partnership (PPP)

The Private Finance Initiative (PFI) was set up in 1993, but initially was not taken seriously, because the Conservatives were believed to be on their way out and because the Labour view of PFI was not clear. There was a 'wait-and-see' attitude. But Labour felt that PFI was the vehicle to regenerate government infrastructure, so on assuming office, they introduced Public Private Partnership (PPP):

> *'PPP is a generic term that covers Competing for Quality (CFQ), the Private Finance Initiative (PFI) and Partnering.'*[97]

> *'Public private partnerships (PPP) have come along and ministers have made it plain that if we're contemplating any significant new capital investment then that will only be funded by the taxpayer if PPP is found to be inappropriate, uneconomic or unworkable.'*[98]

So far, 26 PFI deals in defence have been signed off at a value of £1 billion and deals worth a further £6 billion are in the pipeline. But it is the easy fruit that has so far been picked: new barracks, helicopter and aircraft simulation, army mail; the challenge gets harder.

Many PFI deals are long term. For example, refurbishment of the Main Building is based on a 35 year deal. This removes flexibility from the programmed MOD budget as expenditure is locked in for 30 years or more, hence a ceiling of 15% of the total budget has been set for PFI.

---

[97] MOD's Acquisition Handbook, *A Guide to Smart Procurement,* Edition 1, April 1999, page 21

[98] Peter Ryan, Head of MOD PPP Unit, *Going Private,* Defence Review supplement on Digitization, 1999, page 29

Key Principles of PFI

From MOD's viewpoint, the key principles of PFI are:

- There must be private sector investment and asset ownership.
- The procurement is of a service or bundle of services.
- Contracts are for far longer terms then traditional procurement (typically 20-25 years or more).
- The contract has an incentivised payment mechanism, incorporating a 'no service, no payment' philosophy.
- Risk allocation will show a substantial degree of risk transfer from MOD to the private sector.

PFI is complex. There might be a hundred contracts between the various elements: the loan agreement between the financing agent and the prime contractor (the 'special purpose vehicle'); between the MOD and the prime; between the prime and its sub-contractors; between the prime and the operating companies etc.

Benefits of PFI[99]

Benefits for MOD	Benefits for Industry
Improved value for money	Chance to develop long term business with MOD
Greater visibility of risk	Security of long term income stream
Focus on output & operational needs	Far greater influence on design,
Greater exploitation of private sector capabilities	specification and delivery
Improved service through incentivisation	Opportunity to exploit spare capacity
Long term improvements in service quality	Opportunity to exploit better products in other markets
Greater access to capital funding resources	

PFI Risks

For MOD	For Industry
Contractor will not be there on the day	Large debt at start. Responsibility for delay?
Defining output	Legal advice
Selecting contractor through competition	
Contract negotiation expertise	
Tension between public accountability and	
flexible risk-taking	

99 Bevan Ashford, Legal Workshop, West of England Aerospace Forum Newsletter, July 1999, page 6

PFI in Equipment Procurement

All PFI deals so far have been in the support area – buildings, training, equipment repair and the like. The following are a few examples:

- Joint Services Command and Staff College (£60M).
- RAF accommodation at RAF Lossiemouth (£31M).
- Defence helicopter flying training (£118M).
- Future cargo vehicles (£350M).
- Medium support helicopter aircrew training facility (£100M).
- Skynet satellite communications (£750M).
- Fixed telecommunications services (£70M).

It is more difficult to identify PFI opportunities with front line equipment procurement, but the following have been identified as possibilities

- Heavy Equipment Transporter.
- Hospital Ships.
- Ocean survey vessels.
- Future tanker aircraft.

These are all equipments that operate largely at the back end of operational areas. It probably demonstrates that PFI can apply to support equipment but not to front line equipment *with no other use.*

> Much time is wasted in squeezing out unsatisfactory PPP proposals.

PPP is being pursued dogmatically and much time is wasted in squeezing out unsatisfactory PPP proposals. This should stop and clearer guidelines be laid down governing equipment proposals, perhaps along the lines of MOD evidence to the House of Commons Defence Committee which defined three distinct bands for using private capital:

- If something never moves, the MOD would not see any reason why it could not be provided by Public Private Partnership.

- If something moves but never goes anywhere near the front-line, it would be a serious candidate for PPP.
- If something is in the front line, it is not pursued.'[100]

But the boundaries of the front line are not always clear, so clarification needs to go further if MOD and industry are not to waste precious resources on dreaming up impractical or operationally unattractive PFI ideas.

Sponsored Reserves

Operational equipment, even if only second or third line support equipment, would have to be manned by contractors in a full PFI deal. The whole question of these contractors becoming sponsored reserves is under intensive investigation. Experience of using contractors in the Falklands and in the Gulf suggests that this could work well, once the legal and administrative problems are overcome, as the individuals are happy and employers are happy. The PFI contract would then obligate the contractor to guarantee a service during operations using sponsored reserves where necessary.

Electronic Commerce

The Government has made a clear commitment to electronic commerce, with a target of conducting 25% of all government business electronically by 2002 and, more important for procurement, 90% by volume of routine procurement of goods by central government to be conducted electronically by March 2001.

Within the Defence Logistics Organisation (DLO), electronic commerce is one of the Lean Support first wave projects, and is expected to produce major savings through a large reduction in holdings made possible by:

- Accelerated order times.
- Cheap, automated processes.
- Delivery-focused order management.

---

[100] HCDC 8th Report 1997/8, The Strategic Defence Review, Volume 1, Paragraph 301, 3 September 1998

- Decentralised ordering and direct delivery.
- Better repair loop efficiency.

In fact, MOD is already making significant use of electronic commerce[101] including:

- Procurement of helicopter spares worth £100 million over 3 years.
- Air and ground handling contracts worth about £4 million per year.
- Purchase of aircraft spares worth about £2.25 million per year.
- Vehicle spares for Land Rovers worth about £12 million per year.

Recently completed, a MOD trial of the Government Procurement Card for the purchase of low value, commercially available goods and services showed the potential for major savings. Use of the card cut the average time taken for arrival of commercially available spares from three weeks to between two and three days.[102] The Treasury estimates that the card could cut processing costs by up to 60%. This will be welcome but is not enough on its own, given that the NAO found the average process cost, to purchase locally £51 worth of goods, was £74. If the process cost is reduced by 60%, that still leaves a cost of £30 to buy £51-worth of goods. The US will claim, though on what basis is not clear, that they purchase $1.00 worth of goods for a process cost of 1c. Nevertheless, electronic commerce has a part to play in reducing process costs and improving efficiency.

There has been some nervousness over the opportunity that electronic commerce provides greater opportunities for fraud. However, it has been reported from the US[103] that:

'90% of all items costing less than $5000 are now purchased by credit card, and this has spectacularly driven down instances of fraud.'

---

[101] Defence Procurement Agency Press Release, *Electonic Commerce in MOD,* AW 4/99

[102] *Electronic Revolution on the Cards*, Supply Management, 13 May 1999, page 27

[103] Dr Ken Oscar, DOD, to Conference on *Managing the Revolution in Military Affairs,* RMCS Shrivenham, 11 November 1998

Electronic commerce is not just about credit card purchasing. MOD plans to use the electronic environment to:

- Keep industry better informed through MOD's Internet website.
- Launch guidelines on conducting business by electronic mail.
- Provide the Defence Electronic Commerce Service (DECS) (under PFI) to connect MOD electronically to its suppliers and to facilitate electronic bill payment.
- Provide a Shared Data Environment by means of shared database access.
- Allow submission of tenders by electronic means and creation of contracts 'on line'.

MOD may have started late but its plans appear to be shaping up. We await implementation. We also wait to see whether the plans, when implemented, go far enough.

How Efficient Will We Be?

There is no doubt about the determination of Ministers, and of most senior MOD officials and officers, to make major efficiency savings in the way we procure and support equipment. They have to be if the Defence Budget is to provide the funds for what must be provided to carry out effective defence.

There is no doubt, either, about the progress that has been made in many areas: in PFI/PPP projects, in the use of electronic commerce, in agencies, and not least in the introduction of resource accounting and budgeting. All those should yield substantial year-on-year savings.

But these are all relatively small. There are two prizes which are substantially larger:

- Savings made on equipment procurement costs through radically shorter procurement cycles (say 5 years instead of 15)
- Savings made on downstream service support costs by cost-efficient design in the early stages of the acquisition cycle, primarily in the Concept and Assessment Phases

Here, opportunity is not being grasped. There is too much emphasis on reducing time overruns rather than on radically reducing time schedules: and there is too much emphasis on keeping competition going until the end of the Demonstration Phase when 80% of support costs will have been 'locked in'.

Some of the smaller savings, then, are being pursued energetically. Alas, the biggest prizes seem to be slipping away.

> *Alas, the biggest prizes seem to be slipping away.*

CHAPTER SEVEN

RESEARCH AND TECHNOLOGY

One of the major curiosities of the Strategic Defence Review and of the Smart Procurement Initiative is the lack of emphasis placed on research and technology, yet this is the essential starting point of any procurement or acquisition cycle. The Strategic Defence Review stated that:

'We will harness the opportunities offered by a Public Private Partnership to strengthen DERA's [Defence Evaluation and Research Agency's] ability to provide world class scientific research well into the next century.'[104]

And not a lot else.

The subject of research and technology has been repeatedly ignored during the creation of the Smart Procurement Initiative and its implementation to date; indeed the new Acquisition Cycle starts with the Concept Phase, not with research. Research is not mentioned in the MOD's Acquisition Handbook, and questions on research to ministers and senior officials at a wide variety of seminars on Smart Procurement have been sidestepped. It appears that, while Smart Procurement has been the province of the Under Secretary of State for Defence, the future of DERA and research has come under the Minister (Defence Procurement). Very curious.

Yet Labour in opposition strongly criticised the Tory government on its reduction in research and development (R&D) spending:

'Decline in government sponsored R&D (by more than 17% between 1985 and 1994) has not been compensated for by an increase in civil research, which has indeed decreased at an even faster rate..... Fears that the erosion of Britain's defence capability will become irreversible,

[104] Strategic Defence Review, *Supporting Essay Eleven*, July 1998, page 11-8

and that the UK industry will become no more than an 'offset graveyard' with only a minor manufacturing role in 'off the shelf' orders placed abroad, have been voiced repeatedly.'[105]

The Importance of Research and Technology

The same Labour document undertook to 'address the deeply concerning decline in Britain's R&D investment levels'. They have not done so yet and R&D levels are set to halve between 1993 and 2000.

While UK has been cutting back its research spending, our main competitors in the defence export market have been increasing their spend or keeping it level. They are in no doubt as to its importance:

'... R&D in general is going to be important in the next ten years. Whether the investment grows is one thing, but the importance of the output is a given. Unlike in the past, where R&D met requirements, I think R&D is going to drive a lot of requirements.....'[106]

The position in this country is somewhat different. Buoyed up perhaps by the excellent recent export record of the defence industry, many in government see no reason to spend on research and technology: 'Things are fine, so let's cut the funding', they seem to say. After all, DERA is funded to the tune of almost £1 billion per year and the defence industry is capturing around 25% of the world export market, a performance second only to the US.

The weakness in this argument should be clear to everyone without prompting: current success in exporting equipment lies at the end of a 15 or 20 year procurement cycle and is rooted in the much higher R&D spending of the early to mid-

Current export success is rooted in higher R&D spending in the 1980s.

[105] *Strategy for a Secure Future*, Labour's Approach to the Defence Industry, October 1995

[106] Interview with Frank Fernandez, Director of the US Defense Advanced Research Projects Agency (DARPA), Jane's Defense Weekly, 26 May 1999, page 32

1980s. The damage to our export capability caused by the slashing of R&D spending in the 1990s (and currently projected to continue into the next millennium) will only become apparent in the 2010 to 2020 timeframe. What price 25% of the market by then?

How Much Should We Spend?

Research comparisons are difficult as most figures lump research in with development, and what falls into development is always for debate. Nevertheless figures from Government sources show that UK is way behind other world players as shown in Figure 17.

Country	Total R&D	Civil R&D	Defence R&D
United States	44.028	19.938	24.092
Japan	10.226	9.625	0.601
Germany	9.575	8.632	0.943
France	8.587	6.097	2.491
United Kingdom	5.761	3.616	2.144

Figure 17: International Comparison of Government R&D Expenditure

(£Bn, 1996 current prices) (Source: Science, Engineering and Technology Statistics 1998, Cm 4006, July 1998, Table 7.6)

Moreover the UK trend is in the wrong direction: in a period when UK defence R&D dropped by 25%, France increased hers by 24% and Germany by 35%; and between 1989 and 2002, US will have increased her government research spend (as % of development and production spending) from 8.5% to 10.2%, while UK will have reduced hers from 10% to 6%.

Not all the blame can be laid on the UK government, for the top firms in UK industry invest in R&D only half the average of the G7 nations, while the remainder are considerably worse as can be seen from Figure 18.

	No. of Companies	R&D Spend (£Bn)	R&D as % of sales
All of UK Companies	516	10.5	1.8
Top 19 UK Companies	19	6.3	2.5
Top World 300 Companies	300	131.3	4.6
International	comparisons with G7	countries (ranked by	R&D spend)
USA	133	59.2	4.9
Japan	69	27.7	4.8
Germany	22	14.2	4.3
France	17	7.1	4.1
UK	19	6.3	2.5
Canada	2	2.5	10.8

Figure 18: International Comparisons of Industrial R&D Investment

(Source: Science, Engineering and Technology Statistics 1998, Cm 4006, July 1998, Table 4.13)

It seems, therefore, that we are being outspent by our main competitors. However, if we spend the smaller amount more effectively that will not matter. But do we?

Research and Technology Funding

> *Only a quarter of DERA's budget is spent on generating technology.*

MOD spends £900 million with DERA each year on 'research'. Of this, £250 million goes on test and evaluation of equipment and a further £200 million goes in support of projects in development in the Defence Procurement Agency. Of the remaining £450 million, half is spent on providing advice and carrying out concept studies, leaving only some £225 million per year (a quarter of DERA's budget) available for spending on generating technology. This is simply not enough. It is only 1% of the total defence budget: would it cause impossible budget difficulties if the figure was doubled or even trebled?

Technology Transfer and Pull-Through

The situation is made worse by the poor record on DERA's ability to transfer technology to industry and industry's failure to pull that technology and their own into winning projects.

MOD recognises that technology transfer is inadequate:

'While mechanisms such as collaboration, extramural research and DERA's strategic alignment initiative lead implicitly to a degree of technology transfer, they fall short of what is required..... customers of the research programme have been working with DERA and industry to develop a more formal means of measuring technology transfer.....'[107]

Measuring technology transfer may be useful but it is difficult; what is required is strong action to *improve* technology transfer but this seems unlikely from the output of the Technology Transfer Working Party. Yet it is fairly simple.

Technology can be effectively transferred only in the brain of a scientist or engineer who has been working on a particular technology research programme; it cannot be transferred satisfactorily by lectures, papers or drawings. This suggests that joint DERA-industry research teams should become the rule rather than the exception. There is a need, too, to pull in academia to these teams as well.

> Joint DERA-industry-academia research teams should become

The problem with joint MOD-industry-academia research teams and with pull-through into winning projects is caused primarily by the dogmatic pursuit of competition. Joint research is held to upset future level playing fields while DERA technology may well lose out in a competition to more mature (less risky) technology with a lesser performance, or US technology fronted by a UK firm. Unless the investment in technology generation is protected, if necessary by doing away with competition and mandating UK technology, the

107 MOD Technology Strategy (Issue 2), July 1997, paragraph 31

return on research investment will continue to drop and more reasons will be found to cut research funding.

An interesting light was thrown on this in the aftermath of the ASTOR win announcement:

'[Raytheon Systems Ltd] had been anticipating a request by MOD for it to accommodate Racal into its ASTOR team at the last moment. "We were surprised it never came," a Raytheon official told Jane's Defence Weekly. Racal had bid an advanced synthetic aperture radar/ moving target indicator (SAR/MTI) package, based on more than a decade's worth of UK-funded technology demonstration work, within the rival Lockheed Martin team bid.'[108]

Maybe there were good technical or contractual reasons. But this is the sort of issue which needs more sympathetic consideration.

Weaknesses in Defence Research

The main weaknesses in defence research have been described above and, in summary, are:

- Insufficient MOD investment in research and technology.
- Insufficient industrial investment in research and technology.
- Ineffective use of that small investment, through duplication of effort between DERA and industry.
- Ineffective use of that small investment through imbalance between the spend on technology generation and that on studies, test, evaluation and project advice.
- Inefficient technology transfer from DERA to industry.
- Minimal success in pulling through DERA technology into winning projects.

In any forward look, these are weaknesses that have to be addressed, yet the Strategic Defence Review, the Smart Procurement Initiative and the Future of DERA study, have all failed to do so.

---

[108] Jane's Defence Weekly, 23 June 1999, page 3

Strengths and Weaknesses of DERA

Most, if not all, of the weaknesses above lie in MOD rather than in DERA. DERA has to carry out its customers' requirements and it does so with its own strengths and weaknesses.

DERA Strengths	DERA Weaknesses
Expertise (sometimes world-class) in some	Declining expertise in many areas
areas	Declining technology generation activity
Knowledge of MOD customers	'Not Invented Here' syndrome
Wide technology information base	Lack of expertise in many areas
Dedication of staff	Bureaucracy
	Misunderstanding of technology transfer
	mechanisms

Some of these weaknesses could be overcome if firm action was taken by MOD to increase spending on technology generation and to set up joint MOD-industry-academia teams. Others such as the high bureacratic burden will need separate action.

The DERA PPP Proposal

The Strategic Defence Review set DERA on a Public Private Partnership (PPP) route to the future, though quite why it did so is nowhere explained and is now taken as the start-point: a 'given'.

Industry's views were ignored.

Unlike the Smart Procurement Initiative, where the openness with which it has been conducted is as welcome as it is radically different from former practice, the DERA PPP proposal has been conducted in a most unhealthy secrecy. Industry was 'consulted' in December 1998 and its views seemingly ignored. The old 'tick-in-the-box' mentality was working overtime.

It was not until the Spring of 1999, when industry began to smell a rat, that MOD gave anything away. By then it was a little late in that the list of options had been whittled down to a single proposal and had gone up for Ministerial approval. MOD had seemingly played a game with industry and was able to claim it had been fully consulted.

The proposal failed to address the weaknesses discussed above. What it did do was to set in concrete the low and declining level of research funding and the imbalance in spend between technology generation and project advice. What it did not do was to provide a solid base for a future partnership with industry.

The PPP proposal would create a 'special purpose corporate vehicle containing most of DERA's existing staff and facilities'[109] operating in the private sector with 'mechanisms to preserve its essential character and to protect MOD's interests.'[110]

MOD Customer Needs

MOD laid down the 'eight commandments' which DERA would be required to meet and these are shown in Figure 19.

> *Privatisation is likely to subvert MOD's 'Eight Commandments'.*

Privatisation is likely to undermine impartiality (the ability to provide impartial advice has for long been a raison d'etre for the research establishments), to make collaboration with industry and with foreign government research organisations more difficult, to close some sources of scientific knowledge and to resist the maintenance of facilities without a firm business case, whether or not required by MOD. Privatisation is likely, therefore, to subvert the achievement of the first seven of the 'eight commandments'.

MOD's 'Golden Share'

The proposal invests MOD with a 'Golden Share' which will enable MOD to enforce its own interests and to interfere in the running of the privatised DERA, such as:

- Approval of Board appointments.
- Veto over business which conflicts with MOD's interests.

---

[109] UK MOD Consultation Document, *A Public Private Partnership for the Defence Evaluation and Research Agency*, May 1999

[110] Ibid

MOD STATEMENT OF CUSTOMER NEEDS[111]

1. To provide timely, impartial scientific[112] and technological advice to MOD on policy and on the options for the future equipment programme, through a structured programme of operational analysis, research and technical demonstration.
2. To provide timely impartial scientific and technological advice and professional services to the MOD and associated agencies[113] in support of the procurement, through-life support (including operational support) and disposal of equipment, for example to assist in tender evaluation, acceptance and through the provision of specialist test and evaluation capability.
3. To maintain access to a comprehensive scientific and technological knowledge base at the required level of excellence, including a thorough understanding of science and technology world-wide with potential utility for defence.
4. To foster and develop collaboration with UK industry and academia to exploit commercial technology for defence purposes, to transfer technology to industry and to generate technology within industry for timely exploitation to deliver a battle-winning edge in military equipment.
5. To safeguard, undertake and develop international collaborative defence research activities most notably with the US Department of Defense and other close allies.
6. To provide and maintain up to date any strategic capabilities or facilities required by MOD.
7. To operate, and be seen to operate, with unimpeachable integrity and at the highest security standards (to meet the most stringent needs of Government business), and to be accepted by third parties as formal representatives of the MOD.
8. To deliver continuous improvement in agility, responsiveness, innovation, price and quality with customer/supplier relationships based on best practice.

Figure 19: The 'Eight Commandments'

- Right of audit.
- Inspection of finances.
- Protection of industrial interests, including IPR.

MOD will have a powerful, possibly too powerful, voice in the running of a private concern and will have many strong conflicts of interest. The outcome is likely to be one of the following:

EITHER A depressing effect on the financial viability of a privatised DERA

OR Erosion of the 'Eight Commandments'

Neither would seem to be a recipe for success.

Opposition to the PPP Proposal

Opposition to the PPP Proposal for DERA has been strong and, slightly late in the day, vociferous. Industry is almost wholly opposed to any further commercialisation of DERA as the Defence Manufacturers Association makes clear in its conclusions:[114]

'The DERA PPP as proposed is a high risk option. Industry's concerns over IPR issues and over DERA PPP as a competitor could damage existing DERA/Industry relationships. Existing conflicts of interest between DERA's role of impartial advisor to MOD and its position as a trading fund would be exacerbated under PPP.'

Another view from industry suggests that:

'PPP would provide overseas companies with greater opportunity to team with DERA, which would have the effect gradually of excluding British industry from MOD funded research.'

Many within the MOD customer organisations feel that privatisation will erode their control over the meeting of their research requirements. There is, too, considerable opposition to it from within the scientific community, including DERA.

---

[111] Ibid

[112] Scientific embraces science and operational analysis

[113] Agencies includes other Government departments and their agencies

[114] Comments by DMA on the DERA PPP Proposal, 25 June 1999

'In my opinion, the option outlined in the PPP consultative documents would, in the longer term, seriously impede DERA from meeting or supporting MOD's and UK's defence needs..... the concept of impartiality is incompatible with a private sector company..... the ability of DERA to undertake 'complex' research would be compromised..... restrictions would produce a semi-private DERA, hamstrung by draconian rules preventing it from winning business.....'[115]

And the concern extends to Parliament, where the Shadow Defence Minister said:

'The UK is highly dependent on access to United States technology and, to a lesser extent, to French technology. It is essential that future changes at DERA do not jeopardise that access. The USA and France retain their research programmes in Government-owned facilities. Of course they will be concerned about allowing access to their research for commercial enterprises. If access is denied, there will be a penalty out of all proportion to the short-term financial gain.'[116]

Opposition is based on the following beliefs:

- Competition with a privatised DERA will be difficult if DERA retains its role of giving impartial advice on competitive technical solutions, particularly when DERA is part of one of the teams.
- Exploitation of IPR, some of which has been paid for by industry, will give DERA a winning, and unfair, edge.
- Extramural contracts may be reduced, particularly in areas that are lucrative or have long-term prospects.
- MOD will back maximisation of dividend rather than protect the 'Eight Commandments'.
- Important but unattractive research will either not be done, or be hugely overpriced if DERA is the only bidder.

---

[115] Colin Skelton, CBD Porton Down, letter in DERA News, July 1999, page 14

[116] Hansard, Volume 330, No 76, 26 April 1999, page 67

- Cooperation in research between DERA and industry will become more difficult.
- DERA, with its large bureaucratic overhead, could fail to win enough business to remain viable, unless supported financially, or quasi-financially, by MOD thus making the competitive playing field between DERA and industry even more tilted.
- The 'Golden Share' concept might be illegal.
- The compliance regime will be ineffective.
- In the longer term, takeover of DERA or its component parts by one or more large defence companies.

As a result of the now strong opposition, the PPP proposal seems to be on hold.

A PPP Proposal from Industry

Industry has now begun to develop an alternative proposal for the privatisation of DERA, which would retain around 2000 DERA personnel within MOD to provide independent and impartial advisors to IPT leaders on equipment selection, procurement and support, while the remainder of DERA would be established as a private sector enterprise, with private sector shareholders and a MOD 'Golden Share'. Unfortunately, this just tinkers with the unacceptable MOD PPP proposal and is equally unacceptable for the following reasons:

- To provide expert advice, scientists must carry out research themselves and not just read about it. Separation of the advice and the research functions would very quickly produce inexpert advice in-house.
- DERA research would be carried out in the private sector, and other countries (notably US and France) might well withdraw access for a privatised DERA to their research programme and facilities.
- The viability of a privatised DERA would be threatened by the lack of a considerable part of current income (depending upon what stays, anything between a quarter and a half; and more if

the competed research programme does not result in a very high proportion of DERA wins).

- This proposed split would do no more than the MOD proposal to ensure that the delivery of the 'Eight Commandments' was not eroded.

This is enough to condemn this proposal as a potential disaster, just like the MOD PPP proposal.

Competing the Research Programme

MOD is working on plans to introduce competition for work packages under the Applied Research Programme (ARP) and the Corporate Research Programme (CRP), and is aiming for a trial in 2001/2002. MOD has published on its website a list of potential projects (less than 5% of the total annual defence research programme) for competition in its pilot scheme, and states that:

> *'Research competition is seen as a way for MOD to enhance access to the widest possible body of knowledge. The pilot exercise offers a genuine opportunity for both industry and academia to participate in MOD's research programme, and may be the first step towards an increased use of primary competition for research in future years.'*

This seems like good news for industry, which has been pressing for a greater share of the research funds cake. But is it good news for DERA and MOD. Yes, say some, as it will drive down costs in DERA which are generally reckoned to be too high, largely because of MOD-imposed bureaucracy and unprofitable requirements. But if its costs are too high, will DERA win competitions for the most profitable research work? And if it does not, what then? If DERA needs changing, it is a bit drastic to throw it to the wolves: we cannot go and buy another one.

DERA needs changing, but not destroying. Nor should we take unnecessary risks with its future. DERA needs our support. A government-owned research is vital for the defence community. What to do?

An Alternative Future for DERA

Ministers now need to revise their edict that DERA is to become a Public Private Partnership although there is no need for them to change their ruling that the status quo is not an option. The status quo, with its downward spiral of research spending, its bureacracy, its high costs, its inefficient pull-through of technology into winning projects and its worsening relationship between DERA and industry, is indeed not an option. But that does not mean that ditching the status quo means PPP. There is considerable opinion that the best way forward is for DERA to remain almost a wholly Government-owned agency but with some major modifications to policy:

DERA should remain a Government-owned agency.

- Restoration of adequate research funding.
- Instigation of a true research and technology partnership with industry and academia, including joint research teams in all areas as the rule.
- Formation of a joint MOD-industry-academia research strategy.
- Instigation of mechanisms for the maximisation of pull-through of MOD funded technology to winning projects, including the modification of competition policy where necessary
- PPP of some or all of the DERA test and evaluation facilities.

Similar recommendations were made by the Defence Industries Council in October 1997[117] and the very title – Strength Through Partnerships – suggests a way forward that is in tune with Smart Procurement, rather than the PPP proposal which is in direct conflict with it.

'These measures could transform defence technology in this country. First, DERA would become more and more attractive as a potential collaborative partner for US and European research agencies .... Secondly, industry would be in a much stronger position to win

---

[117] *Strength Through Partnerships,* DIC input to the Strategic Defence Review, October 1997

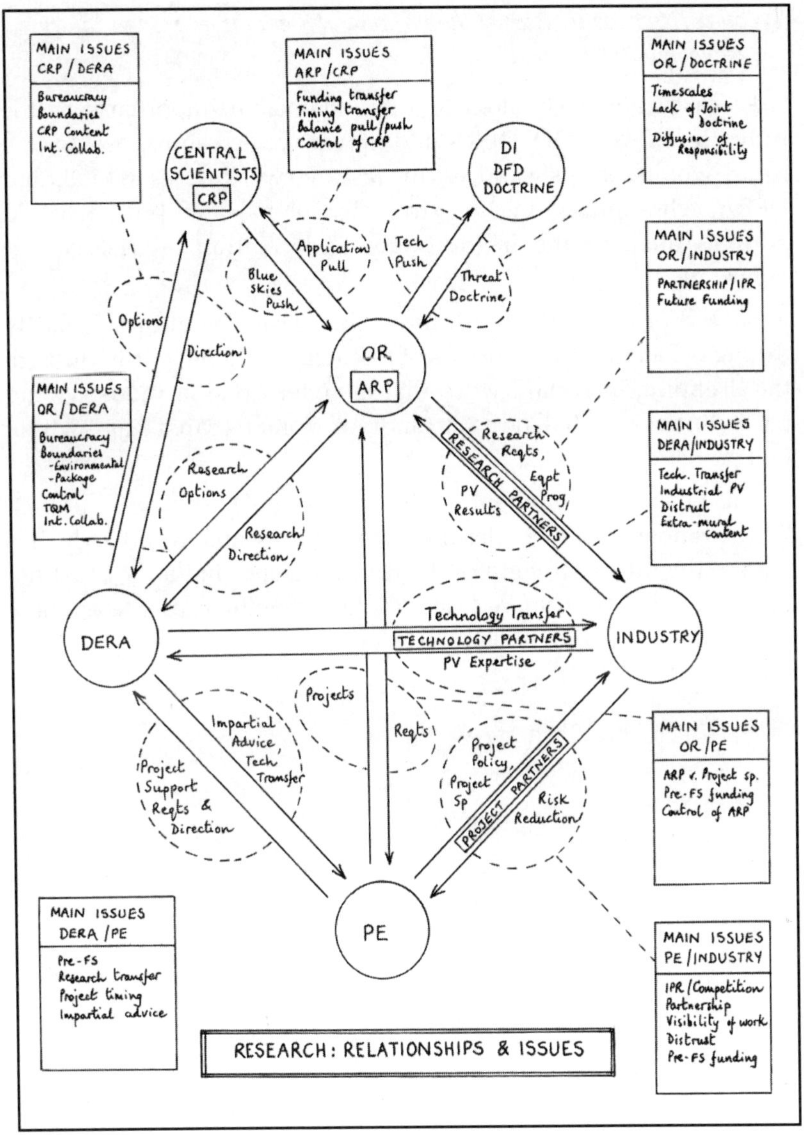

Figure 20. Research: Relationships and Issues

competitive contracts at home and abroad on the basis of the technology it develops.'[118]

Research and technology is of fundamental importance to the future health of MOD, DERA and industry. Such a proposal for the future would seriously address the research weaknesses in MOD and DERA, while preserving the strengths; at the same time it would address most of the major issues and relationships shown at Figure 20.

Such a proposal for the future could easily be afforded, partly through changing the priorities of research spending, partly through the dropping of certain work that is better done in industry, and partly through partial industry funding of joint research teams within DERA.

But it needs commitment on the part of MOD itself: without that, DERA cannot survive under this plan. Our research future, which is vital to the future strength of the British defence industry, must not fall victim to ill-considered dogma. In the opinion of one eminent scientist, the situation is 'close to terminal'.

---

[118] Further details of such an approach can be found in *It's Only R&D, but We Need It*, by Bill Kincaid, Defence Review, Winter 1998, pages 49-51

CHAPTER EIGHT

INTERNATIONAL COLLABORATION

The collapse of HORIZON, the tripartite common new generation frigate, was hardly a surprise after (or even before) the Joint Venture's final proposal came in 20% over budget with an in-service date a minimum of two years late for UK requirements. Secretary of State for Defence, George Robertson, commented:

> *'International procurement must follow the same logic as national procurement – defence can only afford projects which are delivered cost-effectively and on time.'*[119]

Collaboration within Europe

Collaboration with other European governments has not hitherto been particularly successful in terms of delivery within budget or, particularly, on time. There are clear reasons, some of which are:

- Lack of harmony in the military requirement.
- Lack of coincident time schedules and in-service dates.
- Difficulty in balancing international workshare.
- Differences in approach to the procurement process, particularly competition.

While the first two can be overcome with dedicated effort and the passage of a generation or two, and while the third is tending to disappear (or at least to assume less importance), the last has been a major issue since the Levene doctrine took strong hold in UK. Now, just when competition appears to have become a real possibility within Europe, Smart Procurement moves the collaborative goalposts yet again.

---

[119] *UK Breaks up Horizon Consortium*, Military Procurement International, 1999

It is not as if UK has been right all along. Some elements of Smart Procurement, such as partnership with industry, actually turn back on the previous competitive, adversarial stance taken by UK and which UK attempted to force down European throats with greater success in some countries than in others. Now we want partnership with industry. The French will claim they have been in partnership with industry all along.

The French will claim they have been in partnership with industry all along.

Smart Procurement and Europe

Smart Procurement cannot be exported lock, stock and barrel to our European collaborative partners, at least not in the short term. Yes, they are interested, but who would not be interested in a system that promises major savings? The UK government, then, has a dilemma. On the one hand, it can refuse to enter into, or break up existing, collaborative ventures such as HORIZON, on the basis of value for money: as a UK Ministry of Defence spokesman put it when the HORIZON announcement was made:

> *'We considered the risks of the project slipping and cost overruns too great. We decided that the industrial structure of the arrangement was not right and did not offer a value-for-money solution. Unfortunately, in this case, collaboration was not the way to go forward.'*

Yet it had been considered the way forward for more than a decade. So what was new? Two things:

- Smart Procurement with its driving concern to reduce cost overruns and delays.
- Political brinkmanship: the project was allowed to run on under successive Administrations until cancellation, if it was to be made, could no longer be delayed.

Cancellation was inevitable for 'we have always accepted that British Warships will be built in British yards.'[120] Despite assurances

---

[120] Hansard Vol.330, No.76, 26 April 1999, Oral Answers, page 51

to the contrary, the UK government (like its predecessors) has not renounced its interest in workshare.

So on the one hand we have a desire for value for money, limits on cost and time overruns and, in some areas, an (outdated?) concern for workshare. On the other hand, we have a government keen to be operating at the heart of Europe and to be seen as doing so. Nowhere more so, perhaps, than in defence equipment. This government needs European collaboration to reinforce its European credibility.

But these two policies conflict. Collaboration within Europe (with very few exceptions) has been spectacularly unsuccessful. Where is the common tank, or even different tanks which can fire the same ammunition? Ditto small arms. Ditto ships. Ditto surface to air missiles. Ditto missiles of all sorts. Ditto, above all, communications. Yes, there have been a couple of aircraft and, yes, artillery can fire most of each other's (mainly US) ammunition.

> *Collaboration with Europe has been spectacularly unsuccessful.*

Even the tripartite guided anti-tank missile (TRIGAT), to which UK is committed now in the medium range version, is undermined in value for money terms by the huge development spend on the long range version which UK wasted when it pulled out many years ago; we are still paying for development of a system that we are not going to buy.

It is not a happy story, even before considering MRAV, HORIZON, TriMilSat......... Add to taste.

Cost overruns and major time delays have been endemic. Smart Procurement is based firmly on eliminating procurement cost and time overruns, so how can it succeed overall if collaborative projects (which are predicted to increase to 40% of all equipment projects) do not become 'smart' in the near future?

> *How can Smart Procurement succeed if collaboration is not 'smart'?*

It is a major dilemma and not surprisingly the Smart Procurement leaders have not addressed it publicly, except in a low key way to state some, but not all, of the issues:[121]

- Advantages – UK more flexible over trading-off time, cost and performance.
  – Partnering with industry closer to European style than previous arms-length approach.
- Challenges – Tough external targets will make UK less ready to accept risk of overruns.
  – International standards/methods needed.

OCCAR

The Organisation for Joint Armaments Cooperation, OCCAR, was established in 1996 by France, Germany, Italy and UK (Netherlands is about to join) and will have legal status by 1 January 2000. It exists to manage collaborative European programmes under five principles:

- Cost Effectiveness.
- Harmonisation of requirements and technology.
- Maintenance of a competitive industrial base.
- Renunciation of 'Juste Retour'.
- Open to other European nations.

So far around 15 programmes have been allocated to OCCAR, but only four have UK participation: the weapon locating radar COBRA, the medium range anti-tank missile MR-TRIGAT, the multi-role armoured vehicle MRAV and the surviving air defence missile element of the defunct HORIZON programme, PAAMS.

The OCCAR procurement principles would appear to be concordant with Smart Procurement:

- A flexible approach to management.
- Autonomous programme teams.
- Simplified approvals.

[121] Slide, Smart Procurement Implementation presentation, Simon Webb, MOD/DMA Seminar, Didcot, 24 June 1999

- Clearer identification of the customer.
- A through-life approach.
- Fuller planning [funding?] in early programme stages.
- Personnel are a primary resource.

So that's alright then. Or is it? These 'principles' are as yet just good tags. What do they mean to the other nations? What are the expectations and targets? It is too early to say. There is, however, one big cloud on the horizon. Although the aim is to run OCCAR as a business and not a multi-Government organisation, the Board consists of the National Armament Directors of the participating nations. That seems to have the potential to sink OCCAR.

The question is: if projects with a UK participation in OCCAR are seen to be overrunning in time and cost, what will the UK do? There will be a strong (perhaps irresistable?) urge to interfere. If this is resisted, there will be an equally strong urge to pull out, as has happened with HORIZON. UK, with its record of collaboration with US and its history of pulling out of European projects, is already seen as a weak collaborative partner in Europe, and further defaulting will be politically difficult.

The hope must be that OCCAR exceeds public expectations (which are low, because of the poor performances of the previous multinational, slow-moving project offices) by a very great margin.

Collaboration with US

The history of collaborative government ventures with US has hardly been much better, if we disregard the many successful ventures in which we have bought US equipment largely off-the-shelf or bought in to the later stages of development and production. The story of the terminally guided warhead (TGW) for the multiple launch rocket system (MLRS) is a good illustration of one of the difficulties of international collaboration. The MLRS TGW programme, after a slow start, was a great success despite significant re-design and programme re-scheduling as a result of a major change in the Soviet armoured threat. The final prototype test, a single round which went through the complete launch, dispense, target acquisition and target hit process, was outstandingly successful. But, by then, the US had withdrawn in favour of one of their own 'black' programmes. The project collapsed.

But the main problem with collaborating with the US is that of size imbalance. A single European nation will inevitably have a tiny off-take compared with US. Not surprisingly, US expects to dominate the programme and to have a complete assembly line in the US. If you pay comparative peanuts, you'll buy a small share.

Is Government Collaboration Attractive?

Inter-Government equipment collaboration has had a pretty disastrous history, whether it has been the failure of the massive NATO Armaments Group organisation to carry through NATO projects, or of the multi-national project offices to limit time and cost-overruns, or of attempts to agree a joint European procurement policy with each of the leading nations allocated areas of expertise. OCCAR may not follow in this long line of failure, but it is difficult to be sanguine.

So should Governments collaborate? The usual answer given is yes, because we cannot afford to go it alone. That is patently untrue in the case of MRAV, and is likely to be untrue in many other cases: if we can go it alone on a frigate, we can afford to go it alone on most things. In any case, is collaboration between governements cheaper than national procurements? Where are the figures?

Another answer, although less often articulated, is the technology aspect. In some cases we no longer have the technological ability to design and build the whole system; in others, we need access to newer technology (principally US) for performance and cost advantage.

But the real answer, articulated normally only by military users, not procurement managers, is for one very good reason: interoperability. If the future reality of warfare is operational collaboration between Western forces, whether under the UN, or as NATO or in a US-led coalition, then the value of being able to fire one another's ammunition, to have weapons platforms repaired by another nation's workshop, or to share spares depots is an overwhelming requirement. Anything else means colossal added expense.

So we need Government collaboration, but in what way? A general view would be to harmonise requirements. But the NATO Armaments Groups have been attempting this for decades with relatively little success: the projects it starts either collapse after the early stages or are replaced when major nations pull out to pursue bi-, tri-, or multi-lateral projects which in turn frequently fail because the requirements have not been adequately harmonised.

Despite this, collaboration has been and still is a popular theme, at least with Ministers. Why? For a number of reasons, mainly through the perception of the potential advantages. Those advantages, and the disadvantages, were compared by the National Audit Office[122] with those for other procurement routes and this comparison is shown in Figure 21.

These advantages and disadvantages do not tell the whole story, though. In particular, costs of collaborative procurement are inevitably higher, but the supposed cost reductions through economies of scale are usually derailed by overt or covert workshare pursuit, and by duplication of integration lines.

So, if collaboration is not cheaper, we certainly do not want the disadvantages of Government collaboration in the later procurement process. Now that the defence industry is becoming more and more global, why can't each government place its own contract with a prime? Once a prime has a contract with one government, it will be in a strong position to win contracts with several other governments to provide the same, or similar, equipment. If that prime is good enough, it will offer what is wanted at a low price taking advantage of economy of scale.

---

[122] National Audit Office Report: *MOD Defence Procurement in the 1990s,* 20 May 1994, Figure 5

Route	Advantages	Disadvantages
National Development	Control over specifications	Very high costs likely for major platforms
	Control over timescale	Developing a weapon from scratch as opposed to buying off-the-shelf carries greater programme and cost risk.
	Ability to impose UK contractual practices	
		Lack of commonality with NATO allies
	Possibility of overseas sales	
Collaborative Development	Commonality with NATO allies	Risk of compromising on specifications
	Economies on in-service support	Risk of delays through problems in partner nations
	Can lead to net inflow of technology	Difficulties in imposing UK contractual practice
	Cheaper through economies of scale	Imposition of workshare can inflate costs
		May result in net outflow of technology
Individual off-the-shelf	Much cheaper than funding development	Equipment may not meet requirement
	Equipment is proven when purchased	Costly customisation of equipment
	Control over timescale	
	Ability to impose UK contract practice	
Collaborative off-the-shelf	Cheapest owing to economies of scale	Risk of compromising on specifications
	Enhance interoperability with allies	Risk of delays through problems in partner nations
	Cheaper than development options	Difficult to impose UK contractual practices
	Can lead to net inflow of technology	Equipment may not meet the requirement
		Costly customisation of equipment

Figure 21. Comparison of Main Procurement Routes

The Government Collaborative Requirement

What Governments must do is to tackle the interoperability issue. They must agree on the main parameters and enforce them. So far that has happened rarely, although agreement by France, Germany, UK and US on artillery calibre and ballistics has paved the way for true interoperability of artillery ammunition. There are different degrees of interoperability and this can help the process:

- Ammunition interoperability, where one nation can fire another's ammunition from its own guns. This has been successful with artillery ammunitions, but not with tank rounds or small arms bullets.
- Spares and components interoperability, when components can be supplied to one nation from another's resupply organisation.
- Equipment similarity or commonality, when one nation's equipment can be repaired by another nation's workshop.

These are important enough, but even more crucial is the ability to communicate with each other, and to share data, strategic mobility and logistic support. Thus, the most important form of interoperability is:

- Interoperability in enabling technology such as C41, rapid air mobility and logistics.

If Governments agreed interoperability guidelines in all capability areas, they could leave individual nations and industry to procure what they wanted within these guidelines, without the huge and largely unsuccessful effort that currently goes into harmonising requirements, procurement processes, timescales, and contracts.

> *If governments agreed interoperability guidelines, each nation could procure what it wanted.*

This is exactly what is happening with the Conventionally Armed Stand-Off Missile (CASOM). MOD had a requirement which went to competition and was won by Storm Shadow. The French Air Force had a similar requirement and their selected Scalp EG missile is identical to Storm Shadow. Now, both missiles are being produced by Matra-BAe to a merged specification, combining the best features of each requirement. Each country has its own project office and is managing its own project independently. Purchase of the same missile by the two countries brings longer production runs, and should mean lower support costs in service.

The IPT leader said:

> *'the programme had set a new template for international co-operation which did not involve the bureaucracy and complex decision-making processes inherent in traditional collaborative projects.'*[123]

If such processes were to become the norm, the major Western nations within a relatively short time (perhaps 20 years), would be interoperable to a much greater extent and industry would be able to provide cheaper equipment through longer production runs.

Governments' role in collaborative procurement has been one of unnecessary, expensive and unsuccessful control. We need to get rid of the control freaks.

Smart Procurement Export

Not surprisingly, MOD is looking to export its Smart Procurement principles. Certainly, it has aroused interest throughout Europe and in many other parts of the world. But this does not mean those principles will be adopted overnight, or even in the next decade.

Exporting Smart Procurement to the US is unnecessary for it has many similarities with US Acquisition Reform which has been in place for some years, although there are numerous Americans who will criticise its implementation. Nevertheless, results which are quoted are impressive. We have little to teach the US.

Exporting Smart Procurement to Europe will be difficult, particularly to France, with its state-owned industries and its antipathy to true competition, and also to Germany with its close relationship with France and the large number of Franco-German

---

[123] *Preview*, Journal of the Defence Procurement Agency, No 59, 1 April 1999, page 17

programmes. So Smart Procurement can only be exported to Europe, if at all, over a long period. If collaborative programmes do rise to 40% of UK programmes as is forecast by Ministers, the gains made by Smart Procurement in national programmes could be wiped out by cost overruns in collaborative programmes in Europe. This will discredit Smart Procurement and leave a major hole in the savings targets that are an essential part of future defence funding.

Smart Procurement, Collaboration and Interoperability

It seems we can do one of three things if collaboration is not to undermine, or even sink, Smart Procurement:

- Hope OCCAR will work and do nothing.
- Reduce, rather than increase, collaboration with European governments and accept the political penalty.
- Pull out of all further 1980s style government collaboration and concentrate on agreeing interoperability guidelines internationally, while leaving procurement to individual nations with global defence companies.

The third seems to me to be the only practical path. It will bring both cheaper equipment and true battlefield interoperability. Oh, and it will save Smart Procurement.

CHAPTER NINE

SMART PEOPLE AND MOD CULTURE

The need for a major change of culture within the Ministry to make Smart Procurement work has been recognised from the beginning by Ministers and, rather more slowly, by senior officials and officers. A move to proper accountability which is *the* fundamental issue was signalled quite clearly by the Under Secretary of State for Defence very early:[124]

> *'I am not going to accept a situation where no-one is accountable or accepts authority. I want people to have the confidence and authority to do the job and to be clear who is worthy of praise or blame for the outcome.'*

Such a move is indeed a major step forward and is one of the most heartening features of the Smart Procurement Initiative; or will be, if delivered. This caveat is essential because such a change will be difficult to implement and will take many years.

A Start

But a start has been made. Early on, the delegated financial authority levels were increased dramatically:

Category	Procurement Cost	Approving Authorities
A	Above £400M	EAC, then Ministers
B	£100M to £400M	2* group
C	£20M to £100M	1* group

[124] John Spellar, Under Secretary of State for Defence, to a RUSI Seminar on Smart Procurement, 29 January 1998

Regrettably this is partly undermined by the direction that Ministers would have visibility of all submissions with procurement costs over £50M. Apart from the potential for high level interference, this sends quite the wrong signals on the determination to introduce a new culture.

A second move has been the delegation of greater authority to Integrated Project Team (IPT) Leaders and they have responded with initiative and vigour:

> *'The initiative will not succeed unless we change the culture and our people respond to the circumstances we create for them. In the pilots, they did. We have begun to see a culture change in this relatively small group of staff. Our challenge now, and I accept it is a heavy one, is to spread this success throughout ..... the acquisition function and beyond to the rest of the Ministry of Defence. We need to become more flexible, responsive and receptive to new ideas. We need to depend less upon rule books or precedent and more on judgement and experience.'*[125]

Delegation of authority to any significant degree is a courageous decision. It can only be done if those at the top accept that mistakes will be made. The adverse effects of those mistakes can be large, including:

- Exposure of Ministers to embarrassment.
- Inquisition of senior officers and officials by Select Committees.
- Closure of factories and loss of jobs.
- Delay.
- Cost escalation.
- Performance shortfalls in equipment.

But all this happens now with our stifling scrutiny. Can anyone say that delegation of authority will make things worse?

There will, however, be loud calls from all over the place (the media, Parliamentary committees, Treasury officials, the National Audit Office, senior officials in MOD etc) to improve oversight of those making the decisions. It will be tough to oppose these calls. But

---

[125] John Spellar, Under Secretary of State for Defence, RUSI Journal, Vol.144, No.3, June 1999

> *Delegation will then be no more than fancy labelling.*

if Ministers do not stand firm, delegation of authority will be hedged around with more and more checks until it will cease to be anything more than empty labelling.

Of course delegation of authority must be qualified; the trick is to balance the one with the other. Difficult. The good start must not be dissipated.

Implications of the Culture Change

Most people now accept (or at least appear to accept) that such a culture change is necessary. But accepting the need is only the first step, for implementation will depend on two things:

- Creation of a new culture of accountability, including the true delegation of authority (including financial and contractual authority) to those at the working level.
- Development and selection of individuals with the requisite personal qualities, experience and expertise.

> *Officials who believe decision-shelving is more important than decision-making.*

The culture of the consensus committee and the rule book that has existed for decades (centuries?) has developed a type of official who believes that decision-shelving is more important than decision-making, that delay saves money, that initiative is dangerous, that individuals with huge responsibility cannot be trusted to make relatively low-level decisions.

The new culture is almost the diametric opposite, where an Integrated Project Team (IPT) Leader (say Grade 7/Lieutenant Colonel equivalent) becomes accountable for delivering a project within laid-down cost, time and performance parameters and **is given the authority to do so.** He will be expected to make decisions and implement them; to manage his team and motivate them; to think radically about possible programme changes and to make trade-offs within the given parameters; and, finally, to deliver his project within the set parameters at each acquisition stage. And all this, with little reference to higher authority.

This is indeed a challenge to the individual, but it can be done. BP's Andrew Platform integrated management team,

> *'sought to create an environment which encouraged people to come forward with ideas and question proposals in the knowledge that there would be no adverse reaction, no threat to their security on the team. As people realised they were able to behave openly and that Andrew was not constrained by traditional client-contractor hierarchies, their desire to contribute came to the fore – contribution was their ticket, their entitlement to be on the team. This led to a sense of shared ownership of the project which fired their enthusiasm to participate even more. A culture soon developed where people set their own targets and then sought ways to improve on them still further; once success followed, it became a habit.'*[126]

Many of the existing dyed-in-the-wool stately dancers will find it difficult, if not impossible, to make such a major change, and it is depressing to hear how many in acquisition jobs say there is no way they would want to be an IPT leader, which should surely be the plum post for all to aim at. But accountability scares them. If these people amount to 10% of the total, then MOD will not have a problem as they will just waste away. But if the proportion is much higher (say 50%), then they will have to play a major part in Smart Procurement and will have to be changed, or failure is inevitable.

It is depressing, too, to hear an increasing number of people say that greater accountability will actually hinder decision-making. Depressing, perhaps, but not really surprising when accountability has been portrayed by some very senior people as an exercise in getting 'hands round necks'. That surely is part of it, but not the principal part; and it is certainly not a motivating part.

---

[126] *No Business as Usual, an Extraordinary North Sea Result,* by Terry Knott, 1996

There are other people, though, who will welcome the new atmosphere as an elixir of life, transmuting the base metal of the old (dumb?) procurement to the new smart procurement. Some of these will even thrive.

> Others will welcome the new atmosphere as an elixir of life.

But a process or a system is not satisfactory if it can only be made to work by the most able. It must be capable of efficient operation by 90% to 95% of the staff available (the other 5% to 10% will have to be 'retired'), and that means the average or even below-average person must be able to work it. At the moment this would appear unlikely. We need a new breed of 'Smart People'.

Smart People

There is a widespread feeling throughout the defence industry, and to a certain extent within the Ministry of Defence itself, that the average individual in MOD's acquisition chain is of too low a quality to make this change of culture effective.

> *'We have no way of measuring our own performance. How can we call ourselves professional?' A MOD project manager.*

> *'Dealing with certain MOD areas is rather like dealing with Orderly Room clerks.' An ex-military executive in a UK company.*

> *'People are of variable quality in MOD: they are particularly good at project manager level, but particularly poor at desk level.' A manager in a small UK company.*

The last quotation suggests that there is at least some quality in MOD. But it also suggests that some people grow into authority, but very slowly. This is reinforced by the views of an IPT Leader:[127]

> *'I think IPTs will help unlock some of what I believe is a largely untapped resource within MOD – the innovative potential of the*

---

[127] David Brewerton, GBAD IPT Leader, *Preview*, the Journal of the Defence Procurement Agency, No 59, 1 April 1999, page 33

Department's own staff. We need to unlock that talent and create an environment in which it can flourish. I want to develop an atmosphere in which constructive debate is encouraged. This will mean that we do not miss any good ideas and that everyone feels they 'own' the decisions taken.'

What is needed is a scheme to grow individuals more quickly and more certainly. In other words, we must find a way of ensuring that all individuals reach their full potential as quickly as possible. And those that do not measure up must be shown the door early, not left mouldering in dark corners.

So what does our Smart Person need if he is to make Smart Procurement work? He must have:

- The necessary personal qualities such as the ability to think clearly and innovatively; the decisiveness to make difficult decisions and implement them; the determination to deliver.
- The relevant background experience and knowledge gained through a clear career path, managed professionally by a central acquisition organisation.
- The optimal training programme throughout his career, both on-the-job and off-the-job training.

The Requirements 1: Personal Qualities

The most important aspect of Smart People is their innate personal qualities. We do not yet know how many of the existing MOD acquisition staff have the necessary qualities because they have yet to be tested in the new environment, but we can guess from what we have seen in the past. The gut feel is that too many will be found wanting at all levels, partly because the wrong people have been promoted in the past; that is, those who have made the fewest mistakes. This is particularly true, perhaps, in the administrative areas and in the military. As a result the best have gone elsewhere.

If this is so, we shall fairly quickly hit the inadequate level, well before the Wave 2, let alone the Wave 3, IPT leaders have been selected and their teams completed.

There is little that can be done to rectify this state of affairs immediately, but it is vital that urgent measures are put in hand now to reduce the difficulties that will be encountered over the next few years through a lack of the right calibre of person, and to eliminate them eventually. Measures to increase the proportion of staff with the most suitable personal qualities should include:

- Maximum recruitment from industry, including the civil sector. This will be expensive if it is to be successful as few industrialists of high calibre will see a five year stint in MOD as a career-enhancing path. They will have to be tempted financially.
- Increased recruitment of graduates, which again will need financial incentives.
- Improved internal recruiting with clearer career paths to the top for the most deserving, not for the decision-averse.

Recruiting from Industry

It will not be easy to lure the right people from industry. Successful industrialists at all levels will be planning their career and will wish to be free to change jobs at short notice to take advantage of market opportunities. Even if they stay put in one company, they will want to remain in the promotional eye. A move, of even short duration, to MOD will not normally be seen as attractive, either financially or career-wise. A permanent move will not be of interest without very strong financial inducement. Without such inducement, there is a clear danger that industrial recruits will be of the wrong sort.

The difficulty in recruiting from industry has been evident from the efforts by MOD to attract industrial candidates for IPT leader posts. One has been appointed as the team leader of the Future Carrier IPT, but the call for industrial candidates for the IPT leader of the Primary Casualty Receiving Ship had to be extended because of a lack of applicants. MOD has stated a goal of appointing eight IPT Leaders from industry in the Wave 3 IPT roll-out. It will be interesting to see what response is like, in both quantity and quality.

One immediate consequence is the realisation that the desired five year tenure is too long if industrial candidates are to be tempted. As CDP stated recently:

'To help increase the number of applicants [from industry] the tenure of the post needed to be relaxed to two or three years from the five originally planned.'[128]

Quality Versus Quantity

The measures will be financially difficult. However better quality should lead to lower manning levels: one quality individual could often do the job of three low-quality individuals, and do it better. Not only that, but the new streamlined procedures, together with delegation of authority to lower levels, must (if properly implemented) lead to less work overall. After all, two separate MOD studies found that a Project Manager spent 80% of his time NOT managing his project(s), because he was continually engaged on seeking permission from his superiors, consensus from his peers, and authority from the scrutineers.

The Requirements 2: Expertise and Experience

Two weaknesses that are too often evident today are a lack of relevant experience and a lack of expertise. While the best individuals may overcome both these weaknesses within months of assuming a job, the less able will take years. Either way, it is a huge burden to bear and largely an unnecessary one. And it is aggravated by the short time that individuals remain in post, so that it is tempting to skate over the surface and hide behind a mask of procrastination.

Two answers to this lack of expertise and experience would be:

- The creation of a coordinated approach to each individual's career, whether he be military, technical or non-technical.
- The prolongation of an individual's tenure of a post.

---

[128] *Preview,* the Journal of the Defence Procurement Agency, No.63, July 1999, page 18

It is therefore very welcome news that Smart Procurement includes both the extension of tenure to at least five years and also the creation of an Acquisition Stream.

The Requirements 3: Training

Personal qualities, expertise and experience are an excellent foundation, but cannot necessarily produce the finished article in most cases. Hence the need for a much improved system of acquisition training.

> *Currently, training is a hit-and-miss affair.*

Currently, training is a hit-and-miss affair, being carried out at different places under different authorities. Individuals do not always (perhaps only rarely) get the right courses at the right time, and those courses are often inadequate. For example, the National Audit Office has noted, in many of their reports, that better training is required in such areas as technical risk assessment, contracting, financial analysis and accounting.

Training does need to be improved, but so does the system of allotting individuals to courses. Too often, an individual cannot be spared once he has started the job, and cannot be released from his previous job early enough to do the necessary courses between jobs. Even when he can, particular courses that he may need are not being run at that date. On-the-job training should go some way towards compensating for missed or poor courses, but is generally very poor and learning from experience of others is almost non-existent.

Training is a lottery and losers have to find out too much for themselves, without an adequate hand-over period, while they are bedding down in a high pressure job. It is not surprising that so many take refuge in procrastination: it is their only hope of survival for many months, by which time it has become a way of life. Not only do those new in post not hit the ground running, they have to concentrate on not falling flat on their faces. It is only long experience that gives a person the necessary know-how.

Again it is heartening that these weaknesses are intended to be eliminated. But will they be?

The Acquisition Stream

The Strategic Defence Review announced in July 1998 the formation of a special,

> *'Acquisition Stream, encompassing military and civilian staff involved in the full spectrum of the defence procurement process, from the earliest stages of requirement formulation to the final disposal of obsolete equipment.'*[129]

This single Stream will therefore encompass those in the operational requirements and the logistics worlds as well as those in the Defence Procurement Agency (DPA), but not it seems the Defence Evaluation and Research Agency (DERA).

> *'The Acquisition Stream for both military and civilian staff has been created which features long-term sustainability, career paths and an endurable culture of change for all those involved in acquisition.'*[130]

Nothing about quality, you will notice. But perhaps this is implicit? Or perhaps it is not.

The Acquisition Stream comprises all those in acquisition posts. Individuals will often leave the Stream and return later to the Stream when they are posted into another acquisition post. Some, of course, will remain in the Stream for good. Thus, there is at all stages a sideways entry route into the Stream to ensure that the best man for the job can always be selected. Provided, that is, that he can first of all be identified and, secondly, that he is available and willing.

The sideways entry route into the Acquisition Stream is fine so long as there are good people wanting to rejoin from other parts of the MOD and the Armed Forces or wishing to come in from areas outside Government service (for example industry or academia). Empowerment and promotion in post are excellent lures, but they may not be enough to counter the inevitable lower pay compared to outside or the just as inevitable higher level of bureaucracy that will still exist however successfully Smart Procurement turns out.

---

[129] Strategic Defence Review, Supporting Essay Ten, Page 10-7, July 1998

[130] MOD's Acquisition Handbook, *A Guide to Smart Procurement*, Edition1, April 1999, page 25

Monetary incentives are not the answer, except for low level schemes, for they would be very costly if they were large enough; and if they were large enough, they would be dangerous because they:[131]

- Might threaten the UK tradition of virtually incorruptible military and civil services.
- Could distort priorities.
- Could be divisive with different criteria in different areas.
- Could tend to suppress bad news.
- Would be difficult to implement fairly over the long period of a project.

No, monetary incentives are not the answer. So what is? To persuade an industrialist to take risks with his future career, or a serviceman to forsake the delights of real soldiering, there must be a clear promotion path visible to both within the MOD acquisition stream.

Such a promotion path is partly in view with the different levels at which IPTs are managed, from Grade 7/lieutenant colonel equivalent to two-star. But is the pyramid the right shape, or is it just a reflection of the previous manning levels of the old Procurement Executive? The pyramid needs shaping to account for those in other acquisition areas, too.

So far the Acquisition Stream implementation has been slow although, now that a one-star individual has been placed in charge of it, things may speed up. But there are a few knotty issues to be unravelled, including:

- The Acquisition Stream is a virtual one as individuals do not leave the control of their own personnel authority; this suggests that is has no control of its own and can operate only with the consent of many other personnel authorities. A recipe for emasculation?

---

[131] Based on part of a presentation by Dr David Kirkpatrick, University College London, to the Defence Studies Course, Southampton University, 13 October 1999.

- Procurement jobs are not military 'command jobs', yet an IPT leader, of, say, one-star rank may well feel that his job is at least as complex and responsible as many one-star 'command' appointments. Should they so qualify?
- Promotion in post is a feature of Smart Procurement so that individuals are not penalised for longer tenures. Does this mean that only those already recommended for promotion in the future will be eligible for such a post? If so, will this reduce the number of starters? It seems that there will have to be a change in military procedure here.

Training Integration

At present, training is fragmented. Most of the Defence Procurement Agency (DPA) courses are run by the Defence Procurement Management Training (DPMT) organisation, managed jointly by MOD and Admiral, primarily for the benefit of those in the DPA. There are also courses at Shrivenham (the Royal Military College of Science and Cranfield University) which teach procurement, such as the Masters Degrees in Defence Management, Defence Logistics Management and Systems Engineering for Defence, as well as some short courses. And there are courses elsewhere, some of them long courses, with a procurement element, others short courses, some run by universities, some by commercial companies.

Training in the Defence Logistics Organisation is separate again, and not centralised at all as far as is apparent, with training responsibilities devolved to lower budget holders to be done 'internally'. Within the Equipment Support area, schools train against agreed Training Objectives, but are badly undermanned and under-resourced.

Industry, too, runs its own training schemes, some of them effective, some not. These are mostly not open to MOD or, if they are, are not used by MOD. Industry does, however, have some vacancies on certain MOD procurement courses.

So training is fragmented in MOD and is not, generally speaking, carried out jointly with industry.

But training is fundamental to the successful change in culture. There must be a strong case for pulling all the training together into one organisation run for, and jointly by, both MOD and industry. This organisation would be independent of single elements of procurement such as DPA:

> *Training is fundamental to a successful change in culture.*

- A single Joint Acquisition Training School should be established at Shrivenham, for all acquisition training of all in the Acquisition Stream.
- The School should be jointly funded by, and jointly staffed by, MOD and industry.
- The School's courses should cover all aspects of the whole acquisition cycle including capability management, procurement and in-service equipment management.
- All courses should be open to both MOD and industry employees and the aim should be to balance each course between the two.

In this way, joint training with industry will become a reality, which it is unlikely under current arrangements, with DPA making 'places available to industry on IPT members' training courses and on the Smart Procurement Roadshow.'[132]

Until true joint training becomes established, the appalling ignorance of each other that exists in MOD and industry will be perpetuated, to the detriment of both prospective partners. This will be explored further in Chapter 16.

Tenure in Post

One of the findings of the Smart Procurement Initiative was that individuals spent too short a time in post, on average only 2 to 3 years, although the best (both military and civilian) tended to move on even more quickly, while the worst survived longest. It was

[132] CDP to MOD/DMA Seminar on Smart Procurement as reported in Preview No.63 July 1999, page 18

envisaged that tenures would be extended to five years or more, hopefully covering the whole period from Initial Gate to Production, although that period now looks like lasting far longer than five years.

A longer tenure has three major advantages:

- There is a much smaller 'down time' while the individual learns both his job and his project at the start of his tour.
- The individual knows that he will have to live with the consequences of his decisions, rather than leaving them to his successor.
- The individual will get to know his colleagues in both MOD and industry much more clearly, and they will know him. There will be continuity.

But a longer tenure will impede his career, so promotion in post has become a key incentive. Quite how this will work, especially with military personnel, is not yet clear, especially if an officer runs for the post of IPT leader at a higher rank and gets it: what will this do to promotion quotas? The answers are still being worked out.

However, promotion in post is an essential incentive and a modus operandi for both military and civilians can surely be worked out. How sad, then, that there is a general feeling that promotion in post will not happen because of operating cost restrictions.

There is no doubt that longer tenures and promotion in post are essential and it is to be hoped that difficulties arising from them will not debilitate the force of their implementation. It is, therefore, most worrying that, at the first hurdle, it has happened; tenures being reduced back down to 2 or 3 years for industrial IPT Leaders.

Learning from Experience

The Jordan-Lee-Cawsey report of 1987, entitled 'Learning from Experience', recommended a systematic review of the performance of past projects to identify guidelines on best project management practices. This unfortunately was never

> *Learning from experience must be project manager friendly.*

effectively implemented with the result that, in the decade or more since, project managers have remained in ignorance of what their predecessors and current peers have learned. Where project managers have properly documented lessons (a rare occurrence), these reports have lain unread by, and inaccessible to, others.

Yet learning from experience should be a powerful tool for the management of any complex undertaking. There are two essentials:

- The full documentation of lessons as they happen, not at the end of the project when details are less clear and when the reasons for decisions largely forgotten.
- The dissemination of those lessons to all who may benefit from them.

Both are time-consuming and most individuals are time-deficient. The process must be project management friendly. A repeated call for reports and a general order to read reports in a central archive are not going to produce what is required.

What is needed is a small 'learning from experience' cell which is responsible for:

- Extracting lessons learned from project managers/IPT Leaders.
- Collating these lessons into an accessible format.
- Posting the results on the computer-based Acquisition Management System (AMS) which is now in existence.

The AMS does have a 'learning from experience' section and it is to be hoped that it will become a real management aid, rather than the poor relation it has been hitherto.

Learning from Mistakes

Learning from experience is only likely to be fully effective if individuals recognise that they can make mistakes without penalty, provided that the mistakes are not the result of incompetence or thoughtlessness. Until then, most people will hide mistakes and distort the lessons that can be learned.

> *If all mistakes are punished, individuals will become even more decision-averse.*

The existing MOD culture does not like mistakes but, without true accountability, the responsibility for those mistakes is never identified. However, as MOD edges closer to proper delegation of authority and true accountability, mistakes can be traced to one individual. If all mistakes are to be punished, individuals will become even more decision-averse. So it is encouraging that the Prime Minister has publicly recognised that mistakes must be allowed to be made:

> *'We shouldn't be afraid to take risks, even if that means risking failure. If we fail, we should learn from our mistakes. Because if we never make mistakes we'll never change anything. My idea of the ideal public servant is not someone who never fails, but someone who always tries to make a difference.'*[133]

A change of culture indeed.

More Speed, Less Haste

Smart Procurement cannot succeed without successfully changing MOD culture and developing 'smart people'. It is acknowledged that this will take a long time and will be very difficult to implement across the acquisition board. But Smart Procurement may fail if no early results can be clearly seen by those in MOD and industry, many of whom still believe that they have 'seen it all before' and that 'nothing can change'. Early wins are vital, and not just indications.

The major culture change required is only possible with continuous pressure from the top. A start has been made, but so far it is a small step along the road and has been made possible only by strong Ministerial leadership from, until recently, George Robertson, the Secretary of State for Defence, and from John Spellar, the Under Secretary of State for Defence. Now both have moved on and it remains to be seen whether this early pressure will be maintained.

If it is not maintained, culture change is likely to falter and the whole Smart Procurement Initiative undermined. While a start has

---

[133] Quoted by John Spellar, Under Secretary of State for Defence, RUSI Journal, Vol.144, No.3, June 1999, page 75

been made, the step forward is as yet small and, largely, unperceived by the majority. One swallow does not make a summer.

The Smart Procurement summer desperately needs more swallows before individuals believe it has arrived. But the swallows will take their time in arriving. It would be unwise to produce plastic swallows: that is, to neglect the reality for the superficial. Culture change will be slow; it must sit on firm foundations.

> *It would be unwise to neglect the reality for the superficial.*

CHAPTER TEN

WHAT'S IT LIKE SO FAR?

It is now more than two years since the Smart Procurement Initiative was announced by the Secretary of State for Defence when he appeared before the House of Commons Defence Committee in July 1997:

> *'I am therefore launching a major initiative to try and eliminate the kind of cost overruns and delays that have characterised some equipment projects in the past..... So we are looking for 'smart procurement'.*[134]

Regrettably very little was achieved in the following 14 months. True, there was the McKinsey study but that only confirmed what we all knew and what many had been saying for some time. Much of it followed the logic of *A Dinosaur in Whitehall*[135], which it had to do if it was to propose anything with any credibility: the problems were obvious, the options for resolution fairly tightly constrained.

Since the Implementation Team set to work in September 1998, things have speeded up, at least in some areas where some very real progress has been made. But elsewhere there is less (in some places almost non-existent) evidence of headway and, until Smart Procurement begins the advance right across the board, these salients in the enemy territory of old MOD culture are vulnerable to counter-attack or, more probably, to slow expiration through lack of support.

---

[134] House of Commons Defence Committee, *Strategic Defence Review*, Eighth Report 1997/8, Vol.1, 3 September 1998, paragraph 333

[135] *A Dinosaur in Whitehall* by Bill Kincaid, Brassey's, September 1997

Expectations

Progress cannot be hurried too much without skimping on the design of the foundations. Yet Smart Procurement must be seen to be making a difference sooner rather than later, if credibility is to be maintained. Many feel that so little progress has been made in two years that nothing is likely to change radically. They will point, for example, to the most recent National Audit Office report on MOD Major Projects where average delays have increased by 16% over the previous year and cost overruns have decreased only because of favourable movements in foreign exchange rates. If this is progress, they'll say, we've seen it all before. The Royal United Services Institute summed it up:

> *'With six years of accumulated data to compare, the Report makes depressing reading. For the ten programmes common to all six Reports, each year they have continued to slip on average by a further 3 months and increase costs by 2 per cent, excluding Eurofighter. The implementation of Resource Accounting and Budgeting will undoubtedly reveal many more previously hidden costs within the system.'*[136]

The implication is that costs will continue to rise for some years before Smart Procurement has any hope of improving things.

Of course, only the naive would have expected an improvement in the report, which covers the previous year (1998) when Smart Procurement could not have influenced the outcome. Its first effect could only be felt in the 1999 report due out in the middle of the year 2000, and that can only be marginal. So it was, perhaps, foolhardy for MOD to claim that next year's report would be no worse than this year's and that the following one would show an improvement. That is stoking expectation, but hardly as much as:

> *'DPA now matches US in procurement skills.'*[137]

---

[136] RUSI Newsbrief, Vol.19, Number 7, Page 53, July 1999

[137] *Preview*, the Journal of the Defence Procurement Agency, No.62, June 1999, page 6

This of course may be true, although how it is measured is a mystery. But what it appears to do is to suggest that Smart Procurement results are now permeating our acquisition process to such an extent that we have caught up with the US who began their acquisition reform process five years earlier. This is clearly nonsense.

The danger is that hype will engender expectations that cannot be met and consequently disillusionment will follow. Steering a course between the Charybdis of optimism and the Scylla of reality is not easy. Too much in one direction will lead to shipwreck as certainly as in the other.

Hype will engender expectations that cannot be met.

Reality or Cynicism?

The majority know that implementation of Smart Procurement will be a long and very difficult process with a few early gains which may, or may not, have much effect on their own. Their biggest worry is that, historically, initiatives in MOD have stalled after a very few years, and they wonder whether Smart Procurement can be any different as Ministers come and go.

David Davies, Chairman of the Public Accounts Committee, has outlined[138] many factors which would dilute the effects of Smart Procurement, including:

- Inability to identify technical and programme risks at the outset.
- Inability to predict the implications of pol/mil influences on procurement.
- Some elements of Smart Procurement are not new: so why should they work now?
- Quality of industrial competition will decline.
- Management Information Systems in Whitehall are ineffective.

To these can be added others as suggested by a Foreign Office spokesman at a RUSI Seminar:[139]

- No FCO industrial policy.

[138] David Davies MP to the UK Defence Forum, 29 June 1999

[139] Adam Thompson, FCO, The Whitehall Machine, RUSI, 29 June 1999

- No European industrial policy.

All these, and many other, factors will make Smart Procurement implementation difficult and, maybe, less effective than it should be if they are not corrected, or at least given consideration.

The Treasury Targets

The Treasury has provided three years of assured funding for defence, but only on condition that certain conditions are met. These conditions include:

- Performance on major projects:
    - Average in-year slippage (old projects) < 1.0 month
    - Average in-year slippage (new projects) < 0.3 month
    - Average in-year cost increase 0%
    - Performance shortfall < 3%
- 20% reduction in PE/DPA operating costs
- £2bn saving over 10 years

These targets will, at least in the short term, be difficult to meet although some, like the 3% maximum in equipment performance shortfall, will be difficult to measure and some creative figurework can be expected. The expectation is that any extra costs arising from failure to meet these targets will have to be borne by the agreed defence budget. Hence the haste and the hype.

Hence, also, the extremely conservative targets agreed. The MOD has claimed that Smart Procurement is:

> *' a revolution..... a complete cultural change in Ministry of Defence procurement.'*[140]

But if it is to be a revolution in output terms surely we should be looking for medium-and long-term goals which are rather more than:

- Less cost escalation.
- Less delay.
- Less performance shortfall.

[140] Chief of Defence Procurement, Sir Robert Walmsley, *UK Defence Review: A Cut Above the Rest*, Interavia, September 1998

- 4% saving on the overall procurement.

Let us translate these into more meaningful statements. Given that the average length of procurement is 20.7 years, a target of less than 0.3 months delay per annum on new projects translates into a delay of around 7 years. Again, the £2 billion saving over 10 years is equivalent to only a 0.5% increase in productivity within the defence budget year on year. Is this revolution?

What Targets Could Have Been Set?

Stephen Conver, a Vice President of Lockheed Martin and formerly a senior official in the Department of Defense, sees,

> *'No reason why you can't come down from a procurement cycle of 12 years to one of three to five years.'*[141]

These sort of cycle times are fairly normal in the civil sector of industry, even for state-of-the-art major systems. The A340 aircraft was bought by airlines off the drawing board and was in service, on time, within budget in less than four years. BP's Andrew platform came on stream six months ahead of schedule in four years. The car industry just would not function at all on the sort of timescales that are typical of MOD procurement.

Of course, MOD has often been able to produce equipment in such timescales. There were numerous examples in the run-up to the Falklands, the Gulf and Bosnia when Urgent Operational Requirements (UOR) were written, approved and executed all within days in some cases. Why can't this be done in peacetime?

Ah, but it can. A good example is the Experimental Aircraft Programme. Set against the background of AST 403, it was first contracted to BAe in 1982, after ten days of contractual negotiations, and was to be designed, built and flown at Farnborough in 1986. How was this possible? Professor Lynn Davies who was centrally involved in the project says:

> *'MOD laid down the rules and BAe did it. There was no MOD heavy hand. MOD and industry shared the risks, the costs and the benefits.'*

---

[141] Stephen Conver to RUSI, 29 January 1998

In other words, by Smart Procurement.

It may seem fanciful to think in terms of such short design times for routine procurement, but we achieve even better when we need to: that is, in time of war. In the run-up to the Falklands, to the Gulf and in the Balkans, large numbers of projects were upgraded or even designed and built from scratch, sometimes in matters of weeks, or occasionally days. The Urgent Operational Requirement (UOR) process has in-built scrutiny and decision-taking at the appropriate level. Of course mistakes are made, mistakes that can cost money. But prevarication, more unnecessary studies and stifling scrutiny also cost money: lots of it. Why has no-one calculated the cost of delay in the decision-making chain? Major reduction could be made. So, why isn't it? Scrutiny, studies, approvals, competition. In other words, decision-shelving.

Even so, it should be possible, while retaining reasonable safeguards, to halve the length of the procurement cycle, from the current average of 20.7 years from concept to ISD. Although halving development time will not halve development costs as industrial work could not be significantly reduced, the reduction in time would have to come from the elimination of much of the 'down-time' that currently exists while decisions are made in MOD. Nevertheless, this 'down-time' can cost industry £1 million a month on big projects. Saving this 'down-time' will also reduce the risk of requirement and programme alterations, and of changes to the procurement strategy. With fewer and shorter gaps between industrial work, development teams can be kept together and not be broken up as now with costly learning curves when a (not necessarily the) team is reassembled.

So, it is not fanciful to assume a reduction in development costs of 30% when cycle times are halved.

Partnering arrangements should include incentives to drive down production costs, although the amount that will be possible will depend on how early partnering agreements are agreed between MOD and the selected prime contractor: the earlier in development that partnering is begun, the greater the potential for the prime to reduce costs. Firmer and more transparent MOD plans will allow industry to plan production facilities, with in-built flexibility to cope with orders from MOD and abroad. The latter, of course, boosted by the attention that could, and should, be paid to exportability right back in the Concept Phase. A saving of 5% does not seem unreasonable, and it could be more.

The biggest potential cost saving should come in support costs, but is only likely to be optimised by partnering arrangements that start in design and are carried through to the in-service phase with one prime contractor sharing risks and rewards with MOD. The safeguard for MOD is that the contract arising from the Partnering Agreement should specify a reduction in costs of a few per cent year on year (in addition to raising equipment performance). The saving over the equipment life cycle of, say, 30 years could be 100%, but let us be more cautious and settle for 30%.

Halving the procurement time is only possible by stripping out management layers and reducing management and scrutiny functions. The Defence Procurement Agency (DPA) has committed itself to a manpower reduction which will yield £0.2 billion a year, and the old Operational Requirements area has been cut despite taking on more responsibilities. Elsewhere in the MOD Centre, the cuts are less transparent. Even so, manpower reductions could yield a saving of £0.3 billion a year.

Acquisition savings could be £30 billion.

Thus, very rough and simplistic estimates suggest that acquisition savings over the ten year period of the Equipment Plan could be in the ball-park of:

Development Savings:	£6,000M
Production Savings:	£6,000M
Equipment Support Savings:	£15,000M
Manning Savings:	£3,000M
Total 10 Year Savings:	**£30,000M**

An extra £30 billion for equipment every ten years is worth striving for. The trouble is that, if such targets are declared, the Treasury will build them into future defence budgets. Will Whitehall (not just MOD) never learn that confiscating what is saved is hardly the best

> *Is the idea of a 'smart' Treasury an oxymoron?*

way of motivating those involved in making implementation of new initiatives, like Smart Procurement, actually work?

We need a more enlightened approach from the Treasury if the full benefits of Smart Procurement are to be realised. Do we have a 'smart' Treasury? Or is this idea an oxymoron?

The Moving Targets

The possible savings estimated above coincide fairly closely from those that would derive from the early slogan coined by industry, but adopted unofficially for a very short while in the early days:

'On time, in half the time, at 30% less cost.'

This, of course, could not be achieved straight away and was hurriedly dropped. For a while nothing was heard except that 'faster, cheaper, better' of the SDR report. Then the moderate targets agreed with the Treasury (as outlined above) were officially adopted.

The Ministry insists that these targets are just the start and that Integrated Project Teams (IPTs) will be required to better their targets in the 'Breakthrough Process'. So that, in addition to achieving delivery of their project within cost, time and performance parameters laid down by the Equipment Approvals Committee (EAC), IPTs will have Hard Objectives and Stretch Objectives, described as:[142]

---

[142] MOD Acquisition Handbook, *A Guide to Smart Procurement*, Edition 1, April 1999

Hard Objectives	Stretch Objectives
Testing but achievable	Encourage team to think 'out-of-the-box'
Work as a true team to overcome barriers and share ideas	Target is out of reach, but not out of sight
Adopt novel approaches to identify savings	Significantly harder than Hard Objectives
If easily achievable, they are set too low	Requirement and mandate to address all boundaries and constraints, even 'impossible' ones
	Determine 'what needs to come true' and then make it happen

Confused? The example given of Stretch Objectives for a hypothetical project is:

- Reduce in-service support costs by 20%.
- Reduce length of time from Main Gate to the start of production by 25%.

Such targets are nearer to the concept of revolution than those agreed with the Treasury, and will bring MOD's approach more into line with the potential savings estimated above. But the MOD Hard and Stretch Objectives are not yet translated into overall savings targets which are increased year by year.

So far there is encouraging news on savings from the IPTs:

- The VCIO IPT has identified initiatives to achieve a 10% increase in serviceability.
- The Future Offensive Air System (FOAS) IPT is pursuing a 5 year reduction in procurement time.

- The Type 23 Frigate IPT is aiming to cut the upgrade programme schedule by 30%.

All of these lie in the future, and we will have to wait and see whether they will be achieved. Nevertheless the will is there. At the moment.

Target Realities

It is easy for an IPT to cut time out of a schedule years in advance, and meet its targets while patting itself on the back. But are they being realistic?

For years, schedules adopted and endorsed by EAC have proved to be optimistic. The official targets only seek to reduce the effect of such optimism. No doubt Smart Procurement will cope with that. Now Hard and Stretch Objectives are cutting out large chunks from these optimistic schedules. The question is:

> *Will cuts in schedules just import risk downstream?*

Q. Are these cuts based firmly on what Smart Procurement will deliver or are they just importing schedule risk downstream?

A. Until we know more about Smart Procurement across the board, we must wonder whether the net result will be increased schedule risk and consequent escalation in delay.

Exactly what is not required.

This is not to say that hard and stretch targets should not be set: indeed, it is essential that they are if the claimed revolution is to be achieved. But what is disappointing is that the only proclaimed targets are so soft and that there is no increase in the benefits sought year by year. Would it not have cut more ice with the acquisition world at large if progress, year by year, could be measured against set targets? Failure to achieve the targets would not necessarily need to be penalised but would have to be explained.

By not doing so, MOD broadcasts the message that it does not really believe in the revolutionary benefits it claims to foresee.

Profiling the Savings

One problem that has not been addressed, but may be a good reason why harder targets have not been officially announced, is the profiling issue. If Integrated Project Teams (IPTs) are successful in completing projects faster than scheduled, more money will be required in earlier years to pay for them.

'How will the new Equipment Plan, that will replace the Long Term Costings, deal with such procurement success? Will it slow down some projects, so frustrating their energetic teams, so that other projects can come in early, or will it make more money available in the shorter period? Will cash limits be more relaxed in the age of Project Capital?'[143]

The hope is that savings against the envisaged costs will be greater, enabling MOD to pay for both the earlier delivery and the required savings against Treasury targets. The savings will take time to show up, but have already been taken by the Treasury. Any move to bring forward project milestones will demand up-front savings, so how will that be handled?

'In the interim, it seems to have fallen on the DPA to find cash by squeezing programmes in the bid phase. DA [Defence Analysis] has heard of major squeezes underway on such programmes as ASTOR, and up-coming ones on TRACER, MRAV and BVRAAM. The idea is that if DPA can "find" a few extra hundreds of millions, then this will give a breathing space for longer term savings to show up.'[144]

If that hope is not fulfilled, then schedule reductions will have to be limited or new projects will have to be delayed or cancelled. Not very smart!

---

[143] *A Sprinting Start*, by Professor Trevor Taylor, RUSI Journal, Vol 144, No 3, June 1999, page 84/85

[144] Defence Analysis, *Different Hymn Sheets or Different Hymns?* Volume 2, Issue 3, March 1999

Areas of Real Progress

The most striking evidence of implementation (not just proclamation) of change, although not necessarily progress as yet, has occurred in the Defence Procurement Agency (DPA), spurred but not necessarily instigated by the change to Agency status on 1 April 1999. The primary changes made are:

- The setting up of Integrated Project Teams (IPT) on a fast, progressive programme leading by April 2000 to a total of some 90 in the DPA and a further 50 in the Defence Logistics Organisation (DLO).

Smart Procurement Proposal	Achievement
Partnering arrangements with industry	Much paperwork; little clear implementation as yet. Numerous problems to be addressed
Streamlined processes	New acquisition cycle adopted but not yet tested - particularly Initial Gate, Main Gate, and approval frequency
Organisational Changes	DPA now an Agency. DLO now a tri-Service organisation. Future of DERA, Systems area and elsewhere still in doubt
Incremental acquisition	Not yet tested. DPA/DLO responsibilities unclear. Main Gate approvals in doubt
Integrated Project Teams	Pilots, Wave 1, Wave 2 in place. Remainder due in 2000
Delegation of Authority	Happening in pilot IPTs. Less clear elsewhere
Specialist Acquisition Stream	Virtual Stream only. Issues still to be sorted out
Training	No true joint training with industry on the stocks
Capability Working Groups	Not yet in being
Investment increased for early project stages	Not yet in being

Progress Overall

- Increased financial delegation to two-star and one-star officers and officials (see Chapter 9).
- Increased authority, and decreased subordination, of Pilot IPT Leaders.

Progress Overall

While these steps are welcome, they do not in themselves prove that a major improvement in the acquisition system is around the corner. But it is these salients of change which must be supported by the implementation of all the other measures proposed.

It is, perhaps, instructive to list the main Smart Procurement proposals and how they are faring (table on facing page):

The Missing Pieces

Assuming that the above proposals are satisfactorily implemented, and that's a big assumption, there are still four areas which seem likely to prove highly counter-productive:

- While the new Joint Doctrine Centre should in time fill the joint doctrine hole that has bedevilled the justification of capability, its location at Shrivenham rather than in Whitehall is likely to turn it into an ivory tower, working within arbitrary guidelines imposed from London.
- Industrial policy at both national and European level is non-existent, and there appears to be no plan to produce them. This make partnering arrangements with industry difficult.
- The PPP proposal for DERA, however watered down from the April 1999 proposal (see Chapter 7), runs entirely counter to the Smart Procurement aims of partnering with industry.
- Collaboration with other governments may be impossible if Smart Procurement values are paramount. As collaborative projects, particularly with Europe, are forecast to rise significantly, this will undermine the overall Smart Procurement gains.

Revolution or Retrogression?

The first thing to say is that progress has been made. In fact, rather more progress has been made than I would have thought likely two years ago, and that is greatly to the credit of Ministers who have led from the top. However, it must be recognised that the progress to date is patchy and represents only a very small step along the full Smart Procurement highway. It is too early to judge whether MOD will complete the journey, or even a significant part of it.

The output sought from Smart Procurement could be stated as:

'Major reduction in time and cost across all procurement and support, so that the newest technology can be fielded, before it is obsolescent, in equipment that can be bought in sufficient numbers.'

In an increasing number of fields, technology generations are far shorter than procurement timescales. The only way that the above output could be achieved is by reducing procurement timescales to well under ten years (we should be looking at around five) and incorporating as a matter of routine continuous and effective technology insertion or incremental acquisition. Currently the average length of procurement is 20.7 years (concept to ISD), so the aim should be to reduce the average procurement timescale by around 15 years, and insert technology at around five-year intervals.

> *The aim should be to reduce the average procurement time by 15 years.*

We are not yet in sight of this peak; we are still finding our way through the foothills, taken in by false crests all around.

What is clear is that if all the Smart Procurement proposals are fully implemented over the next five years or more to meet the Hard and Stretch Objectives, there will indeed have been a revolution in the way in which MOD acquisition is carried out: streamlined procedures; greater delegation and accountability; smart people; faster, cheaper, better. But the revolution in acquisition processes and organisation will only achieve the real aim of fielding new technology if it is implemented far beyond the targets that are being set now: Hard and Stretch Objectives, while mighty difficult to achieve, fall well short of what is required. The final peak is not in view.

So if full implementation of the Smart Procurement Initiative is achieved, the gain in output may still fall well short of what is required, and further initiatives will be necessary. What is equally clear is that unless Smart Procurement implementation is driven through to the end, it will falter and there will be little or no improvement in output. In this case, the huge investment made in change will have been to no avail and will have served only to divert energy from the real business. The cynics will be able to say: 'I told you so.'

The opportunity to improve MOD acquisition out of all recognition is at hand. It must be driven through with the energy displayed so far until implementation is complete and the whole culture has been changed. There will not be another opportunity for a quarter of a century or more.

We cannot afford to falter after the first few steps.

We cannot afford to falter after the first few steps.

PART THREE:

THE IMPLICATIONS OF SMART PROCUREMENT FOR INDUSTRY

CHAPTER ELEVEN

THE ROLE OF INDUSTRY IN SMART PROCUREMENT

In any relationship with the Ministry of Defence, industry will require to:

- Achieve satisfactory return on investment in the short term.
- Maintain, or improve, their competitive advantage over their competitors.

If these two requirements are not met, industry will find it hard to partner MOD. Yet judging from its view of its new relationship with industry, MOD does not fully understand this as it is asking industry, at least in the early stages of the procurement cycle, to provide input for free and to risk eroding its competitive position by putting its ideas on the table in open forum. And all this without any guarantee, or even suggestion, that such investment of time and taking of risk will be rewarded in any way downstream. There is a stumbling block which will need to be removed.

> *MOD is asking companies to risk their competitive position for free.*

What Industry Can Offer

Industry has much to offer MOD in both the early stages and the later stages of the procurement cycle:

- **Early Stages**
  - Practical advice on technology and timescales, exportability, risks and costs.
  - Identification of knock-on effects of design/concept decisions on manufacture and in-service performance and costs.

- **Later Stages**
  - Identification of trade-offs and their implications in terms of cost, time and performance.
  - Identification and definition of upgrade/incremental acquisition options.

A Closer Relationship

Certainly, MOD is keen to involve industry much more closely in the procurement process, and that is not just the hype from the top. The leader of the Future Attack Submarine (FASM) IPT, Carl Monk, says[145] he is keen to get industry involved in the project which is still in the concept phase. He has set up an industry forum which meets regularly to discuss issues of mutual interest. There is, however, a difficulty in that, at least until the final prime contractor is selected and contracted, input from any one company is unrewarded in the short term and risks undermining its competitive advantage. What is in it for industry?

Not a lot in the short term is the answer. In the longer term, the better understanding of MOD future requirements is clearly an advantage, but one that is shared by all. In the medium to longer term, there is also the probability that greater input in the early stages will ensure a good base for competitive bidding. But again that is an advantage that is shared by all.

The one concession that MOD appears to have made is that, if there are too many potential contractors for the Capability Working Group (CWG), or Integrated Project Team (IPT) Leader to handle, there may be a 'selection process' to reduce numbers but that 'down-selection' will not prevent other companies from

> *'conducting dialogue with the IPT or from competing for contracts later in the project cycle.'*[146]

So, when is a 'down-select' not a 'down-select'? There needs to be more of a carrot than this.

---

[145] Defence Industries Council newsletter, Issue 2, May 1999

[146] MOD Home Page, *The Role of Industry*, page 6, 26 November 1998

Carrots for Industry

There are, of course, other carrots but some of them are not particularly nutritious and others have parts that are inedible. But some are definitely worth buying:

- Clearer understanding of MOD thinking.
- Clearer identification of future competitors and their approaches.
- Clearer view of future teaming partners.

These carrots are juiciest when eaten by those with the least to offer. They will interest the leaders the least. We, therefore, have a situation whereby the least competent in that particular field may be the most ready to input their ideas while the most competent hold back as any down-select will not bar them from future competition. If those who have withheld from inputting to the CWG/IPT in the Concept Phase were to win a future competition, the early industrial input may have been off-beam.

> *The least competent may be the most ready to input ideas.*

Making the CWG Work

So MOD will have to offer better carrots. What it must do is to tie 'down-select' for future competition to useful input in the early stages. This will provide the necessary stimulus and should attract really strong industrial input from the beginning.

'CWGs are a tremendous opportunity. Therefore we must make them work.' A senior manager in a large UK prime

To make them work, he went on to list the major impediments which had still to be overcome:

- Industrial presence and role in the IPT.
- Competition v. partnering.
- International collaboration.
- Incremental acquisition.

- Technology transfer.
- Early selection of the final prime contractor.
- DERA PPP.
- OCCAR and Smart Procurement.
- The gainshare mechanism.

Some of these are being actively worked upon, others are not. But until there is a better view of the likely solutions, industry will inevitably hold back, although there will be some industrial input at all stages. Inevitably, though, innovative concepts and trade-offs, before the final prime contract is awarded, may be rather less than they could be.

So to tap industry's potential input fully, MOD must provide better carrots and work harder at resolving some of the knottiest problems. Then there will be no reasonable excuse for industry to hold back. If they do, they will be cutting their own throats.

> *Then there will be no reasonable excuse for industry to hold back.*

CHAPTER TWELVE

SMART RELATIONS IN THE CONCEPT PHASE

There is confusion over what is meant by partnering and when it starts. For clarity, I am using 'partnering' to describe the activities between MOD and the final prime contractor, and 'smart relations' for the new relationship between MOD and industry prior to that final contract. Partnering may be one outcome of earler 'smart relations'; and partnering arrangements may be one outcome of 'partnering'.

Smart Relations should start in the research phase, but we have already seen that this will not happen under the Defence Evaluation and Research Agency (DERA) PPP proposal. So MOD has artificially limited the potential gains from the early stages of the procurement cycle for both sides.

Smart Relations in the Capability Working Group

MOD wants industrial input to the CWG and I have discussed, in the previous Chapter, the current difficulties for industry in providing that input. But let us assume that work in removing those difficulties and providing enough carrots is successful. How will industry provide that input? Through the Capability Working Group (CWG)? Or outside it, as happens now?

Relatively little information has so far been released on the operation of the CWG, mainly because of the long time it has taken to come to decisions on the Equipment Capability organisation. Nevertheless it seems that:[147]

- Industry involvement will be as one of several stakeholders involving several companies (potential primes and subs).

[147] Colin Howard, *Industry Involvement*, DMA/MOD Seminar on Smart Procurement, Swindon, 2 February 1999

- Industrial support to CWGs will be funded by industry but:
    - This does not inhibit funding from MOD for studies.
    - Industrial commitment at this stage could be an evaluation criterion.
- IPR issues will govern how input is to be made.

IPR Issues

IPR issues dictate that some, or many, bilateral (MOD – single company) discussions will be necessary on, amongst other subjects, innovative concepts, how to amend requirement or other documents to reflect such innovative concepts and the level of detail provided whilst protecting IPR.

Bilateral discussions on these topics, if pursued seriously, will be resource intensive for both industry and MOD. For MOD, this is a critical issue as the resources within the new Equipment Capability organisation are very limited, once the significant slice of staff has been lost to IPTs. It seems that they will have little or no ability to resource work outside the CWGs.

For industry, the resource issue is also serious. In the past, the Marketing Department has tended to front up early discussions with the operational requirements (now equipment capability) staff, but now the discussions, and particularly input by industry, will require more technical, project and commercial representation. Moreover, the detailed industrial input can only be made after some form of concept work and IPR definition, both requiring significant effort, all of it unpaid. It will only be effective and cost-efficient if the right resources are invested. It may be that an industrial organisation will have to change to provide individuals who have a better across-the-board knowledge of technical concepts, IPR and future exportability possibilities. It would seem prohibitively resource-intensive to use many industrialists to provide the necessary input to each of the many CWGs.

IPR is a key. Innovative input must be protected from rivals. But unless the company is clear as to its own IPR position and can detail it to MOD at the start, later discussions are either going to get bogged down in arguments and disagreements, or will be less productive than they could be. But once IPR is clarified, it should be relatively straightforward to see how requirement documents can be written or amended to take account of the company's innovative concepts without undermining its IPR, and to agree the level of detail which can be provided openly or bilaterally to MOD.

Whole-Life Input

MOD wants industrial input on a whole-life basis. It will therefore expect industry to provide, not only advice on innovative concepts, procurement costs, timescales, exportability and fabrication, but also on in-service performance and costs. This is vital at this stage for two reasons:

- The in-service cost is very much greater, over a thirty-plus year life, than the procurement cost.
- Typically 80% of in-service costs are locked-in by the start of full development; i.e. soon after the Main Gate in the new Acquisition Cycle.

There is concern in some parts of MOD that in-service considerations will not be taken seriously by Customer One in the early Concept and Assessment Phases and that he will continue to pay lip-service to the whole-life concept as he has done in the past. This is quite possible although the creation of one logistic supremo, the Chief of Defence Logistics (CDL), is likely to bring greater pressure to bear on Customer One than could the previous single-Service logistics chiefs and their former committee. But more powerful still will be the more accurate information on in-service costs that will be available under resource accounting and budgetting (RAB). Provided that the Equipment Approvals Committee (EAC) does its job conscientiously, equipment design will be closely examined for whole-life cost-effectiveness. And CDL is a member of EAC.

> *In-service support may not be considered seriously early on.*

There are, however, two major difficulties:

- Projecting in-service costs at the concept option stage will be difficult and inaccurate.
- Industrial membership of the CWG will need to have the requisite logistic expertise.

The first needs major work in both MOD and industry if the accuracy of in-service cost is going to be good enough to determine design options. There are procurement cost models but no in-service cost models for use at the Concept Stage. This suggests immediate investment is required both within DERA and within primes if they are to be taken seriously.

The second is linked. Primes will have to develop or buy-in the necessary logistic cost expertise. Again resourcing CWGs suggests that prime contractors will need, at least, to understand projected logistic costs, whether the work is done inside or outside the company, so that a single person can argue them through along with other issues.

Communications within Companies

Communications within large organisations is difficult. Some manage better than others. The Services do it well, MOD less well and industry hardly start. Many individuals within the defence industry have confirmed this and have suggested a reason over and above incompetence:

> *'Information is power. By withholding information from others, a manager can improve his power base. He gets no points for telling people anything.' An executive in a UK company.*

Whether this is as widespread as suggested is irrelevant. Communications within companies are appalling. It irritates many in MOD who give their time to talking to industry and who then see that information not passed on to all those who need to know.

But it is not just MOD which loses. Industry loses out itself and will do so increasingly when it operates within CWGs unless it improves its ability to communicate effectively with all those who need to know within the company. The alternative is to bring along to the CWG all those who need to know, but that would be costly and inefficient. In any case, MOD would not accept this. The CWG will only work if industrial representation is very small (ideally one per company) and expert in diverse areas.

Industrial representation must be small and expert in diverse

Industry has some way to travel if it is to input successfully, or even to listen efficiently.

Capability Working Group Indications

No CWGs have yet been operating officially. However there are a few Integrated Project Teams (IPTs) which have been operating in the Concept Phase and these give a few pointers, as can the Future Infantry Soldier Technology (FIST) group.

The Future Offensive Air System (FOAS) is to start replacing the Tornado in about 18 years time. It appears to be doing work which would seem to be the province of a CWG, presumably because no CWG is up and running. Some relevant points are:

- The range of concepts studied is huge, and includes both manned and unmanned aircraft.
- The concepts are a response to a 'renewal of a capability', not to a Tornado replacement.
- Already some 100 companies in US, UK and Europe are involved.

The Future Attack Submarine (FASM) is a project which is being handled by an embryo IPT 'on behalf of the MOD Central Staffs Maritime Capability Director'. Ten different concepts are being studied for entry into service in the second decade of the next century. The IPT leader states:[148]

'I want to build a closer relationship with industry, and for them to understand better the needs of the project. Getting industry involved

148 *Preview*, the Journal of the Defence Procurement Agency, No.59, 1 April 1999, page 9

so early will bring potentially significant benefits in the identification and pull-through of new technologies. It should also help us ensure those technologies are affordable..... Through life aspects are being addressed more fully than in the past.'

The Future Anti-Surface Guided Weapon (FASGW) IPT has already involved industry in the early development of concepts for the Sea Skua replacement:

'It is essential we have the views of a wide range of potential contractors at this formative stage. We want industry to sit in on the requirements capture – when decisions are taken about the capabilities desired in the new system. Industry can then tell us whether the things we and the Operational Requirements (OR) branch are asking for are already available and can be procured without significant development, whether a significant development cost is attached to a requirement or whether something is frankly unobtainable.'[149]

These Concept Phase IPTs are clearly involving industry much more than has been the case before. While there must be doubts as to how the Defence Procurement Agency (DPA) can resource these IPTs and, even more of a problem, whether the Central MOD Customer can resource the relevant CWGs, to extract the required input from up to 100 companies per project, it is essential that this MOD initiative is not cold-shouldered by industry or inadequately resourced. It is vital that industry:

MOD initiatives must not be cold-shouldered by industry.

- Makes the right individuals with the right experience and expertise available to CWGs and IPTs.
- Goes all out to make substantial input, either in full forum or bilaterally with MOD.
- Listens with understanding to MOD's thinking.

The DPA Concept Phase IPTs appear to be doing what the CWGs, if they had been set up earlier, should have been doing. This absence

[149] Ibid, page 10

of CWGs has caused industry some confusion. At a MOD/DMA Seminar, delegates in one panel were worried about many issues including:

- The lack of planning so far in the front end of the process (i.e. CWG).
- The lack of dynamism.
- The possible tilted playing field as no method of selection of industrial companies is clear.

All the more reason for industry to keep close to both the Central MOD Customer and DPA. A company that understands what is required and demonstrates its willingness to input will not be shut out. But one that sits back and waits to be wooed, may well be.

FIST

The Future Infantry Soldier Technology (FIST) group is neither CWG nor IPT, but an MOD-DERA-industry group managing a technology demonstrator programme (TDP), but it does have considerable relevance to CWGs. The TDP aim was to deliver eight sets of equipment – for one infantry section – for assessment trials in August 1999. The results of these trials will provide the foundation for the design of the FIST 2000 system. More than 150 companies attended the FIST Industry Briefing Day in July 1999.

This points up the concern that many companies will have about inputting early in the process, particularly when they have to pay to do so (FIST TDP is being funded half and half by MOD and industry), when at a later stage the competition (and the ideas) are thrown open to others. This would seem to be a very real concern, as input to a CWG, which comes under the Central MOD Customer, will not necessarily be fully visible downstream to the IPT leader, who is answerable to the Chief of Defence Procurement for propriety, best practice and cost-effective procurement solutions. Downstream reward, for those who input significantly to the CWG or the IPT in the early phases, must be addressed by MOD if they are to persuade industry to provide the expertise MOD seeks. This is not to suggest a cosy 'scratch-my-back-and-I'll-scratch-yours' approach, but a pragmatic realisation that input to the concept and early design can result in huge savings later in procurement and, especially, in-service. That input should be very valuable to MOD, who must make some payment for it; if not at the time, then at least later.

The FIST TDP group has worked well after a slow start. Pilkington Optronics and BAe Royal Ordnance have worked closely with the Infantry Trials and Development Unit, Director Infantry, the Defence Clothing and Textile Agency, various branches in DERA, the operational requirements staff and, now, with the DPA.

FIST has reportedly exhibited many Smart Procurement traits. The close MOD-industry relations and the lack of the usual over-bureaucratic control have enabled decisions to be taken much more quickly; tougher targets to be set and, very often, met; 'thinking-out-of-the-box' to be the norm, not the exception; and individuals to grow into 'smarter people'.

This is good. But what now?

Now, FIST becomes part of the Dismounted Close Combat (DCC) Cluster IPT. Now, FIST will become just a small proportion of the 45 projects within the DCC IPT. Now, there will be a hiatus while MOD ponders the next step. Now, the impetus and team working skills are in danger of being dissipated. The IPT Leader says that:[150]

'The bulk of our work is focused on some 18 projects in the assessment, demonstration and manufacture phases.'

Not FIST.

But FIST could, in effect, become the whole DCC itself, integrating the whole approach to the future infantry soldier as was the original intention. This would ensure that the importance of FIST was recognised and maintained, but it would not necessarily maintain the momentum that has been built up in the TDP phase. It is imperative that the DCC IPT leader finds ways of maintaining the pace of progress and the valuable work that industry has been doing to date in the FIST programme. It is not an easy task.

---

[150] Ibid, page 32

> *Another nail in the coffin of the MOD customer-supplier relationship.*

There is another interesting issue: the CWG stage has been bypassed with the leap from the TDP to the IPT. Admittedly there was no CWG. But, together with the earlier examples of FOAS, FASM and FASGW, the (embryo) IPTs are growing a culture of handling the concept stages themselves and this may become the way of life as it is always difficult to undo what is already being done and what many would see as 'turning back the clock'. With the operational requirements (equipment capability) staff too small to cope with the expanded role they have been given, this return to the original Smart Procurement vision is perhaps impractical.

Does this matter as long as the best-placed group does the job? Yes, it does. It hammers another nail into the coffin of a taut MOD customer-supplier relationship.

Will this worry industry? Perhaps not. But it will surely confuse them. And if they are confused, they may not be best placed to input their expertise. If you don't know which of two targets to aim at, you may miss them both.

Exportability

Nothing from the Concept Phase IPTs/CWGs/TDPs has suggested that exportability is a major consideration, yet this is a critical issue for industry in the long term. However, it is not a critical issue for MOD and is not likely to feature strongly unless pushed by industry. Industry may feel the shorter-term issues are more urgent, but they must put 'exportability' on the agenda and keep it there. It is in the Concept Phase that critical decisions will be made that will determine exportability in the long run. It must feature strongly in the User Requirement Document (URD), which is produced in the Concept Phase, and industry must shape it.

> *Industry must put exportability on the agenda and keep it there.*

Not considering exportability today will not put a company out of business tomorrow. But the lack of investment in research by both MOD and industry, together with a failure to ensure that future MOD equipment is as exportable as possible, might well do so in ten to fifteen years' time. Not BAe-Marconi, perhaps, but many smaller companies.

How Smart the Relations in Concept?

The slow set-up of the Equipment Capability organisation and, consequently, of CWGs has had the effect of switching the lead for the whole Concept Phase to the DPA away from the Central MOD Customer (Customer One). This is not to say that there is not close cooperation between the two, which there is, but the DPA lead means DPA dominance.

That may or may not mean a great deal in practical terms, but it defeats the Smart Procurement theory of the DPA supplier working to the Central MOD Customer. Given the slender resources of that customer, it is perhaps inevitable. MOD therefore needs to consciously revisit the theory or bolster the Customer's resources. The latter seems inconceivable.

As for industry, it must recognise that MOD is actively engaging it this early in the procurement cycle and play its part. It must be willing to impart its knowledge and expertise, either in full forum or bilaterally. Unless industry is proactive in this, and not just reactive to MOD calls, it will lose out.

The Smart Relations theory is being implemented by MOD in the Concept Phase. Let us all make it work; not just with enthusiasm but also with clarity of thought to overcome the real obstacles (resources, IPR, unwieldy numbers etc) that could condemn us to continuing the 'dumb' relations of the past.

CHAPTER THIRTEEN

SMART RELATIONS IN COMPETITIVE PHASES

Once the Concept Phase is over and the Initial Gate is passed through, competition in the Assessment (equivalent to the old Feasibility Study plus elements of Project Definition) and Demonstration (equivalent to the remainder of Project Definition and much of Full Development) Phases will be the rule not the exception. It is here that the dichotomy of competition and partnering is at its most intractable. Probably as a result, there is confusion.

> *Here, the dichotomy of competition and partnering is at its most intractable.*

At the most recent MOD/DMA Seminar on Smart Procurement[151], two conflicting statements were made about industry's involvement in the IPT during competition:

'IPT..... involving industry except during periods of competitive ***tender****.'*

and 'Competition ***phases****..... industry withdraws as formal member of the IPT but dialogue continues with bid teams.'*

So far there is little indication from the IPT Pilots how industrial involvement will be managed, primarily because most, if not all, the Pilots in the Assessment and Demonstration Phases were or are at the bid or post-bid, pre-decision stages.

Still more confusion. At the same MOD/DMA Seminar, the joint MOD-industry panel on Industry in IPTs stated that:

---

[151] MOD/DMA Seminar on Smart Procurement, Simon Webb, Didcot, 24 June 1999

'Industrial membership of an IPT appears to be based on the premise of holding a contract'.

At another seminar, it was announced that:

'During competition, industry are associate IPT members, to be moved in and out of the IPT as necessary.'[152]

The MOD Website[153] states that, in the Assessment Phase,

'it is important at this stage that industry becomes a core member of the IPT.'

It is not surprising if industry is confused. So what does appear to be the MOD thinking?

The Bidding Phase

In the Bidding Phase during competition at any stage, industrial membership of the IPT will be suspended, although 'dialogue will continue'. It has been agreed that the previous practice of copying answers to questions from one bidder to all other bidders will be discontinued because of the greater likelihood of the existence of commercially sensitive information.

Otherwise, the bidding phase is likely to remain broadly similar to previous practice. The actual bidding process is discussed in Chapters 20 and 21.

Industrial Resourcing during Competitive Phases

It has been suggested that MOD might operate with multiple teams, each associated with one competing contractor. This, however, is likely to be too resource-intensive and would be the exception, with only a very few special cases being conducted in such a way; and then with only two teams. The usual form will be for MOD to operate with only one team, establishing 'Chinese Walls' with limited access to sensitive information. In other words, what has happened previously with, perhaps, a little better control.

---

[152] Malcolm Vickers at Defence Net SouthWest, Bristol, 28 July 1999

[153] MOD Website, Home Page, The Role of Industry, Page 7, 26 November 1998

The industrial membership of IPTs needs careful consideration, particularly as industry will have to pay for its own IPT resource. It is assumed that each prime will nominate one person as its IPT member but augment him with other individuals for particular stages to deliver specific expertise, but this augmentation will have to be kept to a minimum or the whole IPT will become unwieldy.

However, it is not only prime contractors from industry who may be represented on the IPT:

> *'Much of the military capability within a contract may be supplied by sub-contractors, rather than the prime contractor. If only the prime is represented in an IPT by virtue of his contract, the MOD may not gain full visibility of the programme for delivery of key elements of the military capability, and may not be able to engage effectively in processes such as gainshare at this level. It is essential, therefore, that all industrial partners to a contract who deliver a significant element of the military capability should be brought actively into the IPT by the prime contractor.'*[154]

There is much to be said for including sub-contractors or even some sub-sub-contractors in IPTs, and small companies will see this as essential if they are to gain their share of the benefits (see Chapter 17). There are, however, some difficulties. Apart from the difficulty of handling what is likely to become an expanding number of industrial representatives in an IPT, MOD will be very wary of becoming involved with sub-contractors, or of being seen to come between prime and subs, or of taking some form of responsibility for the performance of sub-contractors.

The 'Other' IPT

Each prime contractor is likely to run its own industrial IPT to manage its day-to-day running of the project design and prototyping. It will be these prime IPTs which will be at the cutting edge of the project, not the MOD IPT. The 'real life' IPT will be run by industry, therefore, and not MOD. It is unrealistic to see the MOD IPT as 'the'

---

[154] Panel on *Engagment of Industry in IPTs,* MOD/DMA Seminar, Didcot, 24 June 1999

It is inevitable that there will be several parallel IPTs.

IPT as MOD cannot be responsible to industry's shareholders, any more than industry can be responsible for accountability of public funds. It is, therefore, inevitable that there will be two (in a competition more) parallel IPTs. Indeed it is difficult to see what the MOD IPT will be doing for 40 hours or more a week except to work as individuals. It is even more difficult to see what will keep the industrial representative(s) within the MOD IPT for more than a few hours per week. Yet this does not appear to have been considered by MOD, where a full-time IPT seems to be the conception. There will, of course, be periods when the MOD IPT will have a great deal of work to do, but these will be few. It will not be efficient to retain the services of people unnecessarily and it will not be a fair charge on industry.

The ideal person to represent the prime contractor on the IPT is the industrial project manager for he will have the extensive knowledge and the authority to discuss almost all aspects, without repeated referral back, and to make decisions on behalf of the company. But he will be needed full time to run the project in the company and to run his own IPT, so that he will only be available for minimal periods to the MOD IPT.

Given that much business, during competitive phases, cannot be done in a full MOD IPT with competing industrialists present, it is difficult to understand what the industrial representatives in the full MOD IPT will do. In fact the whole conception of the MOD IPT during competitive phases seems cock-eyed.

An Alternative View of the IPT

There seems very little point in having industrial members of the MOD IPT during competitive phases as there will be little business that can be conducted in the full IPT. Much of it will have to be conducted on a one-to-one basis between MOD and each prime, and it will be essential that most of this discussion will require the presence of the industrial project manager if full benefits are to be achieved.

It seems, therefore, that the MOD IPT concept during competitive phases should be altered to provide for:

- A MOD IPT, without industrial representation.
- Routine, briefing meetings by MOD for all participants, including sub-contractors and some suppliers.
- One-to-one meetings to discuss trade-offs and to obtain the best answers from each competitor. These could be regular (say once a week) or as required by either MOD or the prime. These would include sub-contractors when necessary.
- MOD participation in the industrial IPTs.

By ditching the concept of industrial involvement in the MOD IPT during competitive phases, it might well be possible for MOD to attach separate individuals to each industrial IPT. This would build credible Chinese Walls and would make MOD expertise available on a day-to-day basis to industry, to identify problems early and to clarify military requirement, specification and competition issues without the need for a clumsy question-and-answer procedure or time-consuming MOD meetings. This was practised during the BOWMAN competitive demonstration phase and worked extremely well, and it is happening or is about to happen in one or two IPTs now.

MOD could attach separate individuals to each industrial IPT.

This solution would reduce the industrial resource problem, would strengthen the credibility of MOD Chinese Walls, would limit the MOD resource bill and would produce a much better answer overall. I suspect that MOD will wait until various IPTs have taken action before pronouncing its policy. In that case, I would say to IPT leaders with projects in competitive Assessment and Demonstration Phases: 'Give it a go!'

CHAPTER FOURTEEN

PARTNERING ARRANGEMENTS

If Smart Relations during competitive phases are likely to prove little different from what has gone before, the adoption of Partnering Arrangements between the MOD and the selected prime contractor post-competition is predicted to be a major departure from the old ways of doing business. It is:

> *'The commitment by both customer [MOD] and supplier [industry] regardless of size, to a long term relationship based on clear, mutually agreed objectives..... Partnering differs from conventional contractual relationships in that effective communication strategies amongst the partners leads to openness and trust, better and earlier identification and hence management of project issues, particularly risks, and increased value for money being gained in large scale complex procurements.'*[155]

The MOD approach to partnering is discussed in detail in Chapter 5, and it is now time to look at the subject from the point of view of the implications for industry.

It is stated that there are two types of Partnering Arrangements:[156]

- Strategic Partnering, which may cut across a number of MOD budget areas, encompass a number of individual projects and allows MOD and industry to explore and develop technological and strategic initiatives.
- Project Partnering which can provide a confidence-building first step for those procurements considering the partnering

[155] MOD Website www.mod.uk/policy/spi, *Partnering Arrangements between MOD and its Suppliers*, Initial Page

[156] Ibid, Executive Summary, page 1

approach. Single, high value, long-term projects are the most likely candidates.

To date there is little evidence that strategic partnering, as defined here, is being actively explored in procurement; not surprisingly perhaps as it will limit competition. It is more likely where the supply is, and likely to remain, sole-source or where there are major sensitivities, such as in some Special Projects areas. Nevertheless, even here, the wish to maintain competition wherever possible is likely to minimise the possibilities for strategic partnering arrangements.

Most partnering arrangements will, therefore, fall into the project partnering category. There are few examples as yet and none at all in the equipment procurement arena, although that may change very soon. But there is a view in industry that, without strategic partnering, tactical or project partnering is a waste of time, and this might seem to be borne out by the difficulty MOD appears to be having in identifying the difference between partnering and straight incentivised contracting. We shall have to wait and see.

Longer and Firmer Commitment

Longer and firmer commitment by MOD is top of industry's shopping list. But with a MOD policy of maintaining competition for as long as possible in the procurement cycle (normally throughout the Assessment and the Demonstration Phases), the possibility of longer *procurement* commitment is limited to breaking production up into fewer separate tranches, and even this may not materialise.

The big prize would be the incorporation of a good slab of in-service support with the final development and production contract. Again this might not happen for two reasons. Firstly, if spares (the supply of which is a significant element of in-service support) are to be bought from the prime procurement contractor instead of direct from the component supplier as now, MOD would have to accept a mark-up on the spares price if it retains that prime contractor for full in-service support. Secondly, much of the in-service support activity is still carried out by the Defence Logistics Organisation (DLO) rather than industry. This may well change, but it will not happen overnight.

Regrettably, longer and firmer commitment by MOD is unlikely to be apparent to most primes in the near future. Given that his production price may have been cut to, or below, the bone to win the competition in the Demonstration Phase, the prime is, therefore, unlikely to make much profit. He needs that longer commitment to do so. Only then will he be able to take a highly proactive role in pushing gainsharing options.

The New Relationship

The new relationship, if it is to work, must yield benefits. In the civil sector, partnering has done just that; market research between 1990 and 1997 showed that benefits to companies practising partnering were as follows:[157]

- 76% reduced total cost.
- 73% reduced inventory.
- 70% improved quality.
- 70% improved their security of supply.
- 58% reduced development time.

Of these companies, 94% considered partnering to be a success.

To yield benefits, partnering must work, but it will only work if it is not stifled by bureaucracy and dogma: it must be flexible.

> *'Perhaps the real answer is that partnering will never be capable of definition or categorisation and that it will be delivered through a range of different commercial structures. And whilst it is valuable to research and test out various models, there is no value in searching for the Holy Grail of partnering arrangements.'*[158]

Partnering has to be applied flexibly, but this is not necessarily simple. It is not a question of waving a magic wand and watching the

[157] Partnership Sourcing Ltd to the MOD/CBI Seminar, 20 November 1998

[158] Ian Busby, of Delloitte and Touche Consulting Group, to the RUSI Seminar on SDR, 10 September 1998, RUSI Whitehall Paper Series 44, page 39

benefits pour out of Santa's sack; in fact, partnering is not an easy option at all:

> *'Partnering is not an easy option and has its disciplines....It requires the partners to work for the benefit of a project as a whole, rather than concentrating exclusively on their own area of responsibility: this may mean revising programmes and procedures to help a partner who has run into difficulties.'*[159]

Partnering has to be applied

> *'The key factors of [long term relationships] are trust, openness, aligned business objectives, a non-adversarial relationship, a system that incentivises performance and continuous improvement, and working for mutual benefit....Such relationships require a lot of hard work to develop and sustain, but the benefits are significant.'*[160]

MOD perceives the potential benefits, but the required approach may pose them problems; is there any reason to think that it will be any less of a problem for industry? No, it will probably be greater.

Many partnering arrangements have failed in industry, most of them (for obvious reasons) unpublicised. While every project is different, therefore making the cause of failure difficult to pinpoint, it seems that partnering can only work if a common goal can be determined, a key difficulty in MOD-industry partnering:

> *'In the type of partnering envisaged by SDR [the Strategic Defence Review], the parties are not coming together to achieve a common goal. Simplistically, one party is seeking to produce a service or an asset at minimum cost and the other party is seeking to provide the same at the maximum value to shareholders. There is bound to be tension in such a relationship. And some have argued that it is inevitably a zero sum game in the sense that one party can only benefit at the expense of the other.'*[161]

---

[159] Sir James Hamilton, Brown & Root, *Partnering Benefits,* Securing the Future, Newsdesk Communications, 1998

[160] Peter Smart, Brown & Root, *Outsourcing Problems,* Securing the Future, Newsdesk Communications Ltd, 1998.

[161] Ian Busby, Deloitte and Touche, RUSI Whitehall Paper Series 44, 10 September 1998, paragraph 39

We may not agree that it is inevitably a 'zero sum game', but it does point up the difficulties and the traps of partnering.

Whether or not Partnering Arrangements are to be used for the context of the contract with the selected prime contractor, the nature of the relationship between MOD and contractor will change as soon as the contract is signed. Provided there are incentives in the contract, both MOD and contractor should be jointly motivated to meet the in-service date (ISD) within budget and to the required performance. But more than that: both parties should be motivated to examine, and continue to seek, beneficial trade offs in the cost, time and performance parameters that have been laid down.

The MOD IPT Leader, with his Hard and Stretch Objectives laid down, will be highly motivated to find savings in cost and time (not too much at the expense of performance, it is to be hoped), but will find it hard to do so without the help of industry. It is vital, therefore, that industry when negotiating a contract seeks maximum incentivisation and gainshare.

If industry is not properly incentivised, MOD will suffer as will industry who will not be making much of a profit. Properly incentivised, industry can increase their profit margin and help MOD to meet its targets.

Incentivisation

Incentives must not be one-sided and must reflect agreed, achievable targets. The incentive structure must reflect both the value to the customer of the various performance levels and a meaningful incentive for the contractor. Incentives are especially useful in projects that are complex, high cost or have a history of cost overruns or performance problems.

> *'NASA's cost type Space Station contract provides that the contractor will be docked 25 cents for every dollar of cost overrun, but will earn an additional 25 cents for every dollar saved. In addition, all fee payments are provisional and are subject to recoupment if station hardware fails to perform.'*[162]

---

[162] US Office of Federal Procurement Policy, *A Guide to Best Practices for Performance-Based Service Contracting*, Final Edition, October 1998

Incentivisation can, therefore, be induced by both negative and positive methods; that is by stick and carrot. MOD has stated its sticks and carrots:[163]

Sticks	**Carrots**
Liquidated damages	Shared objectives
Payment retention	Shared rewards
Purchase in default	Gainshare
Express warranties	Payment arrangements
	Bonuses
	Longer term relationships
	Options to extend contracts

But the carrots are, in many cases, too vague or are just contractual arrangements. The third and the last two of the carrots in the list above are, however, of major interest. The last two are almost certainly applicable to in-service support or PFI/PPP deals and not to a procurement-only contract because the options for longer term relationships, and to extend contracts in procurement, look likely to fall foul of competition primacy. Gainshare is therefore the only realistic carrot, and therefore very important for industry, in procurement contracts that have no support element.

Gainshare

Gainshare was discussed in Chapter 5. To make it work, industry must take the leading role and not wait for MOD to do so. As it is the major, perhaps only, source of making profit in procurement, industry should need no motivation but they must understand what they are trying to do and, equally, what they should not be trying to do.

Gainshare is NOT about reducing equipment performance, although some small reduction in some parameters may well be acceptable if the gains in cost and/or time are significant. But changes in most performance parameters are, per se, of little interest to the user in the field: what is important to him is the system performance and any significant reduction here is likely to be

---

[163] DG Commercial Policy at DMA/MOD Seminar on Smart Procurement, Swindon, 2 February 1999

difficult for him to accept. He will only feel comfortable doing so if, in return, he gets either very large cost reduction (enabling him to buy substantially more of that or something else) or both a much quicker introduction into service and the prospect of significant incremental acquisition. In either case there is significant gain, too, for industry.

Gainshare IS about reducing cost. But not just cheaper ways of manufacturing or resourcing the programme which, although welcome, will tend to be small in scale. It is almost certainly NOT about major reductions in tests, trials, quality control or other programme management tools as this will normally import risk and, in the end, raise costs and/or delay delivery. The biggest gains are likely to be achieved either by changes which will affect the cost of running equipment in-service or which will allow progressive upgrading of the equipment in-service without major logistic or training implications.

Gainsharing IS about reducing delay and, more importantly, overall cycle time. Time is money. Also an earlier in-service date is usually attractive to the end Service user because it gives him improved performance and reduced running costs earlier. Reducing cycle time can be coupled with incremental acquisition. There will, however, be a profiling problem within MOD: reducing cycle time means bringing funds forward and if all projects are trying to do this, there will not be enough in the defence budget to do so. It is, therefore, very important that any proposals for bringing forward the in-service date are offset by savings in the shorter term, not just in the long term. This will complicate such proposals.

The weakness in gainshare in procurement is that the selected prime contractor may well gain nothing for changes that produce downstream improvements under his current contract. It is notable, for example, that all the examples of gainshare within the Brimstone project (see Chapter 5) concern procurement, not in-service support or future improvements.

Unless MOD finds a way of rewarding the procurement prime contractor for reduced cost or improved performance downstream, it is likely that gainshare achieved will remain well below its full potential. One way of achieving more is to extend the prime contract much further into the support phase. This could produce some cost increase (e.g. spares mark-up) but this extra cost might be much smaller than the overall gains.

The prime may gain nothing for ideas that improve support downstream.

Industry should welcome (although the losers may not!) greater commitment from MOD and longer contracts which extend further into the in-service support phase as the means to unlocking the last two carrots in the list above. However, industry must earn that extra commitment and be seen to do so. Prime contractors will, therefore, have to:

- Improve their in-service support expertise.
- Buy-in or team with expertise in support areas.
- Above all, come up with major gainshare proposals to save costs and improve performance after the equipment is in service.

Finally, gainshare proposals will not be as useful, and therefore as profitable to either MOD or the prime, if the sub-contractors and the rest of the supply chain are not properly involved. But involvement of the sub-contractors and suppliers must not only encourage the identification and definition of potential gainshare opportunities, but must (and this is absolutely crucial) lead to 'flow-down' of the gain to those sub-contractors and suppliers:

'Although Alenia Marconi Systems, the Prime Contractor, signed the Framework Agreement with the MOD, approximately 40% of the manufacture of the Brimstone weapon system is sub-contracted to Boeing. The launcher and sections of the missile buss and associated electronics form the bulk of this sub-contract. It was essential for the success of this exercise that Alenia Marconi Systems were able to encourage Boeing to join them in the gainsharing process.'[164]

And, in the study's conclusions:

---

[164] *Brimstone and Gainsharing,* A Case Study, Alenia Marconi Systems, Page 3, June 1999

'It was essential that the Prime Contractor was able to obtain "Buy In" from its major sub-contractors for future gainsharing initiatives, to motivate them (and ultimately the whole supply chain) to search for cost reduction mechanisms.'[165]

We shall return to the issue of flowing down of risks and benefits in Chapter 17.

It must be re-emphasised that gainshare is, by and large, an industry-led activity. Gainsharing, and industry's profits, will rest to a very great extent on industry seizing the initiative when it is presented.

The Nuts and Bolts of a Partnering Arrangement

Of course, gainshare and the other sticks and carrots listed above can work perfectly well within a normal contract and do not necessitate a Partnering Arrangement. Indeed, it is difficult to see the advantages for either MOD or industry in a Partnering Arrangement, except in a few specialised areas, unless either competition is dispensed with earlier in the cycle or development and production contracts are extended to incorporate in-service support. So far, there are no examples of Partnering Arrangements in procurement; all examples lie solely in support activities.

MOD and the Confederation of British Industry (CBI) have collaborated and agreed a document on Partnering Arrangements.[166] It is not intended to reproduce it here, but a short resume of some of the main points may be useful, particularly for the general reader.

Selection of a Partner in a Competitive Environment: During the selection phase, MOD and industry must engage in the closest possible dialogue to enable both sides to explore the viability and benefits of a partnering arrangement.

A Single Source Supplier: The challenge will be to build in to the partnering agreement, processes for encouraging

[165] Ibid, Page 4

[166] MOD/CBI, *Partnering Arrangements between MOD and its Suppliers*, 1998, MOD Website, www.mod.uk/policy/spi

innovation, continuous improvement in performance and achieving value for money.

Contract length: Contracts will normally be for a longer period than conventional procurements.

Partnering Considerations: Including long term relationship, risk management, industrial commitment, openness, cooperation, understanding and trust.

Stakeholders: All individuals in MOD and the industrial partner(s), who may be able to impact on the process, are stakeholders and must be involved in the integrated project team (IPT).

Partnering Documents: Partnering Principles, Framework Agreement and Tasking Orders (contracts).

Partnering Management: Proposals will have to be developed for change procedures, performance monitoring, mechanisms for problem solving, IPR, exit strategies, risk, management, contract pricing and payments, performance incentives, post-project evaluation.

As has already been observed, it is difficult to see the benefits of applying Partnering Arrangements in procurement (as opposed to in-service support) unless:

- Contracts post-competition are significantly longer, which means the procurement prime is given a large slice of in-service support and/or incremental acquisition.
- Partnering with a single-source supplier begins in research or concept and is continued through to production or longer.

The latter will be a minority opportunity while competition remains industrially viable and continues to be the primary MOD tool. If the former is not acceptable to MOD, nor made practical by procurement prime contractor expertise, then procurement will remain different from in-service support. As one senior logistics officer remarked:

'There is a difference in contracting for procurement, which is a 'telling' activity, and contracting for in-service support, which is a 'collaborative' activity.'

If MOD wishes to avoid this, it must seriously consider more extension of procurement prime contracts into the in-service support phase.

The IPT in the Manufacturing Phase

In the Manufacturing Phase, with competition over, the MOD IPT now unambiguously includes industry as a core member, and pays for the industrial representative(s).[167] Quite how many representatives it will pay for, or from how many companies, is not clear. The Attack Helicopter IPT Leader predicts that his IPT will grow to about 70 members in due course, the Challenger 2 IPT is about 50-strong as is the Nimrod IPT, while the Eurofighter IPT numbers around 100. Many of the individuals are, of course, from MOD but the industrial element is large.

Funding industrial members of the IPT is an important issue. While MOD is likely to fund one or more representatives from the prime contractor from the project, it may have greater difficulty in making the case for funding the regular attendance of representatives from smaller firms in the supply chain. Yet it is the smaller suppliers or sub-contractors who will find the expense of IPT representatives rather more difficult than the prime. It is important that the small boys are not excluded for funding reasons.

This situation will, of course, be further aggravated if the smaller firms have to be represented on a regular basis at both the MOD IPT and the prime contractor's IPT. For this reason, as well as for others, it is important that two isolated, parallel IPTs are avoided. The answer, of course, is to produce:

- One programme team consisting of both MOD and industry.
- A single team located in industry.
- Minimal use of MOD-only and industry-only sub-groups, purely to discuss matters of no interest to the other side

The above has been suggested in essence[168] as has a combination of physical colocation and electronic colocation.

---

[167] Simon Webb, MOD/DMA Seminar on Smart Procurement, Didcot, 24 June 1999

One IPT will not only speed things up and ease the resource problem, but will improve transparency and consequently trust. It will also make it easier for both sides to agree things on the spot, not least for industry. Depending on who is the individual industrial representative(s) in a MOD-run IPT, and what delegated powers he has been given (probably very little), he will be wary of committing, or simply unable to commit, his company to a decision without referring back to at least his industrial project manager. In a single IPT this would not happen.

> *One IPT will improve transparency and, consequently, trust.*

The Nimrod IPT Leader says[169] that MOD is,

> *'acting as an intelligent customer to the prime contractor. But we have to be more than that; we need to be a hands-on project team bringing together technical, programme, support, commercial and requirements staff so decisions that effect capability and delivery timescales are best matched.'*

He will not achieve that hands-on approach without industry. But he would achieve it within a single forum consisting of a merged MOD IPT and industry IPT, located in industry.

Such a single, merged IPT would reduce, or even remove, the need for parallel briefings to senior MOD and industry managers as this could be done to both at the same time by the one IPT, rather in the manner that the separate project reviews within the MOD to the Master General of Ordnance and the Quartermaster General were merged into one project review in the 1980s.

But such a single, merged IPT will only be possible if there is total commitment on both sides to openness and trust, a subject which will be explored further in Chapter 16.

---

[168] Colin Howard, MOD/DMA Seminar on Smart Procurement, Swindon, 2 February 1999

[169] *Preview*, the Journal of the Defence Procurement Agency, No.59, 1 April 1999, page 22

Cluster IPTs

Much of the MOD output and the industrial input on IPTs has concerned those that are to manage single, large, complex projects. However, the majority of projects will be managed by 'Cluster' IPTs, in which one IPT will run between 30 and 60 smaller projects. These Cluster IPTs pose considerable problems:

- **Project numbers.** In the Air Defence Command and Control IPT, a 50-strong team manages 20 projects; in the Dismounted Close Combat IPT there are 45 projects; the Aerial Targets Systems IPT covers 32 projects; the Flight Simulation and Training IPT has 20.
- **Transfer to the Defence Logistics Organisation (DLO).** Considerable effort is needed to ensure that individual projects transfer smoothly to the DLO and that there is a suitable DLO IPT for them to go to.
- **Industrial IPT Representation.** This is perhaps the most important, and most intractable problem as so many companies will wish to be represented that it is impractical to run a Cluster IPT with core industrial membership.

Yet industrial membership is essential – why should it be less important for smaller projects in Cluster IPTs than for large projects in single-project IPTs? So far it seems to have been put in the 'too difficult' tray by both MOD and by those industrial members of MOD Smart Procurement committees.

Understandably industry is eager to participate:

'It is good to see how industry has welcomed the [Smart Procurement] changes and is eager to participate in the IPTs, seeing them as a way of speeding up the procurement process.'[170]

But they must not underestimate MOD's problems:

'One area which is presenting a challenge at present is how the IPT can best bring an industrial contribution into the team whilst maintaining strict commercial confidentiality. To give you an example, we recently

---

[170] Ibid, page 31

had 16 companies and consortia expressing an interest in tendering for just one of our new programmes.'[171]

> Clearly Cluster IPTs cannot operate like a single-project IPT.

Clearly Cluster IPTs with dozens of projects, each one associated with many companies, cannot operate like a single-project IPT. But a solution must be found.

Approaches to Industrial Involvement in Cluster IPTs

The Dismounted Close Combat team has tried workshops:

> *'The problems of competition combined with the numbers of small projects at different stages of the cycle have prevented industry from becoming full-time members of the IPT. Nevertheless, last December the IPT conducted a successful industry workshop, during which key issues were brainstormed. In February, at the bequest of industry, there was a further two-day workshop at Shrivenham.'*[172]

While these moves were welcomed by companies involved, who were heartened by the high standard of debate, a few infrequent workshops are not going to produce the industrial input required, particularly in terms of gainshare proposals.

Another Cluster IPT suggestion is to explore whether an 'independent' company could act as an impartial interface with industry on behalf of the IPT. This appears to do nothing to solve the problem and would probably be more expensive than increasing DPA staff numbers.

But more MOD staff would be politically unacceptable.

Another suggestion is for the formation of mini-clusters to be formed within the Cluster IPT based, it would be hoped, on mini-clusters of projects where the same companies are involved, rather than on any other grouping. The MOD IPT Leader would then run, not one Cluster IPT, but a number of mini-cluster IPTs, delegating

---

[171] Ibid, page 34

[172] Ibid, page 32

powers to his assistants. But again there is likely to be a MOD resource problem.

A better idea might be to form mini-cluster IPTs within industry with MOD providing the necessary MOD expertise (which would vary from meeting to meeting) at the industrial IPT location. This could probably be resourced by MOD although even that is debatable.

No doubt there are other possibilities. MOD has not yet found the answer to operating Cluster IPTs so it is in industry's interests to take this seriously and to provide practical options for consideration. If they do not, MOD will almost certainly find proper industrial participation in Cluster IPTs too difficult to resolve and industry will be left out in the cold. As the majority of projects are to be managed in Cluster IPTs, a major component of Smart Procurement will only be partially applied.

I have yet to see any practical proposals from either MOD or industry. Isn't it time industry took the lead?

Incremental Acquisition

As was seen in Chapter 4, incremental acquisition also poses several seemingly intractable problems, problems which might well persuade the IPT Leader to steer clear of all but the smallest increments:

> *'Whilst incremental acquisition offers a systematic solution to technology refreshment its effectiveness is critically dependent on the ability of the IPT to manage the operational/logistic support implications and costs of fielding differently configured equipments, possibly with interim support and training arrangements.'*[173]

From the MOD standpoint, it should be possible to manage these issues, although they will complicate matters and may well require greater resources in the IPT over the lifetime of the project, compared with a project which does not incorporate incremental acquisition.

---

[173] MOD Incremental Acquisition Model, MOD Website www.mod.uk/policy/spi, page 4

MOD will be critically dependent on industry to deliver technology insertion.

However, MOD will be critically dependent on industry to deliver technology insertion and to manage their side of in-service support of the initial equipment, while continuously seeking gainsharing opportunities. This will be difficult with different prime contractors and a (possibly large) number of sub-contractors and suppliers involved. There is no doubt that this would be eased if the same prime contractor was to be given responsibility for the initial procurement, all incremental technology insertions and in-service support.

MOD might be expected, at present, to baulk at the idea of such a large contract, but many PFI/PPP deals are for 30 years or more, and some are worth several billion pounds. It is in such a long association that Partnering Arrangements can provide the answer, such as is happening with the control of maintenance and upgrades of the Royal Navy's Type 23 and Type 22 multi-role frigates which is in the hands of one IPT, based in the DPA at Abbey Wood:

> *'We have introduced an integrated system of management for the through-life support of these ships and their equipment in a fully coordinated way. In the past, the system split upkeep and upgrade into two separate authorities – the former in Naval Support Command, the latter in the former Procurement Executive..... We are now able to link maintenance periods and capability upgrades in a seamless way..... The benefits of this new combined approach to the through-life support of the ships exemplifies the kind of incremental acquisition of new technology that is one of the keys to the Smart Procurement Initiatives.'*[174]

A seamless link between support and upgrades should bring major benefit.

This seamless link between support and upgrades should bring major benefit to the MOD, but it could also

[174] *Preview*, the Journal of the Defence Procurement Agency, No.59, 1 April 1999, page 39

bring greater benefit to the procurement prime contractor, for if he is to be responsible for manufacture, he is best placed to tender for upgrades. If he is contracted for manufacture and upgrades, he is also best placed to manage in-service support if the above concept is to be efficiently worked.

So there is an example of MOD's willingness to combine support and upgrades; why should it not happen as a matter of policy on the procurement side?

> *'In many cases, incremental acquisition will, by its very nature, mandate the selection of the prime contractor at Main Gate or earlier, who would be expected to deliver not only the initial capability but also subsequent increments.'*[175]

This MOD view shows that it has already contemplated the step, even if it has yet to implement it. For MOD to be able to take it further so as to bring together procurement, upgrades and in-service support, industry will have to demonstrate it has both the support expertise, either in-house or as part of its team, as well as the procurement expertise to deliver the whole.

The prize is large – for the winner; for the loser(s), the implications of defeat in early competition is far more damaging than previously. The implications for the supply chain are significant and will be looked at in Chapter 17.

Incremental acquisition is a fundamental part of Smart Procurement and is in danger of being bypassed because of the difficulties, if the incremental acquisition proposals (proposals which only add up to fairly ordinary routine upgrades) from IPTs so far are any basis for judgement. But the benefits for MOD are large and even greater for industry. Industry needs to propose a clear incremental acquisition strategy (rather than minor upgrades) early in a project's life, say in the Assessment Phase or even earlier; to propose practical ways of achieving it; and to set out clearly the benefits of earlier fielding of the initial capability, of higher performance downstream, of lower risk, of lower cost and of no obsolescence. And to propose ways of satisfactorily managing the more complex programme.

---

[175] Ibid, page 4

To repeat, the benefits of true incremental acquisition are huge. Industry must not miss them.

The State of Partnering

The position so far on Partnering, one of the central tenets of Smart Procurement, is as follows. There have as yet been no examples of Partnering Arrangements being struck in procurement, only in training and in-service support. Industrial representation in IPTs is still unresolved, particularly in Cluster IPTs which manage the majority of MOD's projects. And true incremental acquisition approaches have not yet been tested.

Nevertheless, MOD has laid the groundwork for Partnering Arrangements. It is up to both MOD and industry to use it. This is, however, unlikely unless:

- MOD actively considers contracting one prime contractor for procurement, incremental acquisition and in-service support.
- Industry develops clear incremental acquisition proposals early in the procurement cycle.
- MOD and industry together examine ways of overcoming the many problems which exist, particularly in Cluster IPTs, incremental acquisition, transparency and joint IPTs.

MOD has laid the groundwork. It is up to industry to use it.

CHAPTER FIFTEEN

SERVICE SUPPORT AND PPP

The Chief of Defence Logistics (CDL) has called industrial performance disgraceful:[176]

> *'MOD received a "second-class service" from industry compared with the service commercial customers received..... But he acknowledged this was partly MOD's fault, since there were internal weaknesses and we had become inured to poor service.'*[177]

At the same seminar, the panel on the engagement of industry in IPTs acknowledged this:

> *'On his own presentation to the seminar, CDL highlighted past shortcomings in industrial in-service support for our armed forces in the field. We would not wish to deny that significant problems have occurred, but would claim that many of these have been the result of working to support the contractual requirements of the Ministry's own inefficient in-service support organisations and procedures.'*

While this may be true to a greater or lesser extent, it suggests an industrial reaction which is negatively defensive, and this will in the end be self-defeating.

Two things should be understood by all companies bidding, or intending to bid, for service support contracts of all sorts:

- CDL is committed to making 3% year-on-year efficiency savings, so he will be seeking to eliminate any inefficiencies within his own organisation, including those concerned with contracting procedures.

---

[176] MOD/DMA Seminar on Smart Procurement, Didcot, 24 June 1999

[177] *Preview*, the Journal of the Defence Procurement Agency, No.63, July 1999, page 18

- With the integration of the three, formerly separate, single-Service logistics organisations into a single entity, future contracts are likely to be larger, longer and consequently fewer.

The first indicates that industry will be unable to shelter behind a parapet of 'it's all your fault' for much longer. The second is much more important: if companies are to take advantage, and avoid the disbenefit, of larger, longer, fewer logistic contracts, they must be worthy of them. The companies that get their act together will survive and, probably, prosper; those that do not will be squeezed out of the defence sector altogether.

> Companies that get their act together will survive.

The In-service IPT

Compared to the mountain of papers and words produced on the subject of IPTs in the Manufacturing Phase, very little has been said or written in the public domain on the operation of the IPT after delivery of the equipment to the service user. This is partly because every one of the pilot IPT projects were in procurement or in major upgrades, and not in the apparently less glamorous world of in-service support. There are however a few pointers to whether the IPT will work effectively in the In-Service Phase.

Will the IPTs bring benefit? It is too early to give a definitive answer, but there is some evidence that benefit is beginning to emerge. Stuart Kendall, of British Aerospace, is a member of the Harrier Integrated Project Team, based at RAF Wyton. He is reported [178] to be optimistic because the IPT engenders:

- Much better understanding by industry of the customer's needs.
- Far better communications between MOD and industry.
- Readier acceptance of industrial expertise and advice by MOD.
- Simpler decision making.
- Identification of duplication for elimination.
- Concurrent working.

[178] Defence Industries Council newsletter, Issue 3, Aug/Sep 1999

The Advanced Short Range Air to Air Missile (ASRAAM) is in the Manufacturing Stage, but with the missile in pre-production and nearing full production, the IPT is already investigating Post Design Services and In-Service Support contracts with industry using the IPT's own finance and contracts staff. This suggests quite clearly that a properly functioning IPT will not allow a hiatus to develop around the point at which it transfers from the Defence Procurement Agency (DPA) to the Defence Logistics Organisation (DLO), but will develop policy and implement it as and when necessary for future stages. It does not matter whether the finance or contracts staff are based in the DPA or the DLO provided they are best-placed to handle the job.

As has already been noted in Chapter 4, the Challenger 2 IPT is split between Abbey Wood (DPA) and Andover (DLO) and, despite the geographical separation, there is a close relationship. This geographical separation will end eventually when the IPT is collocated at Andover. As far as the workings of the IPT are concerned, there is no 'Throw-it-over-the-Wall' approach (see Chapter 3), but a seamless progression.

What Does This Mean For Industry?

The obvious point for industry is that the IPT allows the manufacturing prime contractor to be much closer to those who will be deciding on the in-service support strategy and letting the contracts. He should, therefore, be able to influence the outcome to his own advantage and to the advantage of his own supply chain. But he will not do so if he thinks just like that. To gain advantage, he must propose in-service support strategies that are clearly the best and bring greatest benefit to the MOD. He must demonstrate that any 'mark-ups' on spares supply, for example, are much more than compensated by the lower cost or higher performance overall that will result from retaining his prime expertise for the support phase.

He will not do this without logistic expertise. He must, therefore, seek that expertise either in-house or as part of his own team. And he must do so early in the procurement cycle: certainly in his bid for the Manufacturing Phase, but most desirably in the Assessment and

Demonstration Phases when up to 80% of the support costs are locked in by design.

Spares and CRISP

MOD has recently signed a partnering framework agreement with Vickers Defence Systems (VDS) to support the Army's Challenger 2 fleet. It is reported that:

> *'This agreement is the first of its type to be signed for an armoured fighting vehicle under the MOD Smart Procurement initiatives. It aims to reduce the cost of ownership and improve equipment availability.'*[179]

This will change the current system whereby units order spare parts through the army supply system which in turn orders spares from the prime contractor and many sub-contractors, a system which has led to huge holdings, much of it of the wrong types. The Challenger 2 Innovative Spares Procurement (CRISP) programme is designed so that units will order consumable spares direct from the prime contractor via a computer link.

Provided the prime contractor (VDS) performs well, there are large benefits for MOD. To ensure this, MOD has set cost and performance targets. The initial contract will be for seven years, worth around £10M a year to VDS. It is expected that the agreement will be expanded.

While there are no clear examples yet of partnering arrangements in the domain of equipment procurement, this CRISP agreement is one of a number in equipment support that are operating (either in fact or in name) or are promised – Eurofighter support would appear to be the next large one on the cards.

Public-Private Partnerships

Where partnering in procurement is as yet non-existent and where partnering in equipment support is only in the very early stages, PFI contracts in training and construction are much more numerous and are being pushed very forcefully. 26 PFI contracts worth £1Bn have

[179] Janes Defence Weekly, 19 May 1999, page 19

been signed and another £6Bn-worth are in the pipeline. The principles, benefits and risks of public-private partnerships[180] are discussed in Chapter 6.

PFI is a growth area and is likely to continue to grow for the foreseeable future, with some suggesting the original target of £5Bn-worth by 2001 will be exceeded. A growing area of major business worth several billions is an attractive area for industry. The major factors are:

> *PFI is a growth area worth several millions.*

- Long term contracts of twenty, thirty or more years (contract for the refurbishment of the MOD Main Building is for 35 years).
- Contracts are financially large (the tanker aircraft PFI might be worth £9Bn, compared with £2Bn for the procurement costs alone).
- PFI contracts are complex and costly.
- Financial risk is greater.

By committing itself to partnering and PFI, the MOD is meeting one of the major demands from industry which is for greater commitment. But such greater commitment is not limitless as longer contracts tie-up MOD funding for much longer periods: 'Mortgaging the future' as one ex-MOD industrialist put it. For this reason, PFI is limited to 15% of the total funds available. And, of course, the greater the percentage of funds tied-up for a long period, the more difficult it will be for MOD to commit more firmly or for longer either to remaining projects or to support not covered by partnering arrangements. This limit must be recognised.

PFI Complexity

A typical PFI contract may involve a hundred contracts between the players. The main ones will be between MOD and the prime contractor; between the prime contractor and the money lending agencies (e.g. banks); between the prime contractor and sub-

---

180 PPP = CFQ + PFI + partnering according to MOD's Acquisition Handbook, page 21

contractors for the design-and-build stage; between the prime contractor and agencies operating the facility or equipment once built; and between operators and customers.

There is a greater need by the prime contractor for quality advice on finance, contracts and legal aspects and this is expensive. It is essential that experts within the various stakeholders understand the project in all its aspects, and just as vital that those experts, brought in for particular advice, also understand the project in its complexity.

It is also important that those financing the early stages of the projects are fully involved in project discussions early so that they can understand the risks involved. It may well be that the risks they will be willing to accept are very different from those that the prime contractor or operating agencies are willing to accept.

PFI Common Denominators

PFI Common Denominators for success have been listed as:[181]

- Commitment at the highest level in both customer and supplier.
- Establishment of trust.
- Understanding and apportionment of risk.
- Culture and attitude re-inforced by buy-in to the project by all.

> *Why is there an artificial barrier between PFI and partnering?*

These are no different to those required for successful partnering. Indeed, as PFI moves into equipment support and possibly procurement itself, and as partnering in support moves into procurement and vice-versa, it is difficult to see a clear division between partnering and PFI. They are in fact the same. All projects are different, in any case. So why do we need an artificial division, depending apparently on whether third party funding is necessary or on who owns what? Particularly when primes and sub-contractors have much experience of third party funding in procurement projects:

---

[181] *Private Finance Comes of Age*, Defence Procurement Analysis, Autumn 1998, page 19

'We recognise that the provision of finance must be an important part of any substantial military investment. We have long experience of working with leading banks to provide efficient financing mechanisms, with or without the UK ECGD support.' [182]

An artificial division may not seem to matter, but it is likely to make equipment procurement PFI more difficult as the PFI fuhrers scour the field for support possibilities. If there is to be a division, then PFI should be limited to bricks and mortar, leaving equipment procurement, support, upgrades and training to be one indivisable opportunity for partnering managed by the IPT, with proposals and partnering decisions being taken early in the procurement cycle.

It would then be up to both MOD and industry to propose innovative partnering arrangements, rather than (as happens now) hiving off training as PFI and continuing to look at procurement and in-service support in a traditional way.

The PFI Process

The PFI process is well documented, but it may be helpful to list here the stages in brief. They are:

- Advertisement of the opportunity in the Official Journal of the European Community, the MOD Contracts Bulletin and elsewhere, calling for expressions of interest.
- Holding of an industry briefing day to inform industry on the requirement and timetable.
- Issue of a Pre-Qualification Questionnaire (PQQ) to reduce to manageable proportions the list of interested companies, and to supplement the information already held by MOD.
- Select long listed bidders (no more than six or eight) using endorsed assessment methodology, which 'wherever possible' will be published.
- Issue Invitation to Submit Outline Proposals (ISOP).
- Select short listed bidders (three or four) using agreed methodology.

[182] Nick Prest, Alvis, *Making the Difference,* Securing the Future, Newsdesk Communications Ltd, 1998

- Issue Invitation to Negotiate (ITN)[183] which requires bidders to submit formal, fully costed proposals.
- If necessary, request Best and Final Offers (BAFO).
- Select preferred bidder, again using an agreed methodology.
- Negotiate and place contract.

This appears, at first sight, to be a long and unnecessarily complex route. But many PFI contracts are very large and commit both MOD and industry for much longer periods than has been the norm previously, so the process must be one which does not skimp.

There is, however, one real concern: the Outline Proposals required are now very detailed and even the PQQ is getting more and more onerous. At this rate, there will be three stages at which fairly detailed proposals have to be made, and that is:

- Bad news for MOD as three separate detailed responses have to be assessed. This is expensive and time-consuming.
- Bad news for industry, especially the losers; a big PFI contract will be expensive to bid and may well have dozens, or even hundreds of losers down the supply chain.

While all efforts should be made to persuade MOD to reverse this increasingly onerous progression, industry itself must realise the complexity and costs involved.

The Contractor's Burden

MOD will not normally place a contract with companies which are not quality, security or financially sound, although it is possible that, where the contract is to be placed with a 'Special Purpose Vehicle' (SPV) – that is a company specially created for that particular contract – tendering will be allowed provided the parent companies have the appropriate accreditation and that there is a commitment that the SPV will be accredited within a designated period.

A standard PFI contract may include a 'design and build' phase (of, say, a barracks or a training facility) followed by an operating

[183] Also known variously as Invitation to Propose (ITP), Invitation to Submit Detailed Proposals (ISDP) or Request for Costed Proposals (RFCP)

phase. The contractor will usually require third party funding (from, say, banks) and he will have a large debt for some considerable time, which will eventually be repaid through operating profits. However, if he fails to achieve, say, milestones on time, he will face stiff financial penalties from MOD. He will, therefore, need from the outset clear quality advice on finance and legal matters, and this will be expensive.

PFI is attractive, but risks and costs are high.

While a PFI opportunity may be hugely attractive, the risks and costs are proportionally heavy. There is no point in starting the bidding process if you cannot win. Find a prime who can and offer your expertise to him.

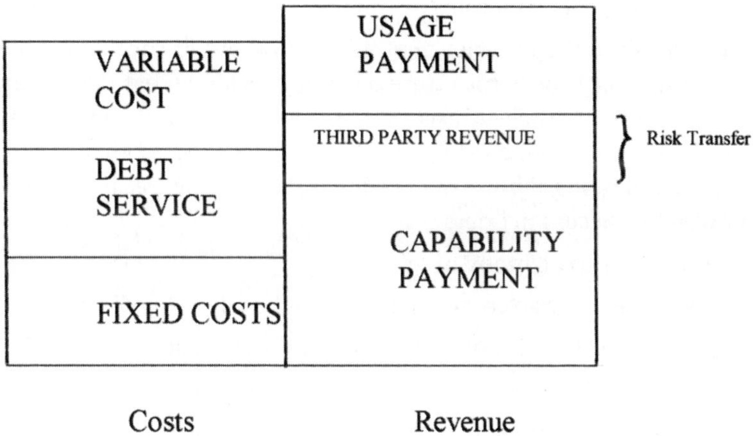

Figure 22: PFI Contractor Costs and Revenue Example

Definition of Output

The final problem is the definition of output. While this is the job of MOD, it is extremely difficult, particularly when both peacetime and operational usage, normally radically different, are both to be catered for under the PFI contract, such as will be the case with operational equipment like the Heavy Equipment Transporter and tanker aircraft. If the definition is not clear, get it clarified; it if is clear, make sure you understand all the implications. Lack of understanding will lead you into a financial mess. That is not MOD's intention. If you need help with understanding the output, ask.

However, that output must not be too rigidly defined early in the process and must be the subject of later negotiations, even when there is no operational aspect to complicate matters. The National Audit Office criticised certain aspects of the PFI deal for the supply of non-combat vehicles to the RAF.[184] The specific criticisms were:

- The contract was more suitable for outsourcing than PFI.
- The procedure limited scope for negotiation.
- The scope for innovation and risk transfer was limited.
- The scope of the project should have been larger to take advantage of economies of scale.

As a result of the experience of this and other PFI contracts, MOD is revising its approach for future deals and exactly what it will come up with is not at all clear, except that it will be subject to persistent change. Nevertheless, bidding companies might expect that some or all of the following will be required if success in competition is to be followed by success in operation:

- Proposals to be innovative.
- Innovation to be a continual feature of the whole life of the project.
- Share of risk and reward to be tied to performance provided.
- Authority to be vested in a single management team.
- Decision-making to be delegated to as low a level as practical.
- Costs and schedules to be continually challenged.
- Transparency of books.
- Incentives to be sized according to the whole project.
- Output to be progressively improved.
- Both sides to understand the meaning of vague terminology, such as 'value for money', before signing contracts.

---

[184] Audit Office report on the *Procurement of Non-Combat Vehicles,* MOD Contracts Bulletin, 8 September 1999

These factors for success are reflected in the experience of Serco, in its partnership with DERA in running the ranges at Llanbedr and West Freugh, where the essential characteristics are listed [185] as trust, commitment, joint management initiatives, mutual planning, performance monitoring and shared risks and rewards. The Target Cost Incentive Fee contract provides a mechanism for sharing, within agreed limits, both savings and costs.

A PFI Case Study

A PFI Case Study on the RAF's accommodation at Cosford and Shawbury was published in the PFI Report in May 1999. Some main points are:

- The Defence Housing Executive (DHE) selected the Riverside Housing Association (RHA) as the preferred bidder.
- RHA will procure the construction of 145 houses and then maintain their availability for 25 years.
- Debt finance was provided by the Royal Bank of Scotland.
- Construction work is to be carried out by Mansell.
- No payment is made by DHE during construction, but a proportion of the unitary charge is paid for each house as it is handed over, less liquidated damages for late delivery.
- RHA grants a lease to DHE for the length of the project and DHE accepts demand risk for the first 10 years, after which it has the right to hand back houses it does not require and, subsequently, for houses to be reinstated.
- The Bank needed to be clear as to how RHA's liabilities were to be capped, and the level of compensation to be paid if the contract terminated early.
- The building contractor was not part of the consortium and was not prepared to accept all the building risks (e.g. the existence of more mineshafts than the surveys indicated), so insurance had to be taken out.

---

[185] Ian Downie, Serco, *Committed to Success,* Securing the Future, Newsdesk Communications Ltd, 1998

- A strength of the project is that it is not led by a building contractor but by RHA whose objective was to provide long term accommodation.

There are plenty more points of interest. However, it should be realised that this £16M project is relatively small in value and far less complicated than the big ones.

Large PFI Projects

Skynet 5 is vastly more complex, with the inclusion of satellites as well as terminals, secure communications and ground stations. It is:

> *'Really pushing the boundaries. In order to ensure ourselves and industry that this is the sensible way forward, we couldn't just leap in.'*[186]

So the intention is a 'sort of halfway house', in which each of two consortia will carry out a study into whether a PFI approach is feasible.

The largest and most innovative PFI project to date is the recently launched request for outline proposals from industry to design, supply, manage, operate and fund a service to replace the RAF's existing air tanker fleet. It is a project that could be worth up to £9 billion over 20 years:

> *'The Future Strategic Tanker Aircraft project is by far our largest and most innovative PFI proposal to date, and offers the opportunity to work in partnership with industry and to show that private finance can work for challenging projects of this nature. The Government will ensure that the RAF operational effectiveness will be maintained, and that the project will deliver real value for money to the taxpayer.'*[187]

A final decision on the way ahead is planned for 2002, and the tanker aircraft could enter service in 2004. A variety of new and second hand aircraft will be under consideration by the six consortia invited to bid.

---

[186] Peter Ryan and Mike Cooper, *Going Private,* Defence Review supplement on Digitization & Communications, Autumn 1999

[187] Baroness Symonds, Minister of Defence Procurement, MOD press release, 333/99, 13 September 1999

> How will third-party use mesh in with operational readiness?

What is new here is not the use of private finance for procurement and operation of operational equipment, nor the size of the project, nor the length of the future deal. The real ground-breaking aspect, as it will be with Skynet, is the operational use of the equipment at very short notice. How that will be meshed in with the essential profitable use by third parties, while maintaining Britain's operational readiness, would seem to be the key difficulty. Writing the exact output requirement, eventually, in such a way that guarantees operational effectiveness without paying over the odds will be a major challenge.

The size of the potential benefits will lure the big industrial companies, but will they be able to manage the risks to the satisfaction of the military?

An Industrial Code of Practice

PFI is just one aspect of the relationship between MOD and industry, and it is a relatively new one. But whether support is through PFI, or more traditional contracts, the judgement of the Chief of Defence Logistics (CDL), that industrial performance during in-service support is 'disgraceful', needs heeding and answering.

The National Defence Industries Council (NDIC) has drawn up a Code of Practice as a public commitment to develop and improve industry's levels of customer service and support. This code of practice will focus attention on the following areas with the following commitment:[188]

- Service, in supporting customers' requirements in communications, defence system and product safety support products, support services, support material.
- Communication: a clear, defined contact plan for communication throughout the support chain.
- Security and Confidentiality of all customer information.
- Safety: immediate response throughout the supply chain.

[188] NDIC Customer Support Code of Practice

- Products, Information and Services: high standards in design, development and support.
- Schedule: timely provision of spares, repair and assets.
- Response: a full, efficient and clear response to all issues.

There is little here that is surprising, except that it does not go further. It is no more than the minimum that MOD might expect as a matter of course. That NDIC has been moved to issue it at all, perhaps underlines CDL's opinion of disgraceful industrial performance in the past.

The question it raises is just how long until we see improvements? Are all companies committed? If they are not, they may soon be in trouble.

A Whole Life Concept

So where does all this leave us? With a sense that the new relationship between MOD and industry in service support, unlike that proposed (although not yet implemented fully) in the procurement phases, is somewhat fragmented. The problem is the usual one of too many chiefs: CDP, CDL, PFI/PPP units, Customer 1, Customers 2 (plural), procurement primes, spares suppliers, PFI contractors et al.

What is required is a much more concentrated approach, at least for all contracts concerning equipment procurement and that includes training equipment, training facilities and in-service support. MOD might be finding it difficult to lead off down the road to huge partnering agreements covering development, production, in-service support, upgrades and training over a period of 25 or so years, but it has made a tentative start.

What MOD needs is the clear support of industry in proposing such arrangements early in the procurement cycle before logistic costs are locked in. Industry must come up with innovative ideas with clear opportunities for large cost reductions in through-life terms without reducing equipment performance. The IPT Hard and Stretch Objectives make it encumbent on IPT Leaders to look for such savings (tens of percent, not single figures), but they cannot do it without the enthusiasm and commitment of industry. While radically innovative proposals in competitive stages will need to be guarded very carefully within MOD Chinese Walls, industry must not allow considerations of commercial sensitivity to stop them innovating.

If winner does not take quite all in a full partnering arrangement, the loser may lose all. And the winner will be well placed to show the Chief of Defence Logistics that industry's 'disgraceful performance' is to be consigned to the past.

> *If winner does not take quite all, the loser may lose all.*

CHAPTER SIXTEEN

CULTURE IN INDUSTRY

MOD has been very open about the need for its own culture change. Industry has been less forthcoming, and many industrialists give the impression that, provided MOD changes its culture, then everything in the Smart Procurement garden will be lovely. Worse, as MOD is incapable of changing its culture, there is no need in industry to change either. That view is continually reinforced by unfortunate statements from all sorts of MOD people. What should we make of this recent offering?

> *'The twin objectives of providing the UK Armed Forces with the best equipment available, and buying the best, good or bad that British industry can supply are clearly incompatible......Yet the present Government seems determined to form a "smart procurement partnership" with this British defence industry which seems to serve our Armed Forces so badly.'*[189]

So, its all industry's fault. No wonder that scepticism is rife in industry about a MOD change of culture.

Of course, there are plenty of more forward-looking individuals in MOD, and there is a number of industrialists who are prepared to believe that, not only will MOD succeed in changing its culture, but that industry will have to change its own culture, too. But in what way? Unfortunately, even those who know that industrial culture needs reforming, find it difficult to be specific about what change is required.

---

[189] Tony Purton, MOD Director of Contracts 1988-93, The Times, September 1999

Shortcomings in Industry

In 1996, Keith Robinson suggested several shortcomings in the culture within UK industry as a whole:[190]

- Historical dependence on MOD sponsorship of research.
- Poor leadership.
- Failure to invest sensibly.
- Risk averse.
- Short termism.
- Slow to adapt to change.

This was very close to my list of failings that I produced for a DMA Seminar in 1994 and which I subsequently reproduced in 'A Dinosaur in Whitehall':[191]

- Myopic higher management.
- Decision-shy middle managers.
- Lack of management expertise.
- No forward strategy.
- Bad news aversive.
- Corner cutting to disaster.

To which could be added:

- Change resistance.
- Backward looking.
- Poor marketing skills.
- Poor knowledge of the customer.

> *Many in MOD have seen little change in industrial culture.*

Many companies will claim that they have moved on from there and some will argue that they have never been there at all. Maybe there is some truth in some of these claims. But only some. Many in MOD will say that they have seen little change, so will others:

'Industry should not focus on maximising short-term gain.'[192]

---

[190] Keith Robinson to UK Defence Forum, 26 November 1996

[191] *A Dinosaur in Whitehall,* by Bill Kincaid, Brassey's, September 1997

[192] Professor Trevor Taylor, *A Sprinting Start,* RUSI Journal, Vol.144, No.3, June 1999, page 84

The Centre for Tomorrow's Company has identified the following problems in industry:

- Ignorance of world-class standards.
- Fondness for adversarial relationships.
- Overdependence on purely financial measures of performance.

A recent article in the Times, based on a survey by the Institute of Directors which canvassed the opinion of 2000 directors of companies with more than 500 staff, castigated half of Britain's industrial directors (not just defence) for having no interest in the Internet and e-commerce:

'What we don't expect is every director and chief executive to be an expert in the bits and bytes of the Internet. What we do believe is they should have sufficient knowledge to understand the implications of technology on their business.....Directors give many reasons for not getting involved in their companies' technological issues, including fear of appearing ignorant; the misplaced belief that the Internet is "all hype"; and a misplaced conception that e-commerce will take years to become a big factor in business.'[193]

So there are acknowledged problems.

What Needs Changing?

A number of defence industrialists were interviewed for their view on industrial culture and what changes were needed. Integration of their views produces a list which, while not all items would have been agreed by all the interviewees, is a reasonable summation of their overall opinions on necessary industrial changes:

- More openness/transparency with customers.
- Better communications both internally and externally.
- Better knowledge and understanding of the customer.
- Improved expertise in many management areas.
- Modification of adversarial approach to, and suspicion of, MOD.

---

[193] *IT Experts Must Spread the Word to Apathetic Directors,* The Times, 6 October 1999, page 38

- More proactive approach.
- Improved decision making.
- Elimination of the fear/blame culture.

The Fear/Blame Culture and Bad News Aversion

Many people have mentioned the fear/blame culture in industry and its corollary of bad news aversion. In such a culture, no-one wants to be the messenger of bad-news, neither does anyone want to hear bad news as he will then become the bearer of bad news up the management chain. But, as John Harvey-Jones put it:[194]

> *'Bad news in all organisations is seldom received with much enthusiasm. The reality of life is of course that it is the bad news man who should be the most prized. It is all too easy to get people who will tell you the nice things..... but those who will stand up without fear or favour and tell you, hopefully tactfully, that things are not really the way that everyone else thinks that they are, are pearls beyond price.'*

This culture makes trust within the company impossible to achieve. Without intra-company trust, what chance trust between company and customer?

Transparency and Trust

Trust will be primarily engendered by two things: transparency and understanding. The latter is very poor but can be improved by joint training (see Chapter 9) and, over a longer time, by prolonged working together with individuals serving for longer in post. The former is less straightforward.

It has been recognised by all that trust between MOD and its suppliers is essential and that trust can only be generated if there is transparency, including financial transparency. Industry must recognise that in a partnering arrangement, MOD must have a greater and more detailed access to its company planning and costings. Even when there is no partnering arrangement, the new

---

[194] John Harvey-Jones, *Making it Happen (Reflections on Leadership)*, Collins, 1988, Chapter 3

relationship between MOD and industry will demand greater transparency than before.

> *'Throughout the life of a partnership, there are likely to be shared risks and common goals. Therefore it is essential to share information and maintain open communication through linked management teams with shared ways of operating. Additionally, there should be visibility of costs and performance, pooling of ideas and joint development of methods and techniques.'*[195]

Opacity will not engender trust.

Industry has been quick to point out that transparency means greater access to MOD long term equipment and detailed funding plans, and MOD is moving a long way towards meeting this request. However, industry has been much more reticent about the transparency which it will provide. It is perhaps here that industry will be required to make greatest changes in their outlook when entering into Partnering Arrangements with MOD. Unless there is a true 'open-book' approach in all aspects of that particular project, opacity and not transparency will be the industrial order of the day. Opacity will not engender trust. Without trust, Partnering Arrangements will be doomed.

But transparency is not only required between industry and MOD, but also within the company. One industrialist interviewed suggested that proper project management tools were not used partly because they force a transparent, disciplined approach which allows managers no place to hide when things go wrong. Transparency within a company is often seen as a threat to individuals, which takes us all the way back to the fear/blame culture. It is a vicious circle.

Short-Termism and Long Term Partnering

Constrained as it is by the next shareholders' report, industry is, perhaps not surprisingly, short-termist. But what is surprising is that too often this short-term approach is not buttressed by a long-term

[195] Ian Downie, Serco, *Committed to Success,* Securing the Future, Newsdesk Communications Ltd, 1998

plan. In the past, the MOD's competitive, fixed-price, short-term contract approach has perhaps reduced long-term planning in industry to a lower importance than it should have but, under Smart Procurement, contracts will become (slowly perhaps but surely) of longer duration and will be planned further ahead. The future prosperity of companies will now start to depend on their long-term plan and their fitness to enter into long-term partnerships with MOD. MOD will not be keen to enter partnering arrangements with a company that clearly still thinks in the short-term.

Joining the relevant Capability Working Group (CWG) must be the basis for a long term approach, for it is here that MOD's future capability requirements will be hammered out. The knowledge and understanding that these will provide should enable companies to plan further ahead than they have done in the past, and this need not be an expensive business. It will certainly pay huge dividends downstream and, if the short-termist accountants are not enthused by that (and they may not be), the direct costs of longer-term planning should be put in perspective.

What costs are there? As a minimum, they are:

- The cost of resourcing attendance at the relevant CWGs. One man (the right man) for each, but very much part-time.
- The cost of paper planning – financial, technical, project management.
- The cost of specific training, if necessary, to fit selected individuals for full contribution to, and extraction from, Integrated Project Teams (IPTs) as soon as these are formed in the Concept Phase.
- Exploratory work on early teaming possibilities.

These costs are all small and, in any case, with the exception of the first, should be done under project funding anyway.

But the above will not necessarily gain you a step ahead of your competitors. What you must be able to do, is to contribute to CWGs and IPTs in the Concept Phase so as to ensure that any early down-selection of contractors for overcrowded CWGs and IPTs includes you. You must demonstrate that you have a lot to offer, whether your contribution is in full forum or one-to-one with MOD.

And what do you have to offer? Well, you may have one or more projects to offer, but this will be of limited value to MOD when they are looking for new options to meet a capability gap. Of more value will be studies that you have carried out into future systems, or technologies that will underpin future systems.

> *For too long, industry has sat back and waited for handouts.*

But you don't do much of that, do you? For too long you have sat back and waited for hand-outs from DERA or for project funding, rather than getting on with your own studies/ technology generation to guide your own longer-term planning, which you don't do either.

At this point I can feel certain chairmen, managing directors, chief executives puffing a little and refuting my arguments: 'That's not true here; others may be like that, but we're not.' Of course, some firms are better than others, but none I believe do nearly enough to ensure long-term prosperity. In the short-term, order books may be full and exports booming, but the run-down in MOD-funded research and MOD project funding, together with the prospect of fewer, longer contracts, make it a bleak long-term outlook for all companies that do not repeatedly win competitive tenders. Future wins will be based on your long-term planning and your work in-house to get you into a winning position.

You will only get to that winning position if you have something worthwhile to offer in the Concept Phase. And it's not only MOD you will be seeking to convince, but other prospective team members. If they are exploring teaming arrangements earlier than in the past, they will be doing so on the basis of your work prior to, and during, the Concept Phase, whether or not MOD is paying for it or contributing to it.

You cannot afford to arrive at the Assessment Phase scrabbling around for team members: you may have little choice.

Of course there is a danger with early teaming. A technology or systems leader today will not necessarily be a leader in five or ten years' time. His edge today may be a millstone tomorrow, but rather than postpone team-seeking, it would be more sensible to select future team players on the basis of their ethos, their attitudes, their innovative track record and their commitment, and not on the one-off technology solution they have today.

Proaction is the name of the game in the early stages – not couch potato-ship. Contribution to CWGs, proposals of joint research or Technical Demonstrators to DERA, in-house technology and systems studies, joint studies with prospective team members are necessary if you are to get yourself into a winning position.

> *Proaction is the game - not couch potato-ship.*

Of course all this will cost money. But, in relative terms, that cost will be small in comparison both with the much larger returns of winning major contracts downstream and also with the damage that will result in the future from losing major contracts. The accountants need to recognise that, under Smart Procurement, there will be fewer, bigger contracts and the penalty of losing will be so much higher.

Can you afford not to put more effort in at the beginning and pay for it yourselves?

The Stakeholder Mentality

Perhaps the first and, possibly, the largest culture change that industry faces is the change from the fixed-price, adversarial mentality to one where risks, problems and rewards are jointly owned with the MOD in either a full partnering arrangement or an incentivised, risk-balance contract. Sitting behind the contract and exploiting the loopholes is not what is wanted in the future. Industry will be a stakeholder and must act like one. The 'them and us' mentality must go, along with the 'you owe us work' approach.

So far, industrial companies, by and large, have not engaged themselves as stakeholders, but have waited for all initiatives to come from MOD. There has been little or no true joint working, except in a very few of the first IPTs. A joint approach means:

- Transparency.
- Joint identification of problems and their solutions.
- Sharing of risks and penalties.
- Sharing of benefits.
- Proaction on both sides, particularly in adversity.

Changing the culture will be neither easy nor quick.

> *'Management research offers the clear finding that cultural change in organisations takes years rather than months to bring about, especially without a wholesale change in personnel.'*[196]

A wholesale change in personnel in the defence industry is not possible without losing technical expertise and is, in any case, unnecessary. What is necessary is a whole new approach to training and education.

Secondment

MOD has launched an interchange programme with industry:

> *'Just as the MOD needs to draw on the best commercial practices, its own workforce represents a unique blend of skills and talents which can be used to benefit your business. We each gain from better mutual understanding. Building links between MOD and industry and commerce via the exchange of people and ideas is the best way to assist this process.'*[197]

The main stumbling blocks have been, first, the unwillingness of industrialists to take a bite out of their career ladder and secondly, especially for small companies, the funding issue. MOD has tackled its own problem with the former through plans that would make it necessary, for those who wish to reach a high grade, to work for one or two years in the private sector. Is industry capable of a similar initiative?

---

[196] *A Sprinting Start,* Professor Trevor Taylor, RUSI Journal, Vol.144, No.3, June 1999, page 84

[197] Sir Richard Mottram, Foreword to MOD's *Interchange*

The MOD Interchange Programme may not solve all the funding problems, but it does state that 'we recognise that in some circumstances it may be necessary to be flexible on costs'.

The interchange programme may build understanding of your prospective partner better than any other way, but the difficulties may restrict secondments to a low level. There need to be other ways.

Training and Education

MOD has its own problem with cultural identities. It has been said[198] that there are three tribes: the civil servants with degrees in acceptable subjects from acceptable universities; the military from an acceptable background often without degrees from any university; and the scientists with useful degrees from unacceptable universities. These three tribes have rubbed along together for decades without fully understanding each other. They have no joint training. Now we have a fourth tribe who is to join them: the industrialists from all sorts of backgrounds with MBAs from all sorts of business schools. What hope is there, without any form of joint training, that they will be understood by, or understand, the other three tribes already ensconsed in the MOD acquisition system?

Joint training of both MOD and industrial personnel is an aspiration of Smart Procurement, but does not seem to have been accorded a high priority despite its obvious importance. A joint MOD-industry panel stressed its importance:[199]

> *'Our final point concerns the importance of industrial education and training for effective industrial involvement in IPTs in both the DPA and DLO regimes. The MOD has itself undertaken a significant training programme for its own staff, and the primary responsibility for industry will be to do the same for its own personnel..... There is concern, however, that the full benefit of Smart Procurement will only be achieved by better mutual understanding of the issues that will face both parties sitting either side of a contract, but with a common aim to*

---

[198] Bill Kincaid, *A Dinosaur in Whitehall,* Brassey's, September 1997

[199] Panel on Industry in IPTs, MOD/DMA Seminar on Smart Procurement, Didcot, 24 June 1999

deliver their programme on time, to cost, and to performance. This can be encouraged by joint training of MOD and industrial personnel, and we look forward to the opportunity to undertake this as soon as the Ministry is able to accommodate it within its schedule.'

As I have pointed out in Chapter 9, joint training is not simply a matter of MOD allotting a few places to industry on its own courses, or industry allowing MOD participation in its own training schemes. What is required is a joint MOD-industry procurement school, jointly funded and jointly staffed.

The benefits of effective training and education are not intangible. A University of Pennsylvania study of 3200 companies found that:

'A 10% increase in expenditure on education produced an 8.5% increase in productivity, whereas the same increase in capital expenditure resulted in a 3.8% increase in productivity.'

Impressive evidence?

It could perhaps be added that, under Smart Procurement, a culture change is essential and this is unlikely to occur without a major investment in retraining. Without a culture change, a company will be less likely to win partnering arrangements or even incentive-based contracts with MOD. The penalties for losing being higher, the company that does not take training seriously will find itself struggling for survival.

When do you begin?

The company that does not take training seriously will struggle.

CHAPTER SEVENTEEN

SMALL AND MEDIUM SIZED ENTERPRISES

Much of the Smart Procurement Initiative has, either consciously or unconsciously, been based on internal MOD change or on new relationships between MOD and prime contractors. Small and medium sized enterprises (SMEs) have felt left out and thoroughly confused by what the implications for them might be. There is a feeling in some quarters that neither MOD nor primes care about SMEs, that the SME base is threatened with extinction, that MOD believes there are too many SMEs and plenty can go to the wall without impact on MOD procurement. And there is plenty to fuel this view. But, like so many other views formed in difficult times, there is both truth and misapprehension here.

Part of the problem is that, for many years, MOD has left prime contractors to manage sub-contractors and suppliers and has hesitated to intervene for clear management and contractual reasons. Hence the persecution view that MOD does not care about SMEs. Equally, primes have often squeezed SMEs for their own benefit, sometimes for all their benefits, if winning a competition can be called a benefit. In some areas where there are indeed too many SMEs, this is only the law of the market place.

> *Many SMEs are lagging in modern practices, investment and innovation.*

But the major part of the problem is that too many SMEs are lagging behind in terms of modern business practices, investment and innovation. Often for the reason that they cannot afford the cost and cannot afford the manpower resources. This is where they need help.

Shortfalls in Performance

A study in 1997 of the supply chain in one particular area – armoured vehicles – drew many conclusions about the state of sub-contractors and SMEs including:[200]

- The failure of defence companies involved to adopt modern business practices capable of increasing productivity and reducing costs.
- The general absence of modern business practices of the type used in other UK industries, especially motor vehicles.
- The lack of IT and the lack of computer links between the prime contractor, suppliers and customer.
- The contrast between advanced and relatively backward firms.
- The use by suppliers at the second and third level of modern business practices but, typically, these suppliers were not defence specialists.
- The treatment by companies with both military and civilian divisions of each as completely separate entities, thereby minimising the opportunities for profitable read-across.

This is all pretty damning. Of course it is not confined to defence. The construction industry appears to be lagging behind the recent changes that have been made within the defence industry. A study on 'Building Down Barriers' states:[201]

'The principle manufacturer should, for example, be seeking opportunities to exploit new technologies or new working methods that the suppliers develop as part of their own efforts to improve their competitiveness through greater innovation. We expect that a similar pattern will emerge in the construction sector, with the demise of suppliers not prepared to invest in the future, as has happened in manufacturing.'

---

[200] *Armoured Fighting Vehicle Supply Chain Analysis,* Centre for Defence Economics, University of York, September 1997

[201] Prime Contractor Handbook of Supply Chain Management, MOD, March 1999

So, we are talking about the demise of SMEs that do not embrace the future. Is that so unfair?

The Impact of Smart Procurement

Smart Procurement is here and it is here to stay. While we are not certain how many of the Smart Procurement initiatives will be implemented or how fully, there is no doubt that most will become reality in some form or other.

'The biggest problem we have at the moment is that some [SMEs] think they can ignore Smart Procurement and it will go away, or it won't effect them.'[202]

> Smart Procurement can enrich some SMEs and destroy others.

Wrong. Smart Procurement has the potential to enrich some SMEs and destroy others. Understanding Smart Procurement and its likely impact on SMEs is fundamental to their future survival.

So what are the likely impacts of significance?

Perhaps most important of all is the possible or even probable increase in size and length of contracts through:

- the integration of the three single-Service logistics organisations into the Defence Logistics Organisation and the consequent amalgamation in many areas of three separate contracts into one.
- the adoption of partnering arrangements between MOD and industry, thereby leading to longer contracts through procurement and into in-service support.
- the moves by primes towards partnership with preferred elements of their supply chains.

Longer and larger contracts are good news for supply chain companies of winning primes, but they are bad news for those in the chain of losing primes. And disaster for those who are in no supply chain at all, except for companies with rare expertise who can sell to anyone.

---

[202] Warren North, Defence Industries Council Newsletter No.2, May 1999, page 6

The next impact is on resources, both financial and manpower as Smart Procurement calls for a much closer relationship between MOD and industry and the participation of elements of the supply chain, not just primes, in Integrated Project Teams (IPTs) and Capability Working Groups (CWGs). Provision of the manpower and the costs of paying them and providing them with greater support (e.g. IT) will fall on the companies concerned. This will be a major burden, but if declined could see the SME excluded from much information and disadvantaged compared with his competitors.

Greater involvement in CWGs and IPTs necessitates input to those bodies, and this raises the difficult issue of Intellectual Property Rights (IPR). For a small firm, IPR may be a matter of survival and could, therefore, make it very difficult to contribute and, consequently, to persuade MOD that the company has both something to offer, and also the right attitude towards smart relationships. IPR will need to be identified clearly and agreed right at the start so that arrangements can be made for its protection. But the IPR factor is not an excuse for doing nothing.

The final major impact on SMEs is the change of culture that is being demanded, not only within MOD, but also by MOD from primes and by primes from SMEs. The move from an adversarial, fixed-price, risk-aversive attitude to one where all elements of the supply chain will be expected to 'own' the output and to contribute to sharing risks and disbenefits as well as benefits, is a major challenge.

> *'The basic principle [of the prime contractor] is to involve anyone from any point in the supply chain if they have knowledge and skills relevant to a particular decision......."concurrent engineering" of product and processes so that problems can be solved earlier and costs "designed out". This of course requires early involvement of the supply chain.'*[203]

Involvement in the whole project is perhaps *the* major challenge for SMEs.

---

[203] *Building Down Barriers,* Prime Contractor Handbook of Supply Chain Management, MOD, March 1999, page 13.

SME Concerns

The potential impact of Smart Procurement has led to the expression of concerns by some working in, or representing the interests of, SMEs. These include:

- Possible exclusion from CWGs and IPTs (particularly Cluster IPTs) because of unwieldy numbers.
- The difficulty and cost of manning CWGs and IPTs at SME expense.
- The possibility that benefits (including gainshare) will not be flowed down the supply chain, while risk and liability will be.
- The cost of new IT to meet likely requirements of e-commerce, MOD or prime standard software formats, better information earlier and earned value management.
- IPR.
- Possible threat to SMEs if the 'big boys' develop long-term relationships with MOD.
- Growth of in-house capabilities within primes to manage longer contracts from procurement into support.

These are all legitimate concerns and have not yet been satisfactorily answered by either MOD or primes. They boil down to two general areas of concern: increasing costs, decreasing opportunities. Together they spell danger. But if the positive, rather than the negative view is taken, Smart Procurement also spells greater opportunities for innovative, go-ahead companies. Unquestionably, there will be a requirement for greater investment and this will only be possible if the company grasps the greater opportunities on offer. Proaction, rather than reaction, is required.

One sliver of comfort (at least I think it is comfort) is the statement by the Chief of Defence Procurement[204] that the 'Defence Procurement Agency (DPA) will need to manage its relationship with SMEs', but this is apparently being opposed by primes. Exactly how the DPA would effect this oversight/managing role, without interfering with the prime/supplier contractual arrangements is not

[204] CDP at the MOD/DMA Smart Procurement Seminar, Didcot, 24 June 1999

at all clear and, as MOD has consciously steered clear of this for many years, oversight without interference is a tricky combination.

A New Culture

If individual SMEs are going to thrive, or even survive, then they must make a major change in their culture which will be difficult and which must be driven from the top. The smaller the company, the easier it will be, given the commitment. That at least is encouraging in that every SME will have a far easier task than primes or MOD itself. But what changes in culture are needed?

First and foremost must be innovation. SMEs that stand still will not offer what primes and MOD want. Innovation, though, comes in two main categories:

- Innovation in product design, so that the company is offering something that others are not and enable the prime and MOD to produce greater performance at the same cost, or the same performance at less cost.
- Innovation in manufacturing methods, to reduce cost progressively over a period of time to meet continuous improvement targets set by the prime and/or MOD.

But an innovative culture is about continuous innovation in design and/or manufacturing methods. If primes are to win competitions for MOD contracts for procurement and support, they will probably only do so by proposing continuous improvements throughout the contract, leading to progressively reducing costs. Primes will only achieve progressive targets with the support and commitment of its supply chain. Hence primes will be seeking innovative companies, not stagnant ones; proactive companies, not reactive ones.

> *Primes will be seeking innovative companies, not stagnant ones.*

Innovation costs money and time. Can small businesses afford it? The answer is, of course, that they must afford it if they are to survive, and there is help at hand. Every Business Link offers an innovation and technology service to the SMEs in their area, to help them recognise the benefits of technology and innovative practice and to apply them effectively. There are awards to develop innovative new products and processes, through grants for feasibility studies and development of pre-production prototypes; there is a scheme to help SMEs to access the knowledge, skills and technology in universities and other recognised research establishments and, possibly, to build partnerships with them; and there are other helpful programmes including Business Incubation, EUREKA, LINK, Foresight, Business and Innovation Centres, the International Technology Service, and UK Science Parks.[205]

Help is around. Given that the company has the basic expertise in its own area, innovation is more an issue of mind rather than matter. Hence a culture issue.

Another culture issue is the change from a contracted supplier mentality to that of a stakeholder. If the prime is to flow down gainsharing and other benefits, the recipient must 'own' the relevant problems that arise and seek remedies efficiently and effectively. This does not just concern problems which arise within the domain of that supplier and which might have been covered anyway in an earlier-style contract, but issues which arise from interface problems or in other specific areas where input is required from all those involved for resolution. If a SME is going to clamour for flowing down of benefits, it must accept a responsibility to help solve problems that arise in and around its area of expertise, whether or not it has caused those problems.

Likewise risk management which needs to be undertaken, not solely by MOD, or solely by the prime, but by whoever is best placed to manage it.

The products and services provided by the companies in a supply chain may account for anything up to 90% of the whole and:

> *'The way in which these products and services are procured – and the way in which their delivery is managed – have a profound effect on the outcome of the project. The performance of the whole supply chain*

---

[205] *A Guide to Help for Small Businesses*, DTI, April 1999

impacts not only contract profitability for all parties, but also the way in which the completed [project] meets the client's justifiable expectations of cost, quality and functionality.'[206]

So if the prime has to change its culture to win contracts under Smart Procurement, it is obvious that the prime will be looking for SMEs that are also changing their culture. And it may well reward those SMEs with a partnership. The others may get nothing.

The SCRIA (Supply Chain Relationships in Aerospace) programme was established in 1995 to change outdated culture:

'SCRIA confronts tired and unproductive working practices. It requires that its participants co-operate to create effective business teams, both between and within organisations. This means open and honest dealings, and a commitment to partnerships........moving from confrontation to mutual achievement.'

This is not just a 'big boys' activity, but applicable to the whole supply chain. In fact, without SME involvement, it cannot work.

'It is widely accepted that effective supply chain management is an integral part of cost and schedule control........SCRIA is the only approach that will provide the training and guidance to make such improvements [in the supply chain].'

It is aimed at setting the highest standards in supply chain relationships[207].

Partnership with a Prime

Primes, therefore, are increasingly seeking partnerships or alliances with supply chain companies:

'Prime contracting replaces short-term, contractually driven, single project, adversarial inter-company relationships with long-term, multiple-project relationships based on trust and cooperation. These

---

[206] *Building Down Barriers,* Handbook of Supply Chain Management, MOD, March 1999

[207] SCRIA is part of SBAC's Competitiveness Challenge programme, sponsored by DTI

long-term, strategic supply chain alliances incorporate continuous improvement targets to reduce costs and enhance quality.'[208]

If primes are seeking partnerships and alliances with SMEs in the supply chain, then it follows that SMEs must seek out such relationships with primes. In some areas, for example the aerospace industry, there is already a burgeoning supply chain relationship, but in others, such as in naval circles where historically sub-contractors and suppliers have been contracted directly to the MOD, there is a much greater need for SMEs to make themselves and their products or expertise known to primes. It is in these areas that the trade associations can play a big role.

Seeking out relationships with primes is not a matter of choice for SMEs, it is fundamental to survival. Clearly, because if all the likely defence primes operating in your area have long-term alliances with your direct SME competitors and you do not, it does not take much analytical thought to arrive at the conclusion that your days are numbered.

But there is a downside to strategic alliances with primes. If the prime is successful in winning contracts, you will be successful, but if he is not, then you may be stuck with a long-term trap. But there is a downside, too, to project partnering because you must then bid and probably compete for every project which is time-consuming and costly, with no payback if you fail to win, or in due course if the prime fails to win. Either way it pays, therefore, for you to do your homework on primes before you commit yourself. You should ask yourself the following questions about each prime you are considering partnering:

- Is he committed to winning contracts in this area, or is his core business elsewhere?
- Is he likely to win contracts at all (e.g. a US-based company looking to prime ship or tank projects)?
- Is his business ethos atuned to both MOD's new Smart Procurement and your own?

---

[208] *Building Down Barriers,* Handbook of Supply Chain Management, MOD, March 1999

- Does he already have your expertise in-house or in his supply chain?
- Does he want you only for competing at supplier level and, if he does, are you confident that you can win some or all of his competitions?

There are probably plenty more such questions. A strategic alliance is only workable if both partners (prime and supplier) understand and respect each other's aims, constraints and ambitions. Without this there cannot be trust. Without trust a strategic alliance or partnership will not work.

Once in a strategic partnership or alliance with a prime, the SME must pull his weight and not sit back and expect the contracts to roll in.

'We have some partnerships with primes and are happy to put our own money into development of a new piece of equipment for a prime provided it becomes a proprietary item.' A managing director of a SME.

BAe has pursued a corporate programme to reduce its sub-contractor base from thousands to hundreds by creating 'full authority sub-contractors' through which BAe can act more efficiently, particularly in its ability to devolve authority and risk.

'It is now three years since the decision was taken to establish partnerships across a broad range of commodity groups making inputs to the Eurofighter programme. Samlesbury's head of logistics, Mick Crowe cites some examples of highly effective partnerships including those for cutting and hand tools and fasteners where the suppliers have been able to bring experience in their own fields into the development engineering phase of the programme.'[209]

Something in it for the prime, then. And for the SMEs?

'Traditional sub-contractors, who have long wanted long term contracts, now find that the partnership approach gives them the stability over the three-to-five years period that they need in planning for the orderly development of their businesses.'[210]

---

[209] Jane's Defence Industry, Vol.16, No.4, April 1999, page 1

[210] Ibid

This is a major change from the past when primes have placed individual, and relatively small, purchase orders for components as and when needed. Now larger and longer orders are placed with the supplier who has to take a greater share in managing the control and delivery of sets of components.

SMEs will need to embrace such a change in management.

'The manner in which BAe achieves its objective will require a re-think of management practices at numerous points in the second, third and fourth tiers of the supply chain, but the indications are that it is confident that it is in the process of creating a supply chain with sharp awareness of what it must do to optimise returns on that which has been invested in product development and transition to manufacturing.'[211]

Primes will increasingly design and develop with the supply chain and will do so with its key supply chain partners through 'Access Points' or 'Full Authority Sub-contractors' or 'Cluster Team Leaders'.

SME Clusters

Small firms are often unable, on their own, to reduce costs by bulk buying. According to the Chartered Institute of Purchasing and Supply (CIPS):

'Small and medium-sized companies annually throw away thousands of pounds each........[An] approach might be for a group of small firms using similar products to form a consortium to buy in bulk. This may have benefits beyond costs......a consortium will hold a single contract with a supplier. Contracts are costly to set up and .... there are considerable savings to be made...... consortia may also elicit an improved service because the higher level of business is more important to the supplier.'[212]

This is a fairly basic solution to a very basic problem, but it points the way to greater benefits and there has recently been increasing

---

[211] Ibid

[212] *Small Firms Can Enjoy the Fruits of Canny Purchasing,* The Times, 28 September 1999

momentum towards forming SME clusters. Sometimes these clusters have no formal bonding agency and are just loose collections of SMEs who may work fitfully together. Others have much stronger cluster bonds. Others may have, within the cluster, the ability to stage competition if that is what a prime requires. These links between SMEs, or SME clusters, should achieve a 'critical mass'.

Momentum towards forming SME clusters to achieve critical mass.

The UK Lean Aerospace Initiative (UK LAI) has recently been endorsed by the Society of British Aerospace Companies (SBAC) as a major driver in the sector's search for competitiveness, and should serve as a model for sectors other than aerospace. Indeed, that move has already begun. UK LAI is expected to deliver significant benefits as a national framework for all related work in aerospace, academia and other industrial sectors. SMEs working within, or to, the aerospace industry would have to participate as part of the prime's supply chain.

Interestingly, a study[213] has shown greater applicability than just that. It concludes that collaboration (clustering) between lean SMEs can lead to:

- The creation of a total package of much higher value and attractiveness on a global basis than the single SME could offer on its own.
- Unique competencies can be built through collaboration with a number of smaller, focused businesses.

However, there is a need for SME clusters to have a focal point or cluster leader(s) to work effectively to a prime to create an alliance, to win a contract, or to get effectively involved in design and development with the prime once the alliance or contract has been created. This suggests one larger SME round which several small SMEs can gather. But that is not vital.

[213] *A Lean and Global Smaller Firm,* Karlsson and Ahlstrom, International Journal of Operations and Production Management, Vol 17 No 10, 1997

[214] Ibid, page 2

A 'cluster' of four Lancashire companies recently won a £12 million contract from BAe for supplying minor sub-assemblies for Eurofighter. The four companies had formed a partnership and a key aspect of their appeal for BAe was their 'willingness to work together' and their close location. BAe considers that the partnership gives a high degree of certainty that quality components will be delivered to time and cost.

A spokesman for the partnership said:

'This new approach is a major cultural change for the companies involved, but it is based on us recognising this major business opportunity. It is a major challenge, but I believe it is also the start of the future for supply chain relationships within the aerospace industry.'[214]

It seems that the basic principles for the relationship between a prime and its supply chain are:

- Establishment by the prime of long term relationships (strategic partnerships or alliances) with key suppliers.
- Management of the supply chain through 'clusters' of SMEs and sub-contractors.
- Involvement of the supply chain in design, development, costing, risk management.
- Development of continuous improvement (cost, time, performance) throughout the supply chain.

SMEs and MOD Integrated Project Teams

If SMEs are to be involved to a greater extent than before in design, development, costing and risk management, they must have a clearer idea of MOD's plans and programmes. This in turn suggests that they need to be involved in both Capability Working Groups (CWGs) and Integrated Project Teams (IPTs), but at an MOD/DMA Seminar it was felt that:

'typical SMEs would not be able to perform well in the role of interfacing on requirements with CWGs or EIPTs (embryonic IPTs), because of their lack of experience in such dealings.'[215]

[215] MOD/DMA Seminar on Smart Procurement, Swindon, 2 February 1999

Nevertheless, SMEs must be involved and must learn from the experience very quickly. The difficulty is not going to be so much a lack of performance in IPTs by SMEs, as a lack of opportunity for them to perform at all. As we have seen in Chapters 13 and 14, MOD is facing difficulties with including industry in IPTs at all in competitive phases and in cluster IPTs, and if primes are excluded, SMEs will have no chance.

A second difficulty is that of protection of IPR. Given that IPR can be the lifeblood of a SME, there are bound to be difficulties for SMEs making substantial input into CWGs and Concept Phase IPTs; perhaps this difficulty is more acute for SMEs than for primes. But difficulties arising from IPR are more often than not caused by the failure to positively identify IPR ownership early in the project, so that the situation is far more difficult to unravel later when funded work has been carried out within that specific IPR area. It is essential to clarify IPR right from the outset.

But clarifying IPR is only the start. As one small firm put it:

'IPR is badly policed and it is often unclear who owns what and who owes what to whom.'

Unless the prime has faith in MOD to safeguard IPR properly, and unless the supply chain has faith in the prime to safeguard the smaller companies' IPR, then IPR will continue to be a big issue. Partnering should resolve this, but it will only do so with clear thought and action.

A third difficulty is the problem of manning IPTs. The smaller the company, the greater difficulty it will have in providing representation at MOD CWGs and IPTs, except perhaps late in the acquisition cycle when the final prime contractor has been selected and representation at the MOD IPT is paid for by the project. Or will payment be restricted to the prime representative? Even if the SME is paid for its representative's attendance at the IPT, there will be difficulty in providing a suitable person as the choice will be limited and most (all?) will be closely involved in making and delivering the components to time and cost, as well as attending the industrial IPT.

So, the likely exclusion of industry from IPTs in the competitive phases and from Cluster IPTs in all phases, the difficulties over IPR that will be posed by input to CWGs, and the difficulties for a SME in manning MOD IPTs when it is invited, all point to a lack of SME involvement in MOD CWGs and IPTs despite the emphasis that MOD is placing on it.

Some of this requires further thought by MOD to:

- Include industry effectively in IPTs during competitive phases.
- Include industry effectively in Cluster IPTs (very important as small projects are the lifeblood of so many SMEs).
- Resolve CWG and Concept Phase IPT methods of operation so that IPR is fully protected and seen to be so.
- Minimise, after competition is finished, the industrial resource requirement by merging the MOD IPT with the industrial IPT, as argued in Chapter 14.

But SMEs must play their part too. They will have to:

- Accept the need to provide greater project funding.
- Find ways of making significant input while protecting their own IPR.
- Use partnership relations with the prime to ensure that SME attendance is only requested when it is in the interests of the MOD, the prime or the SME itself.

SME involvement in CWGs and IPTs is vital. If anything up to 90% of a project is provided by sub-contractors and suppliers, it makes little sense if 90% of the industrial expertise is effectively excluded from the much-vaunted industrial involvement in MOD projects. MOD, primes and SMEs will all have to find satisfactory answers. They are not visible yet.

SMEs and Competition

It is quite possible that SMEs will face more competition in the future: competition to enter an alliance with a prime, competition to remain in the alliance, competition within SME clusters, competition in the supply chain at the behest of MOD when competition between primes is not valid or has been completed. SMEs can thrive on competition (if they have the required attitude and expertise), but competition is costly. While that cost is not usually a fundamental consideration to large primes or to MOD, and therefore is rarely made visible to them, the cost of too much competition could be crippling to SMEs.

Competition within the supply chain must be controlled sensibly.

Competition within the supply chain must be controlled sensibly by both primes and MOD. In particular, MOD must not insist on competition at low levels with primes who have recently held competitions to initiate long-term alliances. MOD needs to accept that in some cases, once the prime has been selected, that he will bring with him a pre-selected group or cluster of sub-contractors and suppliers. MOD seems unlikely to accept this easily, although it has accepted that a code of practice will be drawn up on competition at sub-contractor level, but how far down the chain this will reach is not at all clear. At the very least MOD will require evidence that the marketplace has been thoroughly tested, more so now than ever as mergers and acquisitions may provide 'in-house' capabilities that have not been tested by competition.

> *'But we [MOD] are prepared to be more flexible about how we apply competition on repeat orders, where the performance of the supplier has been proven over time: if we can establish a partnering arrangement with a supplier in which we get continuing value for money gains, we don't feel the need to keep having repeat competitions – but we nonetheless need to demonstrate that any long-term relationship with a supplier is to the benefit of the taxpayer.'*[216]

This suggests a useful shift by MOD. But will it apply, not just to repeat orders, but also to the initial procurement buy?

---

[216] Simon Webb, Head of MOD's Smart Procurement Implementation Team, Supply Management, 13 May 1999, page 24

Costs

The cost of competition, if not applied sensibly, could be crippling to SMEs. But this is not the only increased cost that SMEs face, and unless SMEs pay them, they will be less and less likely to win MOD or prime competitions. Some of the reasons for better IT have been stated as:[217]

- Better information will be required earlier in the project.
- Whole life costs, particularly ILS, will be required and continually updated.
- Introduction of Earned Value Management will mean the requirement for more information.
- Specific regulated formats will be required by primes/MOD.
- COTS equipment will not necessarily provide the information required by primes/MOD (e.g. ILS).
- MOD committed to greater e-commerce.
- Conformance required to certain EDI standard formats (e.g. 'PRO ENGINEER').

The cost lies less in the IT equipment than in the highly skilled, therefore expensive, staff that will be required to use it. This may be significant, particularly for a small company. Nevertheless, SMEs will have to find the resources to equip themselves properly, or they are not going to win partnerships with primes or contracts with MOD.

Again, some Government help is available through programmes and services such as the Information Society Initiative Programme for Business, The Enterprise Zone Internet Service and the Software Business Network.[218]

Nevertheless, the investment in IT will be costly, particularly for the smallest businesses, but companies with less than 200 employees are eligible to apply for a loan under the DTI's Loan Guarantee Scheme to expand or to increase efficiency. However, a loan is a loan and the extra cost of the IT will have to be borne by the company and

[217] Ed Bates, MD Widney Aish, Defence Net South West, 28 July 1999

[218] *A Guide to Help for Small Business,* DTI, April 1999

SMEs will have to consider this as an up-front payment for future benefits from longer-term partnerships. But what are these benefits and how certain are they?

SME Benefits

Ministers have made it quite clear that benefits must be flowed down to the lowest level:

> *'Smart Procurement is not just about prime contractors. Our major companies need, if they have not already done so, to adopt a similar "smart" and open approach with their sub-contractors, so that sub-contractors have a stake in the project and Smart Procurement principles extend right down the supply chain.'*[219]

Good. But will it happen? There is considerable scepticism amongst SMEs.

In theory, of course, it must for unless it does, SMEs will be unable, and very unwilling, to continue to involve themselves in risk management, design and up-front expenditure. And then MOD and the primes will lose out. Therefore primes should ensure that benefits flow down to the SMEs so that further benefits can flow back up to them. But theory is theory and does not necessarily account for realpolitik.

What if a prime sees an overabundance of SMEs in a particular technology area? Will he not take advantage of the prime market and squeeze an SME, discard him and repeat with another? Maybe, but that is life. Survival of the fittest.

MOD has expressed a desire to oversee the prime-supplier relationships to ensure fairness, but primes are resisting such 'interference' and in any case such oversight is bound to cause difficulties between the prime and MOD. It has been said that:[220]

- MOD wants visibility of make/buy decisions to ensure value for money and would arbitrate in disputes.

---

[219] John Spellar, Under Secretary of State for Defence, RUSI Journal, Vol.144, No.3, June 1999, page 77

[220] Ed Bates, MD Widney Aish, Defence Net SouthWest, 28 July 1999

- MOD will want to audit supply chain principles.

But is it doubtful whether MOD will have enough visibility to identify problems or the resources with which to arbitrate or the willingness to intervene in most cases.

The potential benefits that might flow down to SMEs are significant. Innovative thinking throughout the supply chain could reduce project time and cost as well as increase system performance by large margins, often time and again throughout the lifetime of the MOD-industry partnering agreement. The longer the agreement, the greater the benefits that will accrue. In addition, therefore, to the longer commitment that SMEs will obtain from MOD and primes, increasing benefits (usually financial) should accrue to the SME. The size of these potential benefits should not be underestimated, benefits that will be shared between MOD, the prime and the whole supply chain.

Exactly how, is yet to be determined but it is likely to be based on something akin to the principles laid out in Supply Chain Relationships in Aerospace (SCRIA). We can expect a period of trial and, probably, error. Will SMEs be sufficiently motivated to make the whole system of industrial involvement in Smart Procurement actually work?

> *It is asking SMEs to put their money down and leap into the dark.*

I hope so, but it is asking SMEs to put their money down and take a leap into the dark to secure benefits that may or may not materialise. I would like to think that innovative SMEs with the right culture change, in partnership with primes with similar outlooks, will do just that and find their crock of gold. In doing so, they may just secure their future in a much-reduced SME base.

But if MOD and primes do not play fair, the innovative SMEs will go to the wall instead of the reactionary companies, and this will be to the major detriment of both the prime and MOD. This would result in rather more than shooting Smart Procurement in the foot.

MOD will do well to remember this when insisting on another round of competitions in the supply chain. If a SME, which has made considerable improvements resulting in cost or time reduction, is ousted through competition before he sees financial benefit, this will only reinforce the notion that the theory of flowing down benefits will remain just theory.

And without successfully flowing down benefits, there can be no successful flowing down of risk and responsibility. Nor of flowing up innovative thinking.

A SME Success Strategy

Smart Procurement will not succeed without the full involvement of the whole supply chain, and both MOD and primes, as well as the SMEs in the supply chain, have a responsibility for making it work. For MOD, the success of Smart Procurement is at stake; for primes, long-term profit margins are at stake; but for SMEs their very future is at stake. They all need to contribute to an SME success strategy.

MOD must:

- Agree fair supply chain principles with primes.
- Provide clear and free advice to SMEs on such things as contracting, IT and smart thinking.
- Give greater thought to how industry, but particularly SMEs, are involved in CWGs, IPTs during competitive phases and Cluster IPTs.
- Be very sensitive to the effect that badly-timed supply chain competition can have on SME input.
- Identify IPR early and protect it.

Primes must:

- Seek long-term alliances and partnerships with like-minded SMEs.
- Flow down benefits fairly and promptly through the whole supply chain.
- Represent SMEs conscientiously at MOD IPTs if SMEs are excluded or cannot resource attendance.
- Protect the IPR of its supply chain.

And most crucially of all, SMEs must:

- Concentrate on niche markets.
- Attain 'world class'.
- Forge links or form clusters with other SMEs to achieve 'critical mass'.
- Seek long-term alliances and partnerships with the 'right' primes, be they UK, US or European.
- Accept risk and equity sharing; and undertake to provide more up-front funding.
- Get as involved as possible with CWGs and IPTs to acquire knowledge of MOD plans and requirements and to input innovative ideas.
- Recognise that winning competitions will be more vital than before, as contracts are likely to be larger, longer but fewer.
- Accept that greater benefits will only be realised by greater involvement, input and self-funding.
- Put innovation and proaction at the top of the list.
- If active in different areas (particularly in the civil as well as the defence sector), make sure they read-across the lessons learned in each sector.

Do all this and you will thrive. Don't do it and you may die. Unless, of course, you are 'world-class' with no competitors. Then you can dream on!

SMEs must put innovation and proaction at the top of their list.

CHAPTER EIGHTEEN

VERY SMALL ENTERPRISES

Small and medium-sized enterprises (SMEs) have largly been ignored by MOD in the Smart Procurement Initiative and its implementation. True, a SME representative sits on the MOD-industry committee, but his concerns seem to have fallen largely into the 'too difficult' tray, or have been opposed by the industrial big boys. The term SME includes the smallest companies but it is worth considering the very smallest, for the impact on what I shall call Very Small Enterprises (VSE) has been ignored by everyone: by MOD, by primes and by SMEs.

VSEs are companies with total employees in single figures; often the total work force is only two or three. VSEs are very different in many ways from SMEs and neither MOD nor primes should ignore them; indeed they should be looking to shore them up, keep them in being and to use them whenever suitable. There are very good reasons for doing so because they are:

- Highly motivated.
- Highly innovative.
- Uniformly expert.
- Have low overheads.

At the same time, they need sensitive handling because they:

- Are highly vulnerable.
- Cannot implement expensive procedures.
- Cannot afford contract lawyers.

Insensitive handling can destroy VSEs very quickly, and their death can be a serious, if generally unrecognised, setback to MOD and primes.

Motivation

Every single member of a VSE is as highly motivated on behalf of the company's output, as are only a few key directors, and few others, in primes and SMEs. The majority of the latter's workforce is motivated by personal considerations which is rather different. The vast majority of non-VSE employees will leave the company at short notice if they find a better opportunity elsewhere; this is not likely to occur in a VSE for a number of reasons, as the individual may:

- Have sunk money into the enterprise.
- Be an expert in a very narrow field with limited or zero opportunities elsewhere.
- Be far happier in a VSE environment.
- Have the office in his home.

Failure of the VSE, therefore, may lose him money, enjoyment, future prospects and even his home. This is powerful motivation and applies to every single member of the VSE's employment roll.

Expertise

A VSE will probably be founded by one, two or three individuals to carry out more efficient exploitation of a particular opportunity that has been frustrated by, or not been possible in, their former situation. The step in losing the security of a position in the Services or a large company is risky, and will only be taken by those who have:

- Confidence in their own ability to manage.
- Confidence in their own expertise.
- Confidence in the need of others for their project.
- Confidence that they can manage the technical risks.

Those whose confidence is misplaced will not survive for long. The survivors will be expert, with expertise that will be uniform throughout the company, and they will have something of importance to offer.

This is why they should be given every opportunity to compete on a level playing field.

Innovation and Overhead

Experts are usually innovative. But innovation can only be effected in the right environment. A bureaucratic environment, long delays in decision-making processes, superiors and colleagues who are not technically expert, can all dull and dissipate innovation.

VSEs by their very nature will be innovative. They have to be if they are to survive, for they cannot depend, as can larger companies, on buying-in innovation when they need it, from further down the food chain. VSEs are at the bottom of the food chain. All their energy goes into devising solutions to improving existing solutions or finding new solutions.

Very often, the VSE will produce a piece of software or hardware which is financially too small for a larger company to bother with, but is of importance either to a prime or directly to MOD. His low overheads (no secretaries, marketmen, posh offices) will ensure that he can offer high performance at a low price. If he operates through a prime, that price will escalate, perhaps ten-fold. He may offer the product to MOD for £20k, but many primes would not get out of bed for a contract less than £250k. So the difference becomes the mark-up. Massive.

Vulnerability

It makes sense to use VSEs within their areas of expertise because of their unique characteristics. But they must be handled sensitively because of their vulnerability. We all know that SMEs are more vulnerable to cash-flow problems than to lack of profitability, but VSEs are more vulnerable still.

VSE contracts are usually small (if they are not, they rapidly become SMEs), so VSE income is small, but this is balanced by their low overheads. However, this balance can easily be upset by high costs imposed by MOD or prime, through complex procedures, through protracted and repeated competition, and through decision delays. In such cases, a VSE may collapse or may choose to vacate the defence sector, in either case to MOD's or the prime's disadvantage. Their vulnerability must be understood.

This is not to suggest that VSEs be given cosy relationships or contracts that they do not deserve. But if a VSE has something worthwhile to offer, it makes sense to take it and guard the goose that lays the golden (or at least the silver) egg. What can be done?

VSE Requirements

The first thing that VSEs must have is prompt payment against sensibly arranged stage payments, which should be more front-end loaded than with bigger firms. This is not a gamble as VSEs are acutely conscious of the next contract and therefore of producing customer satisfaction in a small project. Poor performance will be fairly rare (probably much rarer than the average for larger firms), and the amounts involved small. Too often, VSEs suffer because stage payments are not negotiable, or are too late, leaving the company no option between borrowing (and increasing costs) or refusing the contract that both sides want.

The cost of competition can be crippling for a VSE.

Competition is clearly going to be applied, and VSEs will normally welcome it, as they will be able to offer a good, compliant solution at a low price. But competition is costly, and repeated competition can be crippling for a VSE. Worse, the long decision-making schedules while competition is evaluated can create difficulties in accepting other work in the interim, thereby extending the period of no income and the difficulties of cash-flow. Even when the competition is awarded, there is often a long time-lag before the contract is signed. With the same effect. Then suddenly, it is 'start tomorrow'. Equally difficult after a long period of uncertainty.

Repeated annual support contracts are expensive for a VSE to manage. But gathering them together into, say, a five-year contract might take it over the EU limit for compulsory competition. And competition for continuation of an existing contract for the support of a specialised project, at low price, often achieves little other than delay and unwelcome expense for the VSE, and inflated costs for MOD.

What VSEs often have to do is to start work before a contract is signed to fill an otherwise work-free hole, but are then vulnerable to changes in the requirement, the funding, or the schedule.

'We kept being told by MOD that a contract was one month away, and were asked to keep on working. This went on for 18 months. Then MOD informed us that they could not contract direct to us and told us to find a 'front company'. We did and the price was racked up by 30%. The 'front company' then went bust, and we had to pick up the pieces.' A director in a VSE.

Another example is that of the VSE which was asked to do immediate work on an urgent operational requirement (UOR) for Bosnia. After two man-months of effort, MOD said that they would not pay as the contract was not approved by a set date.

MOD finds it difficult to do business with VSEs, usually because they are not quality cleared to ISO 9000. Yet accreditation only signifies that quality is uniform to the required standard across the company. In a VSE, it would be normal for only one or two experts to work on a specific contract, and those experts should be known through the company's product or proposal. Does ISO 9000 add any guarantee in such a case? Except to add cost?

VSEs are often told that they cannot bid unless they are ISO 9000, but this is not so as there is flexibility in MOD (one-star agreement); but this seldom seems to be applied for, or granted. Complex procedures should not be applied to VSEs. The resource cost of, for example, ISO 9000 accreditation is very large for a VSE and often not realistic. Similarly, ILS documentation.

Another factor that persuades MOD to eschew contracts with VSEs is that, in such a small outfit, the one expert in a specific contract could disappear, leaving both VSE and MOD in disarray. But a small specialised contract in a large firm may only be understood by one or two experts, and the disappearance of them may be just as disruptive. While the VSE experts will be as vulnerable as their large firm counterparts to being run over by a bus, they are less likely to leave the company for a job elsewhere, are less likely to be redeployed to other projects, and are less likely to have their ideas or designs adulterated by bureaucracy.

The Impact of Smart Procurement

Smart Procurement may have little impact on VSEs:

- The new MOD customer-supplier relationships is unlikely to make contracts easier to strike, although this is likely to depend on how the Defence Logistics Organisation (DLO), Customer One and Customer Two take wing.
- The new Acquisition Cycle will make no difference to VSEs.
- VSEs will not normally be invited onto Capability Working Groups (CWGs) or Integrated Project Teams (IPTs).
- The new relationship with industry is unlikely to make a difference as MOD has difficulties with dealing with anyone other than the prime.

In a few areas, Smart Procurement may have some adverse effect:

- The PPP future of DERA will complicate relations with industry at all levels.
- Partnering between MOD and primes may lead to extended contracts for primes in the support phase, squeezing out separate support contracts with small firms.

And in one area only might there be improvement:

- Empowerment of individuals in the Defence Procurement Agency (DPA) and in the DLO could produce the required flexibility in handling VSEs.

But this will only happen if the individuals are aware of the special nature of VSEs, ditch preconceived cultural attitudes and are not hemmed in with rigid 'guidelines'.

A VSE Solution

If VSEs are going to flourish and provide what MOD and primes require without threatening larger companies, then they must be treated differently. The main bones of a satisfactory solution should:

- Realise that VSEs are good value for money in some niche areas.
- Relax the rule book for contracts below a certain ceiling; say, £20,000.

- Waive competition where this is clearly not disadvantageous to MOD/primes.
- Minimise decision-making time and contract quickly
- Contract support activities for several years.
- Set stage payments with more front-loading than normal.
- Pay promptly (MOD are now good at this).
- Consider strategic partnerships with successful VSEs (based on track record).

This may seem to be a solution all in favour of the VSE, but it is not. VSEs are cheap, expert, innovative and highly motivated, thereby providing good value for money. It is, therefore, to the advantage of MOD and primes for VSEs to flourish, so any help for them is mutually beneficial. It is the essense of partnering.

If VSEs are to flourish, they must be treated differently.

CHAPTER NINETEEN

POLITICS AND INTERNATIONAL COMPETITION

Is there a level playing field in this country for international competition for defence contracts? This is a question which is asked and debated endlessly, but never clearly answered to everyone's satisfaction. Some of the many views given to me recently are:

'No, the playing field is not level because the US government gives advice to US bidders.' A senior executive in a UK prime.

'It's level at the start – before the politics cut in.' An ex-MOD industrialist.

'The Government tips the playing field against British firms.' A manager in a foreign-owned, UK-based company.

'Why do we let foreign companies, particularly French, into our competitions? Their playing fields are not level.' An executive in a UK company.

'There may not be pre-meditated bias, but bias can develop. It is difficult to sell missiles in the UK.' A manager in a US-owned company.

'With the merger of BAe and Marconi, can you win anything when they prime?' Another manager in another US-owned company.

Many of these are standard moans which could have come from a host of other executives in a wide variety of different companies. If both UK and foreign companies think the playing field is tilted against them, surely MOD has it about right? Well….. yes and no.

A Level Playing Field?

There are some areas, such as ships, missiles and tanks where British design and manufacture is largely mandatory, so that foreign primes are bound to lose. The field here is definitely tilted against foreign firms, but would any tax-payer really worry if UK firms employing tens of thousands of employees have some advantage? I doubt it. But MOD and Ministers will have to realise that tilted playing fields will inevitably lead to reduced competitive fields. Will that worry MOD? I expect so. But it shouldn't for the simple reason that it would push MOD and the British companies involved into long-term partnering arrangements early in the procurement cycle to their immense mutual benefit. In fact, this may be about to happen now with Vickers Defence Systems and MOD in the tank field.

But in other areas, the playing field is either level or tilted against British firms because foreign firms have the benefit of Government money (as in France) or the advantage of huge domestic production runs and widespread leading edge technology (as in US). Here, British firms face an uphill struggle to win and very often do not. MOD will, with some justification, point to poor tenders, poor delivery records, and lack of innovation from UK companies: indeed the Chief of Defence Logistics has referred to the 'disgraceful performance' of industry in service support contracts.

Industry therefore should stop moaning about a lack of MOD sympathy and take the matter by the horns. They should not be in the business of 'postponing death' but should be making provision for a healthy future. Almost all companies have a lot to learn.

> *Industry should not be in the business of postponing death.*

What is a British Company?

I have asked many people for the definition of a British company and have received a surprisingly wide range of answers from 'no-one knows' to 'British owned, based, manned'.

Many would accept the definition put forward by most people in UK-based, foreign-owned companies as ones which employ British workers and pay British taxes. That includes, inter alia, Raytheon, Lockheed Martin and Thomson. Others would not accept such a definition because their long-term future in this country is dependent on decisions made in other countries, taking into account factors which have nothing to do with UK industrial health and performance. These would tend to accept a company as British only if more than 50% of its shares were owned by British people, although whether that is a very practical definition in today's volatile industrial world, I do not know.

'I well remember the late 1980s, when we were considering a new anti-radar missile. On offer were the HARM high speed anti-radar missile from the United States and the ALARM air-launched anti-radar missile which was promoted by British Aerospace..... I was in favour of the ALARM project simply because, if we had bought HARM, we would not have had access to the head technology. By developing our own technology, we made sure that we would later be in a position to keep up with the rest of the world.'[221]

Is this a reasonable position to take? We seem to be in a repeat position now with the battle between the Anglo-French Matra-BAe Meteor missile and US Raytheon's advanced AMRAAM for the beyond visual range air-to-air missile, a battle between the latter's apparently cheaper, incremental solution and the former's which is claimed to meet threats that the other does not.

The recent announcement that Boeing has joined the Matra-BAe team has, perhaps, undercut high level US lobbying and could have dealt the Raytheon bid a mortal blow. But it may have additionally muddied the waters. One strong reason for Europeans to prefer a European solution for this high-tech missile system for Eurofighter and Rafale is to prevent US Congress from limiting potential exports of these aircraft. Will Boeing's presence in the team put this risk back into the melting pot?

---

[221] Gerald Howarth, MP for Aldershot, Hansard, Volume 330, No 76, 26 April 1999, page 104/105

It does appear that in certain fields (missiles, tanks, ships) political considerations take precedence over a level playing field for international competition. But not in others. It is not clear whether this will change in the foreseeable future, but I think not. Competition may be the primary tool but the demise of HORIZON, and the clear Government statement that:

'We have always believed that British warships would be built in British yards.'[222]

suggests that level playing fields will continue to apply in some areas only. Of course there may still be competition at sub-contractor level and below and, of course, non-British companies are highly likely to be involved as team members, sub-contractors and suppliers.

There is little doubt that tough international competition produces value-for-money and that more purely nationalist competition, if foreign-owned companies were excluded or significantly discriminated against, would be less advantageous to MOD and the tax-payer. Yet, as I have argued in Chapter 5, the losses through absence of competition should be compensated (more than compensated in many cases) by the striking of early partnering agreements with the preferred prime contractor. Competition may be MOD's primary tool of procurement but it must not be dogmatically or blindly applied.

As John Spellar, Under Secretary of State for Defence, said: 'Oranges are not the only fruit.'

A Two-Tone Policy

However, it would seem that, in the foreseeable future at least, MOD and Ministers will follow the present unstated, two-tone policy:

- In some fields, such as missiles, ships and tanks, competitions if held will go to a British-owned prime, with foreign firms limited to sub-contractor or supplier status. This will be so for as long as British-owned firms can come up with solutions which are perceived by MOD as reasonably cost-effective.

---

[222] John Spellar, Under Secretary of State for Defence, Hansard, Volume 330, No 76, 26 April 1999, page 51

- In all other fields, the competitive playing field will be more or less level and many prime contracts will be awarded to foreign-owned companies. This is likely to be the case until Ministers perceive overwhelming erosion of the British defence industry and/or there is a lack of genuine competition.

The biggest political failing is the refusal to decide at the very start of a programme whether political factors will dictate a procurement strategy. Decisions to go national are left until far too late in the procurement cycle to avoid considerable damage to international relationships or major time and cost overruns or complete waste of major investment or a combination (e.g. HORIZON, Challenger 2, MLRS TGW). Likewise, political decisions to collaborate rather than go national are made too late and can cause major cost, time and performance penalties (e.g. MRAV).

> *Political decisions are left far too late.*

In most 'non-political' competitions, the only political issue that will surface is that of UK jobs, particularly in marginal constituencies or depressed areas. Again this political factor is hardly straightforward as 'metal-bashing' jobs in marginal constituencies can, and perhaps sometimes do, override the importance of creating 'high technology' jobs elsewhere. Northern Ireland, too, creates special consideration and the inclusion of, say, Short's in a consortium gives a considerable advantage politically.

Jobs and Northern Ireland

The issue of jobs will surface in the evaluation of the tenders and not before. In the vast majority of competitions, the jobs issue is not a significant discriminator, different solutions providing roughly balanced job opportunities. But occasionally, jobs may turn the result.

> *'Spellar made much of the fact that RSL's [Raytheon Systems Ltd] ASTOR programme would create and sustain jobs at Bombardier Short Brothers in politically sensitive Northern Ireland – a "key discriminator" that was exclusive to the Raytheon bid and one that may well have helped tip the deal in its favour.'*[223]

Given that the ASTOR competition was close, jobs in Northern Ireland may have swung the decision, although the MOD project manager has stated that the recommendation that went up to Ministers was based on both financial terms and technical capabilities:

'From our assessments it was quickly clear to us what the pecking order was and that we had a clear winner.'[224]

So perhaps Northern Ireland did not swing the decision.

Very few competitions are decided on political grounds and it is difficult to think of even one recent one that clearly has. Political decisions, if never made early enough, are usually made before that stage and result more often in a change of direction (e.g. HORIZON and MRAV). Nevertheless, tenders must cover the jobs issue properly and make the greatest possible case for that particular solution.

The European Dimension

Nowhere is politics more dominant than in European collaboration. In the past, that momentum has been towards collaboration between governments for jointly developed and manufactured equipment. Apart from several successful Franco-German projects (propelled by the strongest political directive), there have been few successes: a couple of aircraft, the COBRA weapon locating radar, medium range TRIGAT anti-tank missile and not a lot else.

The 'successes', including the several Franco-German projects, are now to be managed by the Organisation for Joint Armaments Cooperation (OCCAR) which is to be headed by a Board of Supervisors consisting of the National Armaments Directors from each participating country. The grandest of all the European government collaborative ventures.

But OCCAR is probably the last hurrah of the old government-led procurement initiatives, even if it succeeds and that is doubtful, at

[223] Interview with John Spellar, Under Secretary of State for Defence, Jane's Defence Weekly, 23 June 1999, page 3

[224] Chris Trout, ASTOR Project Manager, Preview, Journal of the Defence Procurement Agency, No 63, July 1999, page 13

least in terms of cost and time parameters. More and more, the initiative is being taken by industry, quite rightly, and this is being supported by governments as evidenced by the Letter of Intent signed by the Defence Ministers of France, Germany, Italy, Spain, Sweden and UK in July 1998 for the establishment of a cooperative framework to facilitate the restructuring of the European defence industry. The merger of British Aerospace and Marconi, although not quite what the signatories had in mind, has created the second biggest defence company in the world and further European defence industry consolidations can be expected, albeit in rather slow time.

As I have argued in Chapter 8, global companies have the potential for designing a system for one government and offering it to others at a very competitive price, thereby obviating the need for time consuming, ineffective, government-led attempts at harmonising requirements and timescales, agreeing on mutually satisfying procurement strategies and insidiously protecting national industrial positions leading too often to collapses late in the procurement cycle (HORIZON) or delivery of late, even obsolescent, equipment (MR TRIGAT).

For the moment however, we try to achieve a 'have our cake and eat it' policy: that is to collaborate with other European governments but to obtain value for money primarily in terms of minimising cost and time overruns. The two do not go together. Hence the Strategic Defence Review prediction that collaborative programmes will account for 40% of projects looks unlikely to be achieved.

> *Our collaborative policy is to 'have our cake and eat it'.*

HORIZON may spell the beginning of the end for widespread UK involvement in European collaborative projects for two reasons:

- The priority accorded to reducing time and cost overruns will not be met by European collaboration because OCCAR is unlikely to be able to perform to cost and time as effectively as our own Defence Procurement Agency.

- No Integrated Project Team (IPT) Leader is likely to recommend European collaboration (and therefore OCCAR management) for a large project as it will do him out of a job.

But we cannot admit to this.

PART FOUR:

WINNING PROPOSALS

CHAPTER TWENTY

THE MOD'S TENDER PROCESS

Smart Procurement is unlikely to change the MOD's competitive tender process to any significant degree. The biggest change will be the greater reward for winning in terms of longer and larger contracts within, it is envisaged, a partnering arrangement covering final development, production, a significant slice of in-service support and, possibly upgrades and incremental acquisition. And the corollary to greater rewards for winners is greater damage to the losers.

> *The corollary of greater rewards for winners is greater damage to losers.*

Although there is unlikely to be significant change to the tender process, there will need to be change to the way companies approach the early stages of a tender process. In the past, many companies (particularly those with limited contact with the defence sector) have waited until they see an announcement in the MOD Contracts Bulletin and, while this has a section on possible future purchases, it is probably already too late to do the necessary preparation for submitting a winning tender in due course, unless the company is fortunate enough to have something in existence that exactly matches the eventual specification at an 'affordable' price. This will be rare.

Companies need to be ahead of the Contracts Bulletin, and MOD is keen to help them to get ahead with understanding the future requirement.

'Get inside the minds of MOD staff at an early stage.' A former MOD procurement director.

Smart Procurement will help them do just that through membership of the Capability Working Groups (CWGs) and Integrated Project Teams (IPTs) in the early stage of the project. But not everyone will be invited into these teams and it is important that you make every effort to flag up to MOD what you can contribute now, not just what you will do downstream if you win the final contract. Company marketing material is not required; ideas are (see Chapter 16).

But all is not lost if you are not invited into a CWG or IPT: if you have something to offer, MOD will still be pleased to discuss possibilities outside these teams on a one-to-one basis, but again only if you have positive expertise and ideas to offer. Alternatively, you can seek to team up with a company that is already sure of CWG/IPT membership.

MOD is making a huge effort to involve industry early and to use their ideas in shaping the User Requirement Document (URD) and, later, the Systems Requirement Document (SRD):

> *'We need to discuss our ideas with industry and to allow industry to input. This will clear the minds on both sides and lead to better understanding.' A current project manager/IPT Leader in the Defence Procurement Agency.*

Awareness of Opportunities

Most defence companies are well aware of the MOD opportunities and process (even if understanding is, in some surprising cases, rather limited), but for those that are not, the Defence Procurement Agency (DPA) has set up the Defence Suppliers Service (DSS) which consists of a small team of 'experienced staff' which acts as a focal point for prospective contractors looking to supply goods and services not only to the DPA, but also to other areas of MOD and various defence Agencies which have purchasing functions. The DSS:

- Produces a booklet entitled *Selling to the Ministry of Defence*, summarising how a supplier may become a defence contractor at Prime, Sub-Contractor or Local Purchase level.
- Produces the MOD Contracts Bulletin fortnightly (in paper or electronic form and is available on the Internet) with sections on Possible Future Purchases, Tenders Invited, Competitive Contracts Awarded, Single Source Contracts Awarded, an

advertising section for sub-contractors capabilities, plus various MOD announcements and reports.

- Is the UK's Focal Point for the Western European Armaments Group (WEAG).

Companies are unlikely to be invited to tender unless they are quality certified. MOD is now using the Department of Trade and Industry's UK Register of Quality Assessed Companies, which lists all businesses that have received a formal quality assurance certification to the BS EN ISO 9000 series. MOD operates a policy of 'No Appropriate Certification – No Contract'. This raises several issues for very small companies and these have been discussed in Chapter 18.

Understanding the Opportunity

The importance of investing in early work to get your company represented in the Capability Working Group (CWG) and the Integrated Project Team (IPT) in the early Concept Phase has already been stressed in Chapters 12 and 15. Just as important is participation in the applied research stage, either through extra-mural contracts from the Defence Evaluation and Research Agency (DERA) or, better still, through participation in joint research teams or technical demonstrators, although both these may well have to be funded partially by your company. Nevertheless, successful participation in a technical demonstrator should give you entry to the CWG and IPT, although whether this will necessarily be the case with Cluster IPTs we shall have to see. FIST will be a good test case, as was discussed in Chapter 12.

There is also the Pathfinder Process whereby DERA seeks proposals from industry for MOD funded applied research packages of work. After a poor start, this has grown into a useful mechanism for MOD-industry research collaboration.

Pathfinder, joint research and technical demonstrators, extra-mural research contracts, the CWG and the IPTs should provide participating companies with an unprecedented understanding of future requirements. On top of these, one-to-one discussions with the equipment capability (that is the operational requirements) staff and with the project management staff in the DPA will fill in any gaps in understanding and provide a way of discussing commercially sensitive matters outside the fora where your competitors are assembled.

If you fail to get anywhere with the above opportunities, you **either**:

- Have nothing of interest to offer MOD.

or

- Have failed to make a good enough case.

Either way, it is back to the drawing board of future planning and in-house studies.

To Bid or Not to Bid

Bidding is expensive and might cost millions or even tens of millions of pounds, although for the smaller projects it will be correspondingly cheaper. Nevertheless, there is much to be said for a hard-headed look in slow time at the chances of winning. Bidding without a realistic chance of winning is a waste of time and money, except possibly as a loss-leader learning exercise. Even bidding with a good chance of winning can lead to large nugatory expenditure for the eventual losers. If losing becomes a habit, you may go out of business. But, conversely, not bidding means no chance of a win.

It might be wise to work through a check-list such as this:

- What expertise, development work and/or studies can I bring to MOD's table, either as a prime or as part of a team?
- What do I know about MOD's plans and thinking in the Capability Area?
- What do I know about the project and its context?
- Who are the likely competitors and what are their strengths and weaknesses?
- Who can I team with or sub-contract?
- Can I afford to bid?
- What can I do in the time available to fill the holes?

This is, of course, pretty basic stuff but it is surprising how many companies do not go through this process (or something similar) before the decision to bid is made. Indeed, some of the above are not considered properly until the bid is being written. Presumably business cases are made up the management line before bidding but, judging from first drafts of some bid proposals that I often see, they cannot have been done very thoroughly.

> *Often, business cases cannot have been done very thoroughly.*

Pre-Qualification Questionnaires

Usually MOD knows who the real industrial players are but, to make sure that a likely contender is not missed, will normally issue a pre-qualification questionnaire (PQQ) or sometimes a Request for Interest (RFI) or a pre-ITT questionnaire. The object of the exercise is to identify the starters and whittle them down to manageable numbers, say no more than six. There is no set format for such a questionnaire but it may well ask the company to:

- Confirm that it will comply with certain aspects of the design specification and the laid down tests and trials.
- Supply specification detail in some areas.
- Detail its familiarity with interface specifications.
- Confirm its quality certification.
- Identify sub-contractors and suppliers.
- Show that it has suitable design and development capabilities or current products which meet the specification.
- Supply financial and commercial information, including sales and turnover figures and details of major orders.
- Supply indicative prices.

Some of these will be difficult or impossible to supply at this early stage, and this may explain why replies vary from one-liners to 60 pages or more. Clearly a company which does business with MOD regularly in that area does not have to be as persuasive as a company which is unknown to MOD. For the latter type of company, the response is critical; it must clearly show MOD that you are to be taken seriously.

The Draft Invitation to Tender

The PQQ has another value to MOD: that of seeking suggestions from industry, but it is not normally successful in this. To do this more effectively, MOD often circulates a draft Invitation to Tender (ITT) which:

- Seeks feed-back from industry, including suggestions as to where the specification might be altered for mutual benefit (time, cost and/or performance).
- Gives industry the chance to clarify (prior to the competitive tender stage) points which are not clear.

This draft ITT circulation is perhaps most important where there are large numbers of potential competitors for a small project. For example in Cluster IPTs with, say, 50 small to medium-size projects:

'The problems of competition combined with the numbers of small projects at different stages of the [procurement] cycle have prevented industry from becoming full-time members of the IPT..... For the IPT we learnt, for some probably re-learnt, an important lesson; namely to improve our communication with potential contractors prior to the issue of the Invitation to Tender (ITT). Early sight of draft ITTs and the opportunity to attend a briefing on the project has ensured that potential contractors understand fully our requirement.'[225]

Industry Briefing Day

More often than not, a briefing for industry is held prior to the issue of the ITT. This is usually heavily attended by all those with any realistic interest. It was reported that 20 companies attended the briefing day on the Future Command and Liaison Vehicle while around 100 attended the TRACER day some years ago.

---

[225] Leader DCC IPT, Preview No.59, 1 April, page 32

Some of these briefings are done well, others less well. But even the best are unlikely to cover ground which is new to serious contenders, although updating (particularly on projected dates for the issue of the ITT and the various stages of the project) is useful. It is also an opportunity to ask questions of clarification, but few attendees do so in fear of giving away something to the massed opposition.

It is, of course, the chance to assess the competition that exists at this stage. But they will not be asking questions either.

Invitation to Tender

At some stage after all these preliminaries have been concluded, MOD will issue the ITT to the half-dozen or so selected contenders. Again there is no set timescale and all projects are different, but it should be understood that the replies from the PQQ and/or draft ITT circulation will have to be assessed and the draft ITT amended. This will take time. A recent example of timescale is given by the Future Command and Liaison Vehicle project:

- PQQs submitted by industry February 1999
- Industry briefing day May 1999
- Intention to issue ITT mid-2000

Whether Smart Procurement will shorten such timescales remains to be seen.

Whether or not it does so, much work can be going on within the company once the shortlist of bidders is selected by MOD, although progressive companies will have got ahead of the game by a considerable amount of planning and initial study/design work before their participation is announced. There is no doubt that time spent in preparation is worth its length in gold. For once the ITT is issued, there is never enough time. Or so I am told by industry. Probably because of a lack of preparation.

> *Once the ITT is issued, there is never enough time.*

CHAPTER TWENTY-ONE

THE TENDER FROM INDUSTRY

The Invitation to Tender (ITT) has arrived. There are four months until your bid is due in the MOD. It seems a long time and there are other wolves closer to your sledge. As John Spellar remarked:

'The pressures of the immediate tend to override the important.'[226]

So the bid gets off to a slow start. Mistake Number One. Whenever I have been called in to 'red team' a tender, I have been amazed at the way everything is left to the last minute with the result that the standard of the bid, on which the future of the company could depend, is well below the standard that it could be and should be. Does this actually matter? Sometimes not. But sometimes it does. MOD will not consciously throw away a better bid that's packaged badly, but when there are plenty of bidders it will be looking for reasons to fail some of them. If the assessors cannot easily understand what you are offering, would you be surprised if you got the chop?

Often the bid is well below the standard it could have been.

Some companies will assemble a bid team of experts, many of whom will be from outside; in one case I know of, 95% were external to the company. This has weaknesses because, financially, it is difficult if not impossible for them to be retained once the bid has been submitted and follow-up questions from MOD are then difficult to handle by those who have not been involved in the bid.

At the other end of the spectrum, a bid team will be assembled entirely from within the company. The weakness here is that many, if

[226] John Spellar, Under Secretary of State, MOD/DMA Seminar on Smart Procurement, Didcot, 24 June 1999

not all, will be dealing with other important issues until well into the bid period. Time passes.

But let us assume that a bid team, including only one or two bid experts from outside, has been assembled in advance of receipt of the ITT. What does it do? The whole bid can of course be designed, in skeleton, before sight of the ITT (it is likely to be based firmly on the draft ITT if that has been circulated) with the aid of a little intelligence and a little experience of other ITTs which the company will hold. The company may, of course, have a 'house' style which lays down the format of the response and which, although there is a danger which we will come to later, will constrain the bid leader quite tightly.

The ITT arrives. What is the first step?

Understanding the ITT

The first thing to be done is to read the ITT very carefully indeed. Do not assume you know what is in it because you read the draft ITT and attended the industry briefing, because things have a nasty habit of changing. You must:

Understand what they think they want.

'Understand what they think they want.' An ex-MOD commercial director.

This is not necessarily the same as understanding what they actually want, and is almost certainly not the same as understanding what you think they want. You have to understand the ITT as written and what it calls for. If you do not understand certain statements, contact the project team for clarification.

The next step is to list the essential requirements (the 'shalls' or equivalents) and the desirable requirements. It is astonishing how often this is not done at all, or at best is done at the end when the compliance matrices are being filled in. There may be 'shalls' which you had not been anticipating and which your technical solution is not compliant with. By identifying these right at the start, you can decide what to do about them: change your concept or remain noncompliant. But if you do not know what you have to be compliant with until the last minute (or even then), you are taking grave risks.

Coordinating the Bid

Except for the smallest projects, ITTs are large and the answering bid must be large. The biggest projects require huge proposals of many volumes. Whatever the size, the writing of the bid must be properly coordinated and overseen, and the selection of the person to do this is critical. It could be the project manager, it could be a marketing man or it could be an outsider. But whoever it is must ensure that:

- The bid answers what is asked for.
- The bid is clear to those in MOD who will read it.
- The bid is concise without unnecessary paperwork (it is big enough anyway).
- The bid makes as strong a case as possible without over-egging it or glossing over obvious weak areas.
- The component parts of the bid are available for integration into the whole document weeks before it is due to MOD.

The best bids achieve the above, although few manage the last one. Too many fail on several counts. With a week to go, a sizeable proportion will have failed to achieve any of the above, and the ensuing rush may only serve to make matters worse by introducing conflicting statements between one part and another, or between the executive summary and the main volumes.

Too often, the bid preparation is distorted by a mania for win strategy, win themes, PEST and SWOT analyses and such like. These all have their places but:

- Should come well before the start of the bid writing phase (ideally before the decision to bid has been made).
- Should not disrupt the preparation of the clearest possible document (they are of course of no interest to MOD).

They have their uses of course and should provide a useful context for the bid, but they are no substitute for clear management and coordination of the bid itself. Do not let yourself be seduced by the sexy ideas thrust upon you at great expense by management consultants. Plain packaging and clear contents make a better package than glossy packaging and smoke-and-mirrors inside.

Aiming Your Bid

Few bid writers or bid managers are clear as for whom they are writing the proposal. Who will read it? The usual view is either the project manager or the contracts man. But it is no use writing the technical solution for the contracts man when it is going to be evaluated by scientists in DERA. Nor is it of any use aiming your management plan at the DERA scientists who will be evaluating the technical solution.

The truth is that many people will read parts of your tender, and most will not have access to all of it.

- The technical volumes will be evaluated by DERA and be examined by the project management staff, the logistics staff, the requirements management staff (alias operational requirements), the central scientific scrutineers and the equipment capability staff (military and scientific).
- The management volumes will be examined primarily by the project management staff, but also by financial, contractor and specialist procurement staff (e.g. reliability, QA).
- The commercial volume will be confined to the commercial staff in the DPA.
- The executive summary may be widely seen (but it may not); it may be used as a briefing tool at senior levels, or as an aide-memoire (particularly if there are many bidders).

There is, therefore, a wide audience and each part needs to be written so that it is clear to all likely readers. Knowledge on the part of the reader must not be assumed without good reason.

Marking the Bids

The bid will be marked under an assessment methodology which has been agreed and endorsed within the MOD well before the bids are returned. But it is impossible to devise a perfect marking scheme and, as a result, MOD normally withholds both the scheme and the marks, although the scoring system and sometimes the weighting factors are being increasingly released to industry. If you do not receive it, ask for it. You may be lucky.

MOD also provides less information on its Cost and Operational Effectiveness Investment Analysis (COEIA) than industry would like. MOD will normally provide an outline of the approach, the type of data used and the concept of analysis. What it will not do now, and is unlikely to do in the future, is to provide the models it uses to industry 'because it is analysis, not modelling, that has to be done.'

However, the lack of complete MOD data does not hinder, and should actually stimulate, contractors from carrying out their own cost-effectiveness studies with their own models and their own system expertise. While these models will not necessarily mirror the MOD's modelling results, they should give as clear an indication to the company of cost-effectiveness of the system that they are proposing which, together with earlier synthetic prototyping, hardware and software testing, risk reduction exercises and read-across from other related projects or sub-systems, should provide MOD with a clear, full bid. Such modelling and testing should not be aimed at second-guessing MOD's eventual choice, but on presenting a winning case.

Perhaps the biggest difficulty lies in the determination of costs: not so much the procurement costs of the technical solution being bid, but the downstream in-service costs. These are much more difficult to determine accurately and will vary enormously according to the input assumptions. But, the whole-life concept being central to Smart Procurement, this needs to be attempted, whether or not the contract is for procurement only.

It is surprising how few companies attempt to model system cost-effectiveness, how few have an in-house ability to do so, how few use specialist modelling companies to do it for them. Smart Procurement demands a re-think.

Few companies attempt to model system cost-effectiveness.

MOD marks the bids under three headings:

- Technical. If the MOD is looking to reduce the number of bidders, then non-compliance is an easy way to do so. So the first hurdle is compliance. But when bids are compliant, they often attract identical technical scores, unless there is one that is clearly inferior.

Those that clear the technical compliance hurdle are then marked for:

- Management or their ability to deliver, taking into consideration the overall project management plan, development plan and milestones, quality assurance, risk assessment and management, integrated logistic support, reliability and maintenance, tests and trials plan, safety, EMC, system integration and demonstration, software plan and often much more. Increasingly, the past track record of the Company is being taken into consideration as are the sub-contractors, individual managers and general 'feel' of the proposal in terms of delivery ability.

There is often a divergence in the marks here and it is here that a proposal may be lost. Those that are clearly management strong, will then be marked for:

- Price. This has often, in the past, been the determining factor and, if less often, still is. Clearly if several companies produce compliant bids with strong management 'feel', then price will continue to be the determining factor.

It has always seemed to me that the first objective is to submit a bid compliant in all aspects; if you achieve that, unless your solution is technically far inferior to your competitors so that it shows up within the COEIA modelling as such, you will have cleared the first hurdle – the technical one. The next stage is much more likely to dump you – that of management of the programme. Here there is less certainty, less 'proof', more gut-feel. Can you deliver what you are proposing? Can you do better than your last rather mediocre performance? This is where many more bids are lost, but not necessarily won.

Where the bid will finally be won will be on price, assuming that more than enough contenders are left in the race. The race, therefore, is a two-hurdle race (technical and managerial) and once safely over those, the order-of-finish (price) determines the winner(s). Fallers at the hurdles are out.

The MOD Approval

The result of the early competitions (in the Assessment and Demonstration Phases) will underpin the MOD Business Case that will go to the Equipment Approvals Committee (EAC). The Business Case must convince the members of EAC, and their staffs, to approve the next stage of the acquisition cycle and the consequent spend. If they are not convinced of the merits of proceeding, they will not approve the Case.

The MOD staff, who are instrumental in writing the Business Case, must therefore have been convinced by the winning bidder in all respects. Much of the winning bid is of direct relevance to the Business Case: it is the winner's technical solution, the winner's management plans and the winner's price that is the subject of the Case. It may help, therefore, if the main elements of MOD's submission to EAC are listed here. They are:

- The User Requirement Document (URD) at the Initial Gate.
- The Systems Requirement Document (SRD) at the Main Gate.
- The time, whole-life cost and performance envelope within which the capability manager (for Customer One) and the IPT leader undertake to deliver the project.
- A cost range for the resources to be consumed by the project.
- The procurement and support option to be pursued.
- The Combined Operational Effectiveness and Investment Appraisal (COEIA).
- Risk reduction.
- Delivery programme and quantities.
- Key performance parameters.
- Industrial issues.
- Financial and scientific scrutineers' comments.

Attached to the main document will be several supporting documents, including:

- A programme responsibility matrix which will identify the programme cost elements and the responsible budget(s), will link to the Master Data Assumption List, will state actual and forecast costs, and will compare these with the provision in the Equipment Plan and the Short Term Plan.
- An Issues Checklist.
- A Risk Management Plan.
- A support strategy and logistic support analysis.
- Balance of investment studies, requirement definition studies and COEIA reports.
- Acceptance plan.

It can be seen, therefore, that many of the elements of the MOD Business Case are built upon the winning bid's solution. If that bid is not clear, how can MOD produce a clear Business Case and how can EAC approve it? The selection of the winning bid is only one element in the whole process.

Lobbying

While this long, tiring hurdle race (more a snail race than a horse race) is slowly unfolding, politics will creep in: both politics in the Whitehall sense and politics in the inter-company sense. The first has been explored in Chapter 19; the second manifests itself mainly in the form of lobbying. The more intense the competition, the greater the effort that is put into lobbying. Does it work?

In my opinion, lobbying can equally as easily work against a company as for it. Intense lobbying in the ASTOR competition deflected the project team from their 'real' work and caused delay. Ill-directed lobbying or ill-timed lobbying can be extremely irritating within MOD and, while doing no good at all by focusing on the wrong target at the wrong time, it can easily create a negative feeling in some sectors of the tender evaluation team. In a close-run competition, a negative feeling can be decisive. One MOD procurement director told me that:

'Lobbying does not do any harm, unless it is too intense.'

> Lobbying needs to start early and be selective.

Lobbying needs to start early in the process, well before the bid evaluation stage and it needs to be selective. A plan is required to target the many different people involved:

- The project manager and the working level.
- Operational requirements.
- One and two stars in the procurement system.
- Members of the Equipment Approvals Committee (EAC).
- Members of Parliament.
- Ministers.

Quite simply, lobbying is an activity that takes place in a well-concealed minefield: a false step and you could be critically injured. The only advice is to steer clear and let the bid document make your case, or employ the experts. It depends whether you want to be negative or positive about lobbying.

Learning from Experience

Lobbying may be the final activity which crowns a successful bid. But it marks the end of the road for the losers. End of the road? Yes, too often. There is, however, one further activity to be undertaken seriously: learning from experience. As the Department of Trade and Industry make clear:

'Ask for – and learn from – feedback if your tender is unsuccessful.'

It is Government policy, therefore, for Departments to debrief losing competitors and MOD will normally debrief bidders without request, but if necessary, ask.

A bid is always lost for one or more very good reasons, although not always for reasons that are under the control of the bidder. Usually, though, there are many reasons for losing a bid and it is important that these are identified and used to effect at the next attempt. But, contrary to what is claimed, MOD may not provide the

The reasons for losing a bid must be correctly identified.

complete story. Non-compliancy, price and technology immaturity are normally incontrovertible and will often be the reasons given, but more subjective judgements such as confidence in the bidder's ability to deliver, technical and programme risk, track record and system cost-effectiveness are all much more open to challenge and are consequently often suppressed.

It is, therefore, vital that the bid team holds its own post-mortem and seeks out those things which were done well and, even more important, those that could have been done better, with reasons for why they were not. This must not be used as an exercise in blame or the lessons will not come out; nor should it be an exercise in finding ways in which to belabour MOD through the local MP, press or official demands for reassessment.

A specialist bid advisor, if he has been involved, will be invaluable in tabulating lessons learned, but it must not be left to him alone as he will almost certainly suppress his own shortcomings! It should be an open, team activity. Learning from experience should be as structured as any other bid process. It is vital for the next bid.

But marking the bid, learning from experience and much of the lobbying lies in the future. For the moment, the effort must be put into the writing of the bid.

CHAPTER TWENTY-TWO

WRITING THE BID

Writing all but the smallest bids is a large job, and it requires time. That is why an early start is essential. There is never enough time and a late start invariably breeds too much haste, which obscures clarity of thought and objective assessment. Without these, the clarity of the bid will be obscured. An obscure bid is a bad bid however good the technical solution and the management plan.

Some of the major weaknesses that are repeatedly displayed by companies in the final draft stage, and often in the final document, are:

- The technical description is illogically-ordered, badly worded and assumes knowledge that the reader may not possess.
- The management volumes are incomplete, unconvincing and appear to have been done without too much thought.
- The executive summary has no impact or, worse, the wrong impact.
- The whole document is laid out in such a way that it is difficult to match to the ITT, with no cross-referencing.
- Compliancy matrices are incomplete.
- Illustrations are on the wrong pages and/or show nothing useful, and/or are indecipherable when copied.
- Meaningless adjectives, such as 'considerably increased, virtually undetectable, significantly reduced, highly reliable', are used widely.
- The document does not answer the questions set.

This is all pretty basic stuff, yet time and again documents are served up with some, or all, of the above weaknesses. Why? Probably for one or more of the following reasons:

- Running out of time through not starting in earnest early enough.
- No single capable person supervising all aspects of the writing and integration.
- No objective appraisal either of the whole or the parts.
- No document plan at the beginning.

Proper planning at the start would produce a better answer at the end.

What is so silly is that proper planning at the start would overcome all these problems, would save time and would produce a better answer. Planning and execution needs to take account of the following factors.

Layout

There is only one rule for the layout of the document and that is clarity. MOD needs to see that the bid answers the ITT and will not want to spend time trying to decipher it. By all means use colour-coordination, different print sizes for impact, pictures and pithy catch-phrases but these will be worthless without:

- Aligning the bid to the ITT as closely as possible.
- Cross-referencing from one part or volume to another when more detail is needed.
- Using clear, explanatory diagrams or pictures where they are needed, and on the same page as, or facing, the reference text.
- Indexing and contents listing.
- Keeping each part/volume complete in itself so that the readership of that part does not have to refer to another part/volume which he may not have.
- Eliminating the unnecessary.

Do all these properly and you will have an admirably clear layout. But it is worth testing it out on someone who has had nothing to do with the bid document's gestation. See how long he takes to find his way around. No doubt he will have recommendations for improvement. The more experienced he is, the more observations he may have. But do not take them all on-board unless you are convinced: seek a second opinion. And this is where an outside 'red team' is so valuable if it is drawn from a completely different part of the company or from outside the company altogether.

But do allow time to incorporate the 'red team's' recommendations. I have often been called in only to find that the bid is due to MOD by Monday and it is already Thursday. Not much time for any significant changes.

Language

Use ordinary, everyday words in short, unambiguous sentences to say what you mean. One of the usual weaknesses is in the use of rambling sentences which say very little and leave out or camouflage the major points. I have often asked what a particularly obscure paragraph means, only to be given a lucid verbal explanation. So why was it not written like that?

The use of meaningless adjectives is commonplace. These must be replaced by adjectives which mean something which, admittedly, is often difficult but not usually impossible. Better still to replace 'high reliability' with 'a reliability of 99.6%'. Do not fight shy of using figures, as long as they are readily understood, even in the executive summary. Sloppy adjectives suggest either imprecise knowledge of what is actually being proposed or an attempt to camouflage a lack of background work, and either will undermine the whole bid.

Finally, do not claim provenance if it is not justified. If a parameter has not been determined by earlier work, say so and say how it will be determined during future work and what the confidence basis is for achieving it.

The Technical Volumes

As might be expected, the technical solution put forward by serious contenders is generally compliant and practical. What a pity it is so often presented badly. The key things to get across are:

- **Description of the solution.** It is essential that the solution is presented in a logical order; do not start with the safety and arming unit of a round of ammunition or the wheel configuration of a vehicle. Use clear diagrams to save word description. Include all the relevant features, but give emphasis to the most important from MOD's point of view, particularly where innovative technology or concepts have been used, saying why it is important in system performance terms. And while component or sub-system performance is important, it is the system overall which MOD is going to evaluate. Help them.

- **Compliancy Matrices.** Design these to match the ITT and fill them in completely, using a comments column to expand on, or caveat, the compliancy statement and to cross-reference to detailed technical descriptions elsewhere. If you are not fully compliant, say so and cross-reference to where the work-around is described.
- **Basis for your claims.** Your claims for performance must be based either on work that has been done earlier in that specific project or other projects or on work that is to be done in the proposed schedule. Unsubstantiated claims are worthless and may suggest ignorance or short cuts. When reading across results from other work, make sure it is valid to do so or qualify it with a statement of further proving work in the bid.

I am told by many MOD procurement managers and directors that the technical volumes are usually well done, if badly written. That is my impression, too, with lack of clarity, illogical order of descriptions and incompleteness in parts being the major shortcomings.

The technical solution is so often presented badly.

The Management Volumes

The same sources suggest that the management volumes are done far less well. Many management plans are not properly defined, with some lacking even the most rudimentary detail. It is this which rings MOD alarm bells. It is no good contracting a supplier who has a good solution, if there is no confidence that he can deliver what he proposes to time and cost. Of course, this has happened in the past where time has become apparently less important; where cost to MOD has been constrained by fixed-price contracts; or where MOD is desperate to find enough starters to hold a worthwhile competition. From what has been said, this will not happen in the future. Past performance and confidence in the ability of a company to deliver will be all-important.

So what are the main weaknesses? They are:

- The programme plan often shows tests and trials but no development milestones, or even development activities.
- Risk is assessed well, but risk management and risk reduction are poorly presented, sometimes not presented at all. This is perhaps the most important flaw of all: if you do not manage and reduce risk effectively, you will not deliver.
- Integrated Logistic Support (ILS) is usually very weak indeed, despite the MOD pressure over the last few years. Copious ILS specifications are not broken down and meaningfully flowed down the supply chain. ILS managers are often quality assurance managers with no ILS training, interest or motivation.
- Resource allocation, particularly at the start of a programme when recruiting may be necessary and key personnel are involved in other projects, is a difficulty but must be covered with fall-back plans.
- Executive visibility is often not covered, yet this can show company commitment more than any other single management tool.
- Management of sub-contractors and the supply chain is often not covered, yet the prime cannot deliver to MOD without sub-contractors delivering the required sub-systems/components up the chain. MOD must be confident that the prime can manage its sub-contractors.

The management volumes usually proclaim quite clearly that insufficient time and thought has been devoted to them. If this is indicative of the time and thought that has actually been devoted to management issues and plans, then MOD cannot be blamed if they go elsewhere. The management volumes must convince MOD that

> *The management volumes usually proclaim insufficient time and thought.*

the company will deliver what it promises and what MOD wants within the laid-down time, cost and performance parameters.

This being so, it is worth expanding a little on a few of these management aspects.

Integrated Logistic Support

Integrated Logistic Support (ILS) is concerned with the balance of investment between acquisition costs and through-life cycle costs and has been a high priority in MOD for some time but with only very limited results. Under Smart Procurement it is set to become still more important. ILS should cover, amongst other things:

- Analysis of the intended operational use of the specific technical solution and its impact on in-service support.
- The support implications (particularly cost and manpower) of the technical option(s).
- Through-life costing
- Design of maintenance tasks to support the evaluated availability, reliability and maintainability of the option(s) once in service.
- Support equipment required, including training.
- A training needs analysis.

Some of the ILS requirement will be provided in the ITT, but some may not. It is not sensible to leave out key ILS responses because the ITT may be deficient. It can either be corrected through discussion with MOD or, if this fails to produce the right data, the tender can provide the ILS answers based on common sense and cross referral to othe project documents. The key thing is that the in-service support implications of your technical design and your mangement plans are clear to the reader.

But ILS is an onerous process and costly. The requirements are flowed down to a certain level, but below that there are often not enough resources to flow it down further. The MOD 00-60 is tailored for the prime but will need considerable work at each level to flow it down in a relevant, meaningful manner. Very often, below the prime and sometimes within the prime, there is a lack of knowledge and understanding of what is required.

The problems have been articulated by CTP Information Management Ltd as:[227]

- Lack of ILS understanding at senior level.
- Lack of motivations and direction at prime contractor level.
- The design philosophy imposed (LSA tasks) were already being performed.
- Constant comparison with large civil projects where there is no formal ILS.
- Expensive software required to produce an LSAR.
- The data required within the LSAR would not normally need to be derived for that type of programme.
- Consequential resource impact in a 'lean and mean' company.

They go on to recommend replacing DEFSTAN 00-60 with an ISO specification; the use in smaller projects of Microsoft Excel or Access tables in preference to expensive LSAR software; and the elimination of duplication of data.

Whether these recommendations are acceptable to MOD, or are even the most effective and practical possibilities, is not known. But what is essential is that the ILS process is made more user-friendly to the lower levels of the supply chain and less resource-heavy.

Reliability and Maintainability

In July 1997, the Chief of Defence Procurement made the following commitment to providing equipment with high reliability and optimal maintainability:

> *'The Services demand, and are entitled to expect, dependable, battle-winning equipment of proven performance. At the same time, all project managers must keep the whole-life costs down. And, of course,*

---

[227] Rory Lipington, CTPi, 5 March 1999

an equipment's operational availability and its cost of ownership are both driven to a large extent by its reliability and maintainability. The Services' annual bill for spare parts and for industrial repair support alone is nearly £2.5 billion which represents a staggering 25% of total procurement expenditure. That is why our procurement policy calls for R&M issues to be given equal priority with the achievement of performance, cost and project timescale.'[228]

It is rare (unknown?) for a bid to give as much weight to R&M as to performance, cost and time, yet clearly it is being treated with much greater importance than previously. Of course, like all system aspects it needs to be balanced with other parameters, and the scrutineers in MOD will assess the R&M plan as to whether it:

- Reflects the operational reqirement.
- Is achievable.
- Is affordable.
- Is demonstrable.

And in contracting a company, MOD will look to ensure that:

- The concept is capable of meeting the use to which it will be put.
- The contractor is competent in the technology involved and has the necessary resources.
- R&M is a specific condition of contract.

As MOD is seeking confidence that the competitor is competent in the above factors, a clear R&M analysis, strategy and plan are essential, together with a progressive framework to meet major R&M milestones, which themselves must be tied in to overall project milestones. All this must convince the tender assessors that the equipment will work reliably in service. If it does not do that, a very serious question mark will have been placed over your ability to deliver.

---

[228] Introduction to DPMT's handout for their Reliability and Maintainability Seminars

Reliability and Maintainability: Progressive Assurance

It has been common practice to wait until the completion of a project to measure the reliability and maintainability (R&M) of a product, but this can result in modifications which will be more expensive than remedial work undertaken at an earlier stage; in any case, uncertainty about the system's compliance with the R&M requirement is becoming less and less acceptable as the emphasis on whole life costs increases.

Progressive assurance is aimed at giving the best possible estimate of the system's R&M at every stage of the project. The level of assurance will depend on the accumulation of evidence at a particular stage and should improve progressively throughout the procurement cycle. The achieved R&M should be progressively plotted against the plan for R&M achievement to log the progress made towards the required levels. By the end of the procurement phase there should be sufficient evidence to demonstrate that the R&M requirement has been met, and this will be invaluable when the project comes up for Acceptance.

The Progressive Assurance process is illustrated at Figure 23.

The Progressive Assurance document should be an overview, summarising the contractor's approach and the framework in which evidence can be placed. Traceability is essential and reference must be made throughout to lower level documents, to other management plans, trials and analysis. Evidence that can be used would include:

- Initial estimates.
- Modelling results.
- Benchmarking and comparative studies.
- Suppliers' data.
- Test results from all stages of the project.
- Read-across (where relevant) from other projects.

The MOD will expect to see:

During the Tender:

- Outline of the analysis, strategy and plan for R&M achievement (assessment and management).
- Progressive evidence framework and timing of events to provide alignment with major project milestones.

During the Contract:

- Periodic submissions of updates to the top level summary document.
- Development of progressive assurance in accordance with the Acceptance Framework.

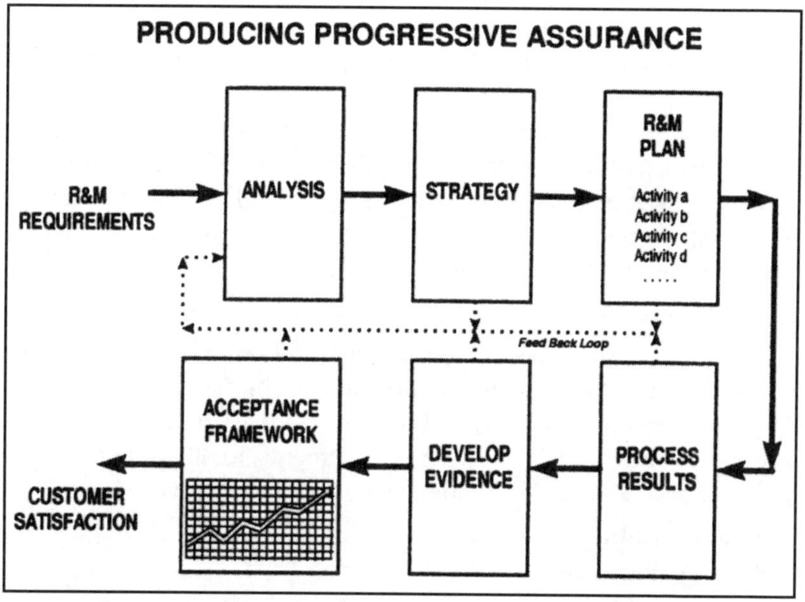

Figure 23: The R&M Progressive Assurance Process

The MOD view is that:

'Progressive Assurance reflects what the contractor should be doing already and should not add significant costs to the project.'[229]

[229] Head of Reliability, MOD(PE), DGLS BD2, 24 February 1999

That may be so, but whatever the costs they need to be built in to the bid. This will, in any event, be far less than leaving it to chance, for the MOD has said:

'In the event that the product fails to meet our R&M requirements, the contractor shall undertake remedial work at their expense and demonstrate the effectiveness of such work.'[230]

There have been plenty of examples of such remedial work being required before an equipment is accepted, almost all being costly, some of it very costly indeed.

Risk Management

In a survey of 28 projects, the National Audit Office identified that:[231]

- 23% of risks identified on 13 projects matured into technical difficulties.
- 61% of technical difficulties occurring on 14 projects examined were not identified as risks at the outset.

This shows quite clearly that identification and management of technical risks are very poor. Technical difficulties result in cost increases (an average of 3%), performance shortfalls (55% of projects examined), and delay (54% of projects averaged 11 months delay). And those figures relate only to technical risks. It is not surprising, therefore, that MOD attaches great importance to identifying, assessing and managing risk.

Identification and management of technical risks are very poor.

It is essential that risk assessment is undertaken early and:

'The identification and analysis of risk, coupled with sound fall-back plans, will be taken into account when evaluating the realism of tenders.'[232]

[230] Ibid

[231] NAO Report on MOD, *Initiatives to Manage Technical Risk on Defence Equipment Programmes,* 10 May 1996, pages 17 to 21

[232] MOD, *Risk Assessment for MOD Contracts,* AD/EMS Business Support Group, March 1998

MOD states that, as part of the tenderer's submission, the following shall be provided:

- A Risk Assessment from inception to completion of production to include as a minimum:
  - Completed risk questionnaires detailing project risks with fallback and containment plans.
  - A high level network with associated three points probabilistic activity durations, critical path(s) and ordered activity criticality index.
  - Cumulative probability distributions of the project timescale for each key activity.
- A Risk Management Plan in two parts:
  - Risk Assessment Procedure.
  - Risk Management Procedure.
  - The Plan should include reporting procedures, methodology, risk management activities, tools and techniques, a risk register, definitions and identification of key risk areas.
  - If the terms High, Medium and Low are used for probability of occurrence and/or impact on schedule, cost or performance, these terms must be more tightly defined in the plan.

The quoted document gives further detail on the above. Also, most ITTs are quite specific on what is required.

One important aspect is the integration of the risk management plan into the overall project or programme plan so that any change to the programme can be easily translated into impact on risk. And vice-versa.

Software Development

There have been many examples of software development impacting adversely on programme cost, time and performance parameters. Bidders are now expected to supply answers to a software development questionnaire with their bid.

This questionnaire consists of a number of sections, including:

- Software development scope covering the software elements proposed and their price.
- The software development environment under which the supplier proposes to execute the work proposed.
- Software system characteristics as determined by the supplier based on the requirements set out in the ITT.
- Software development practices which the supplier is to use in undertaking the proposed development.
- Software development staff experience.
- Software development time and size range as estimated by the supplier either as a range or by functional sub-systems of the proposed development.
- Supplier's previous projects, requiring data for previous projects undertaken of a similar nature and size to that proposed.

The MOD questionnaire is DEFFORM 143 and is generally self-explanatory.

Gainshare Proposals

It is quite likely that future ITTs will call for detailed gainshare proposals, although no clear guidance on this seems to have appeared recently. In many ways, it would be simpler for MOD to start gainshare discussions once the final prime contractor has been selected. However, this could lead to the selection of a winner who subsequently is unable or unwilling to take an innovative approach to gainshare, so that MOD (and of course the selected prime and his supply chain) loses much of the potential fruit of partnering. It is, therefore, of paramount importance to both MOD and industry that the outcome of the competition favours the one with good gainshare proposals. Each competitor will want to keep his proposals from the other competitors, so MOD's Chinese Walls will have to be seen to work.

The actual proposals for gainshare will centre around cost (both procurement and support) and performance as discussed in Chapter 14. They may necessarily, at least in part, be immature at this stage, but they can be refined in later negotiations with the winning prime or team. What the MOD will probably want to see is:

- The scope for gainshare.
- The innovative approach of the bidder.

Both are vital if MOD is to be able to judge correctly the ability of the bidder to deliver, not just the proposed equipment or service, but the benefits that will accrue to MOD if that bidder is selected.

Of course, gainshare could be done in one-to-one discussions between MOD and each bidder separately during the evaluation of tenders, rather than in the tender itself. But for industry that is a minor issue; the major factor is that during the production of the bid, gainshare proposals will have to be worked out in some detail. How those are communicated to MOD will be decided by MOD, either in the ITT instructions, or after prompting by an ambitious bidder.

If a new relationship with industry is to mean anything in output terms, gainshare proposals will have to be given high priority in the marking scheme. But, so far, gainsharing has only been officially pursued in the IPTs of projects in the Manufacturing Stage once competition is over.

The Executive Summary

An executive summary is not essential. But it is an opportunity.

The executive summary is not essential, but an opportunity.

There should be an identifiable, recurring theme throughout the Executive Summary that imparts confidence in the reader's mind: confidence in the proposed solution, and a confidence that the bidder has the ability to deliver. It should, therefore:

- Emphasise the positive aspects, although major weaknesses should be covered stressing the work-arounds.
- Define the attributes that make this proposal so good.

- Use figures selectively rather than meaningless adjectives and emphasise relevant work that has already been concluded.
- Describe succinctly the technical design, the system performance, the major management (particularly risk reduction) issues, and commitment to delivery.
- Use a small number of clear diagrams/pictures where this will shorten substantially the number of words used, or clarify description, or build confidence in the reader's mind.
- Keep it short (say 5-10 pages) but bear in mind the wide readership of the Executive Summary and do not either assume knowledge that they will not have or 'talk down'.
- Produce impact.

MOD requires industry to propose trade-offs where this will result in cost or performance benefit. Industry may also wish to propose trade-offs in their proposal to overcome a lack of compliancy or to reduce cost to a winning margin. Trade-offs should not be confused with Innovative Bids which must be the subject of a separate bid in addition to the core bid against the ITT as written. These will be looked at later in this chapter.

One factor that must be borne in mind with trade-offs is that they must not obscure the clarity of the core bid. Too often it is difficult, if not impossible, to understand exactly what is the core bid, and what is a potential trade-off. Keep trade-offs separate in the document.

MOD is unlikely to be interested in trade-offs unless they:

- Offer almost as much performance at very much less cost, or
- Offer a great deal more performance for no more cost (this will be difficult to make convincing, but not impossible), or
- Offer a great deal more performance for only a little extra procurement cost.

Extra cost will be difficult for MOD to accept if it takes the total above what is already authorised by EAC or other approval bodies. If you know how much this is, you should be able to keep the extra cost of a trade-off within that ceiling sum. It would be nice to think that, if you were able to propose a trade-off that covered significantly higher procurement cost by much lower downstream costs, MOD would jump at it. But this will not necessarily be so: in theory, they would like nothing better, but in practice the limiting factor will be the provision of higher up-front funding.

You may be better off waiting and proposing such changes as part of the gainshare discussions. Assuming that you win the contract, of course.

Innovative Bids

An innovative bid is defined by MOD as:

> *'imaginative or novel solutions made in response to an invitation to tender but not necessarily in a way envisaged in the tender document'.*[233]

and will be considered under the formal tender evaluation process.

An innovative bid against an ITT must be separate from and complementary to a compliant bid. It must:

- Be to the same standard of detail as the compliant bid or it will be rejected as lacking validity.
- Be fully costed.

Innovative Proposals

Innovative proposals are unsolicited suggestions or ideas made before MOD has launched a feasibility or scoping study, or outside a competition or other acquisition process. The MOD undertakes to acknowledge all Innovative Proposals within 10 working days, inform the proposer within another 10 working days whether the proposal will be further considered, and provide a full response within three months.

MOD will reject or not appraise Innovative Proposals only if:

- There is no MOD need.
- Procurement is already in progress.

---

[233] MOD Guidelines for Industry 12, *Code of Practice on the Handling of Innovative Proposals,* MOD website www.mod.uk/policy/spi, 24 February 1999

- The proposal is not new.
- No funding is available.
- There is insufficient information in the proposal.

And will hold a debriefing meeting, if required.

An Innovative Proposal should contain:

- An explanation of what the proposal is.
- A clear statement of what the perceived MOD requirement is and how it would be satisfied, identifying clearly the innovative features.
- Price, payment mechanism, key cost drivers and variables, and estimate of other resources required.
- An outline of commercial arrangements.
- A Statement of the company's experience in the area.
- Background financial and business data on the company.

The Impact of Smart Procurement

In theory, Smart Procurement should eliminate the need for both Innovative Proposals and Innovative Bids as the more extensive and much earlier collaboration between MOD and industry should unearth all possible ways of meeting a user requirement. In reality, even supposing that Capability Working Groups (CWGs) and Integrated Project Teams (IPTs) function as successfully as is hoped and Intellectual Property Rights (IPR) issues are satisfactorily overcome, it is unlikely that any one (relatively small) group of human beings could explore or even identify all potential options. Moreover, technology changes so fast in some areas that new possibilities or practicalities can surface at any time.

It is, however, likely that the opportunities for Innovative Bids will reduce with the incorporation of industry within CWGs and IPTs provided that there is the envisaged industrial input at all stages. The opportunities for Innovative Proposals should also reduce but perhaps not by as much. The potential for a completely new way of meeting a requirement, or indeed of radically changing the requirement while still meeting the capability needs, will remain either because of technology progress or threat/concept changes or funding realities. This will be particularly so when projects fail to pass through the Main Gate. At that point, Innovative Proposals would be valuable and, I would hope, most welcome.

The problem with both Innovative Bids and Innovative Proposals is that they are resource-heavy. Producing a compliant bid is usually a time-constrained nightmare, so producing a parallel Innovative Bid to the same standard as the compliant bid would be beyond the capability of most companies. And it would have to be excessively attractive (primarily in price) to override compliant bids. Such a bid is more likely to succeed when MOD is selecting three or more companies to contest a competition, rather than as the sole solution for final development and production. Apart from the 'comfort factor' which would favour a compliant bid, the difficulties that MOD would face in selecting a sole winner that was not compliant would pose all sorts of problems in explaining the decision to the compliant losers, their MPs and the media. Ministers are likely to fight shy.

It is, therefore, more likely that MOD might include an Innovative Bid as one of, say, three solutions to take forward than as the one selected winner from a field with several good complaint bids. In the latter situation it might be better to save the Innovative Bid until after your compliant bid has won, then introduce it as part of subsequent negotiations. Of course, you might not win. Fine judgement is required.

Getting the Bid(s) Right

The writing of the bid, its integration and objective appraisal, the decision as to whether to add an Innovative Bid to the complaint bid, and the understanding of the bid's readership, points to the need for expertise of a wider ambit than that required for the technical design, the management plan and the pricing methodology. This wider expertise is essential to you if you are to win. It can be:

Management of the bid requires expertise of a wider ambit.

- Provided in-house, although this may only be possible in large companies where bid experts can be gainfully employed on a full-time basis because bids are continuously being made.
- Brought in from outside through individuals as part of the bid team, but their expertise will disappear when the bid is completed.
- Bought in on an as-required basis from a specialist company who will have much wider experience than individuals and will be available for advice on a regular basis between bids.

Whatever solution is adopted, the bid experts must be available early.

Bids that Win

Bids that win are clear, concise, convincing and comprehensive (the four Cs). They must be clear so that MOD knows what is being offered and how it meets the 'shalls' in the ITT; concise because MOD does not want to wade through unnecessary or long-winded material; convincing enough to persuade a wide variety of readers to go along with you; and comprehensive so that all that is asked for in the ITT is provided.

Make it reader-friendly. And make sure you demonstrate your mastery, not your ignorance.

> *Bids that win are clear, concise, convincing and comprehensive.*

PART FIVE

CONCLUSIONS

CHAPTER TWENTY-THREE

CONCLUSIONS 1: MOD

Defence equipment procurement has, for generations, been characterised by high cost and long gestation periods, together with significant time and cost overruns on original estimates. Much effort has been made over the years to correct the problems, but real progress has been elusive.

The Smart Procurement Initiative promises revolution in this field, and its main features lie encouragingly in the right direction. Implementation, however, is the real test and already many serious problems have been encountered, with few of them being overcome satisfactorily and others in danger of being placed in the 'too difficult' tray.

Nevertheless, much change and a little real progress has been made, thanks largely to the strong Ministerial leadership provided by George Robertson and John Spellar; changes and progress which were considered by many as inconceivable two years ago. But the limited success must be a spur to further progress, not a halt for back-slapping.

The situation as at November 1999 can be looked at separately as it applies to:

- MOD internally
- MOD-industry partnering
- Industry internally

Within MOD, implementation can be divided into:

- Progress
- Weaknesses
- Issues for Further Thought

PROGRESS

Genuine progress is relatively sparse. There are three areas alone where clear progress has been made, and even here there is a strong possibility of recidivism.

Initiatives. The Smart Procurement initiatives are good and lay out a clear direction to the final objective, although the exact path to be followed is lost in low-lying mist for most of its length. The main initiatives are:

- Personal accountability.
- Partnering with industry.
- A through-life systems approach.
- Incremental acquisition.
- Streamlined procedures.
- Taut customer-supplier relationships.
- Greater investment in early project stages.

The one disappointing aspect is the lack of an effective policy for research and technology.

Empowerment. Personal accountability is only possible if individuals are empowered, so that they have the authority to match their responsibility. Progress has been made in two areas.

- Financial delegation limits have been increased significantly: to £100M for a group of one-star officers/officials and to £400M for a group of two-stars. However, this is undermined by the retention of oversight by Ministers for all decisions above £50M.
- Management of projects is to be much less overseen by a management chain above the Integrated Project Team (IPT) leader. This has worked well with the Pilot IPT leaders reporting direct to CDP, but this cannot work with 90 IPTs.

Creation of IPTs. The creation of 150 IPTs in the Defence Procurement Agency (DPA) and the Defence Logistic Organisation (DLO) by April 2000 represents the implementation of the biggest change to date. In many ways, this is only formalising the previous system and in itself is unlikely to improve output, but:

- Empowerment, as discussed above, will give the IPT leader and IPT members greater ability to make and implement decisions.
- Incorporation of industry has the potential to avoid contractual stand-offs.

There are, however, serious difficulties with the latter, and these are discussed in Chapter 24.

WEAKNESSES

For every piece of progress, there are four glaring weaknesses in the implementation of Smart Procurement.

Research and Technology (R&T). The plan for R&T and the future of DERA has been handled separately from Smart Procurement and the PPP proposal (temporarily on hold at the time of writing) works in the opposite direction from all other Smart Procurement initiatives. The plan negates many of the current R&T strengths and accentuates the weaknesses:

- It will endorse the continuing decline in R&T spending, its inefficient use for technology generation, ineffective technology transfer (TT), minimal pull-through into winning projects, and multiplication of work within industry.
- It will limit or deny UK access to foreign R&T, particularly French and US.
- It will undermine the achievement of seven of the 'Eight Commandments', laid down by the MOD customer.
- It will place a PPP DERA at risk by limiting its commercial potential.

PPP DERA should be dropped in favour of a new Government-owned DERA plan which would:

- Restore adequate MOD research funding.
- Instigate a true R&T partnership between DERA, industry and academia, with joint research teams the rule, under a joint research strategy.
- Keep together DERA's research and technical evaluation functions as they are indivisible.

- Institute mechanisms for the maximisation of TT and pull-through of technology into winning projects.

Under this plan, PPP of certain Test and Evaluation facilities should be investigated.

Internal MOD Customer-Supplier Relationships. The plan for implementing taut relationships between Customer One and DPA, and Customer Two and DLO is based on too simplistic a view of the whole acquisition process and will not work in practice. In fact, the two customers (one of which is split into three or more) and the two suppliers are locked into a close relationship throughout the whole acquisition cycle.

It is essential, therefore, that:

- The 'four-horned monster' approach (Chapter 3), or a variant of it, is adopted and the operating costs and other administrative difficulties overcome.
- Customer One is adequately resourced in manpower or much of his work (and therefore his authority) will be misappropriated by DPA.
- The Chief of Defence Procurement (CDP) and the Chief of Defence Logistics (CDL) be replaced as members of the Equipment Approvals Committee (EAC) by Customer One and Customer Two.

Incremental Acquisition. Apart from what would amount to small in-service upgrades, incremental acquisition poses several problems which are severe enough to sink this intiative. These include: the unattractiveness of introduction of a much lower capability in a not much faster timescale; the difficulties attendant on the managing of major procurement increments by an IPT in the DLO; and the problems of funding approval of later stages before those stages are defined. If the latter enforces repeated returns to EAC, timescales, bureaucracy and costs will escalate.

A workable solution for incremental acquisition, where the increments are major improvements, must ensure that:

- The whole project is approved at Initial Gate and Main Gate without subsequent returns for each increment.

- The initial capability is fielded in a much reduced (halved at least) timescale.
- Later increments are largely transparent to user and maintainer.
- Later increments can be introduced without marked loss in availability.
- Funding for later increments is protected.

These are all major challenges which have yet to be addressed.

Positioning of Main Gate. One of the few differences between the new Acquisition Cycle and the old Downey cycle is the apparent reduction in the number of times a project is submitted to EAC for approval: twice instead of thrice. But in the past, most projects have returned to EAC many more times. It is to be hoped that this will not happen in the future, but the positioning of the Main Gate (Chapter 4) is too early for us to be confident. It is prior to the Demonstration Phase (equivalent to Downey's Project Definition) when cost, time, performance parameters and the procurement strategy will all be immature. Competition will not have been completed and no useful gainshare negotiations will have taken place. **The Main Gate must be:**

- Moved to later in the cycle, to a point where competition is complete.

Or:

- Retained where it is and:
    - The Acquisition Cycle changed to split the Demonstration Phase, the first part of it being incorporated with Assessment.
    - EAC must accept they will be taking greater risk when approving.

Cluster IPTs. Most projects will be bundled into Cluster IPTs with anything up to 50 projects in each. Apart from the difficulty of one IPT managing so many separate projects, individual projects are to be moved at the In-Service Date (ISD) from its DPA Cluster IPT to a 'suitable' DLO Cluster IPT. So the risk and hiatus in moving at ISD from DPA to DLO is heightened by the change of IPT. This will be even further aggravated if that project is an incremental acquisition project.

There is no simple solution. However, if the 'Four-Horned Monster' approach is adopted, there would be no need for a change of IPT at ISD. The Cluster IPT will almost certainly be broken down into mini-clusters, or even single projects, so the selection of personnel to work on each is not a major issue and can be retained to smooth progression of each project through the whole Acquisition Cycle.

The difficulties of incorporating industry in Cluster IPTs will be covered in Chapter 24.

Smart People. The 'smartening' of the MOD acquisition workforce requires the improvement of personal qualities and a major change of culture. This will take time and will require strong leadership from the top over a long period.

In particular, smart people will not be created unless:

- Individuals are empowered.
- Individuals feel that they can make honest mistakes without penalty.
- Learning from experience is effectively introduced and tenures are lengthened.
- True joint training (DPA, DLO, Customers One and Two, DERA, users, industry) is instigated, preferably at Shrivenham.
- Individuals are properly incentivised by empowerment and promotion in post.
- The newly created Acquisition Stream has full (not just virtual) responsibility for the career of every acquisition post-holder.

Collaboration. The creation of OCCAR is unlikely to improve the appalling record of cost and time performance of collaborative projects within Europe. This will ensure that collaborative projects dilute, or even negate, the gains made by Smart Procurement.

Export of Smart Procurement principles and their adoption by other European nations will be a slow and incomplete business. Collaborative projects (except for buying off-the-shelf) should therefore be reduced, rather than increased in number and the political penalties accepted.

Reduction in Cycle Time. The key element in Smart Procurement should be a major reduction in acquisition cycle time. Reduction in time would bring commensurate savings in cost and would allow the use of maturer technology, thus reducing risk and further reducing cost and time. The time factor circle needs breaking into and the cycle time reduced from 20 years to 5 years.

The implementation of Smart Procurement, as it is envisaged at present, will not bring about this drastic reduction in cycle time, although it may reduce time and cost overruns. Thus the big prize, a genuine resolution in acquisition efficiency in output terms, will elude us.

ISSUES FOR FURTHER THOUGHT

In addition to these weaknesses, which need rectifying, there are several issues which need further thought if they are not to develop into yet more weaknesses.

Merger of CDL and CDP. The awkward change in responsibility at around ISD when the project IPT moves from DPA to DLO or, worse, when the small project moves from one Cluster IPT to another in the DLO is potentially inefficient and costly in time, performance and money. Although it would create a monster post, the merger of CDP and CDL would eliminate this difficulty.

Mergers of Customers One and Two. Likewise Customer One and Customer Two could be merged and the joint customer function for procurement and support of equipment undertaken by a four-star officer in MOD Centre reporting directly to CDS who has, or should have, the ultimate responsibility for provision of field force, including equipment.

Reporting Lines. The new organisations are still bedevilled by the conflict between solid and dotted lines of responsibility. This is particularly evident in the operation of the IPT where the IPT leader has line management of his team, some of whom have functional lines of responsibility elsewhere. And the team leader himself is 'answerable' to Customer One and 'accountable' to CDP.

This conflict between solid and dotted lines requires rationalisation.

Delegated Authority. Two figures of delegated authority require a rethink:

- Ministers should not have visibility of decisions as low as £50M. This should be revised upwards to more than £100M, preferably £400M.
- Customer One, headed by a three-star officer, should have greater powers to commit funding prior to Initial Gate. Funding should be already allocated in the Equipment Plan and should be relative to the size of the whole project funding. His current £5M limit should be changed to 5% of total procurement funding.

Up-front Funding. The recommended amount for the Concept and Assessment Phases is up to 15% of total procurement funding. Early year funding is notoriously difficult to introduce, so this must be inserted in the Equipment Plan and the Short Term Plan right at the start of the Concept Phase before the project is formally commenced.

Whole Life Concept. As 80% of procurement costs are often locked in by the end of the Assessment Phase, support concepts and costs must be a high priority in the Concept and Assessment Phases. Options to reduce support costs, even if they increase procurement costs, must be seriously considered by Customer One and Customer Two in tandem, despite the fact that the bulk of the savings will lie outside the Equipment Plan timescale while the whole of the costs will lie within it.

Modelling of whole life costs needs major improvement.

Profiling. Shortening equipment procurement timescales markedly will bring large sums of money forward, which will be impossible without larger savings in the early years as well as later years. This problem may well mean that many projects have to be delayed if others are to be accelerated, which is not the intention of

Smart Procurement. The profiling issue needs review so that it does not negate progress that might be possible.

IPTs in the DLO. Once IPTs have transferred to the DLO, it is said they will become smaller and will be manned at a lower level. Given that support costs are very much larger than procurement costs, this seems to be illogical. The difficulties of incremental acquisition, if later stages are of any size, reinforce the view that IPTs in the DLO need to be a continuation of IPTs when they were in the DPA, with only a shift in the proportion of DPA to DLO personnel.

Public Accountability and Empowerment. The view that public accountability and empowerment are incompatible is wrong. However, empowerment of individuals to make decisions is bound to come under attack when mistakes are made. If empowerment is to be more than an initial advertisement without long-term foundation, then Ministers and their top officials must educate the Treasury, the Public Accounts Committee and others that the gains are greater than the losses. This must be placed on the agenda of 'Joined-Up Government'.

PFI Guidelines. Clear PFI guidelines, on the lines given verbally by MOD to the HCDC, must be promulgated so that industry and MOD IPTs do not waste time and money on chasing impractical ideas.

Collaboration and Interoperability. Given the huge effort that has been put into international collaboration within NATO and Europe together with the extremely limited achievements that have resulted, inter-government collaboration on defence equipment procurement should be discontinued. Instead, governments should agree interoperability guidelines and leave it to individual governments to procure equipment within them. Global defence companies winning contracts for similar equipment from different governments will, through economies of scale, be well placed to harmonise individual nation's requirements. Future interoperability would be assured and commonality would be slowly achieved in most areas.

Targets. The Treasury Targets are far too lax. The IPT Hard and Stretch Objectives are more challenging but there are no aggregated targets which get progressively more demanding year by year in terms of cost, time (not just overruns) and performance (not just shortfall). By setting progressive targets, year-on-year, major changes should be achieved within a decade which will otherwise not be sought. In addition, relatively small steps of, say 5% per year in cost or time reduction, would avoid the importation of major risk that current measures (e.g. 30% removed from procurement cycle in one go) are likely to accummulate and, thereby, increase overruns in due course.

IMPLEMENTATION IN MOD

The above conclusions show quite clearly that:

- Real progress is so far very limited and is subject to recidivism.
- There are many real weaknesses in how Smart Procurement is being implemented, and these will constrain, or eliminate, the possibility of significant benefits.
- There are numerous issues that need resolution and/or further thought and work.

Smart Procurement has correctly identified the objective. The path that implementation is mapping out will only be in the right direction and will only reach the required distance if the weaknesses are eliminated and the immature issues are resolved satisfactorily.

CHAPTER TWENTY-FOUR

CONCLUSIONS 2: MOD AND INDUSTRY

One of the central themes of Smart Procurement is the forging of a new relationship with industry, including partnering. If this is to become a reality, there are many issues that must be resolved between MOD and industry, to the satisfaction of both.

PROGRESS

There has been little clear progress in establishing the new relationship in procurement, in contrast to the progress that has been made in PFI in support.

Longer, Firmer Commitment.

PFI partnering deals over 20 to 30 years (or even more) have become increasingly common in the support area. While the impetus has come from the PFI/PPP initiative, it has been extended from facilities and training into equipment support, a good example being the seamless support and upgrade of the Royal Navy's Type 22 and 23 frigates.

Industry in IPTs

Industry has been welcomed into IPTs, particularly where competition has been completed, and a closer relationship between MOD and industry has been fostered. MOD and industry together have shaped gainshare, explored and agreed trade-offs in cost, time and performance parameters, and have replaced adversarial distrust with a degree of trust and transparency.

This new relationship, however, is not yet in evidence where competition is under way or anticipated in the future; where a project sits in a Cluster IPT; in the Concept Phase; or in research.

IPT Leaders from Industry

Leaders have been sought from industry for a number of IPTs, and individuals have been appointed. It is too early to say how successful these individuals will be, but the principle is right and must lead in time both to a welcome input of quality and cross-fertilisation of business and MOD ideas, approaches and culture.

However, the take-up by industry has been slow, partly because of short notice given by MOD, partly because the posts have not been widely seen as career-enhancing. Hence terms for industrialists have been reduced from five years to two or three which is a serious step backwards. Unless these posts carry better incentives, there is a real danger that they will either not be filled by industry, or will be filled by the wrong people.

ISSUES FOR FURTHER THOUGHT

The tentative progress so far is outweighed by many problems which need further thought for resolution. Most of them are potentially serious obstacles to a new relationship which works.

Competition

There must be a balance between competition and partnering: too much or too prolonged competition will reduce, or even negate, the fruits of partnering. Competition therefore must be:

- Dispensed with where there is no clear indication that its benefits will outweigh the benefits of a longer partnering period.
- Completed earlier than the end of Demonstration: by Main Gate or earlier, unless there are clear indications that partnering benefits will be minimal.

Unless this happens, partnering in procurement will be largely still-born.

Partnering Arrangements

Partnering arrangements can only be initiated once the final prime contractor is selected. Benefits will accrue slowly but with increasing pay-off. Thus a partnering arrangement will only be really successful over a long period of time, such as 20 to 30 years as has become commonplace in PFI contracts.

Such lengthy periods can only be achieved if procurement contracts include a large slice of in-service support, together with upgrades and incremental acquisition, for it is in support that most of the large gainshare opportunities are likely to arise. Conversely, without the inclusion of in-service support, the prime will not be motivated to seek support savings if he cannot benefit; indeed he may well seek only procurement benefit which could well increase support costs downstream.

If competition is dispensed with, or completed very early in the acquisition cycle, the prime can optimise design to minimise support costs, something which he is unlikely to achieve if competition is retained too long.

Incentivisation

In a procurement contract, the main incentive will be gainshare which can be maximised over a long partnering arrangement. In addition there are two other major considerations:

- Industrial input while competition is in process or in prospect must be rewarded in some way, or that input will be of limited value to MOD and, subsequently, to industry. Down-selection of those companies that provide the best input at each stage would seem necessary.
- Exportability of the equipment defined in the Systems Requirements Document must be considered seriously in the Concept and Assessment Phases.

Sharing of Benefits and Disbenefits

Sharing of benefit through Gainshare has been enthusiastically promoted by MOD and industry. However, the sharing of disbenefits has not, although better risk apportionment and management has been accepted.

What does not seem to be accepted by either side is the need to work together to resolve issues jointly, even where a problem has been created by one partner. There is still a clear 'them and us' culture which must be eliminated.

Intellectual Property Rights

IPR is a thorn, although the latest DEFCONs reduce the problem.

What is required is that:

- MOD understand, and be seen to understand, the importance of IPR to companies.
- MOD protects IPR of companies throughout the acquisition cycle.
- MOD and industry detail IPR from the start of every project. Early definition is vital.

IPTs in Competitive Phases

A single IPT in competitive phases will not work and neither MOD nor industry could afford to resource more than one, except in exceptional circumstances. The answer is to ditch the Smart Procurement idea of industry participation in IPTs during competition so that:

- The MOD IPT consists of MOD personnel only.
- Each team or consortium be left to run its own industry IPT.
- MOD place one project individual in each industrial IPT.

The last point should ensure that MOD 'Chinese Wells' are credible.

IPTs in Non-Competitive Phases

In non-competitive phases, MOD and industry IPTs should be merged into one joint IPT in industry. This would ensure that:

- Transparency is maximised.
- Trust is engendered.
- Resource requirements are minimised.

- The IPT has the key decision-makers (MOD and industry) within it.

Joint Training

Trust is unlikely to be created without each partner having full knowledge of each other's processes, culture and organisation. This can only be obtained through much improved training, and is unlikely to be really successful without true joint training. It is, therefore, essential that:

- One acquisition training establishment be set up at, say, Shrivenham.
- This establishment to be funded and staffed jointly by MOD and industry.
- All acquisition training be carried out there.
- All acquisition personnel in MOD (DPA, EC, DLO, DERA, Customer Two) and industry be trained there.

SMEs

Small and medium-sized enterprises are both valuable and vulnerable. Together MOD and primes must:

- Agree fair supply chain principles.
- Oversee their flow-down.
- Find satisfactory ways of including SMEs in IPTs without straining SME resources.
- Agree sensible strategies for supply chain competition.
- Protect SME's IPR.
- Recognise that very small enterprises (VSEs) represent excellent value for money, but are extremely vulnerable: take steps to use them considerately.

THE NEW RELATIONSHIP WITH INDUSTRY

Implementation of the new relationship with industry is slow and uncertain:

- Progress is limited and some can be reversed.

- Areas for further thought and resolution are numerous.

Unless the problems are resolved, progress is likely to falter or even go into reverse, destroying progress to date.

However, if the problems (none of which are insuperable) are satisfactorily overcome, the limited progress made to date will be reinforced and accelerated.

CHAPTER TWENTY-FIVE

CONCLUSIONS 3: INDUSTRY

While MOD has put huge effort, and quite some thought, into implementing Smart Procurement (admittedly with limited results so far in terms of output), industry has done very little indeed to further the process. Indeed, too many firms have done nothing except keep their head down and hope it will go away. Very few industrialists have appreciated the huge benefits that could accrue to them and even fewer have done anything to seek those benefits.

PROGRESS

Nil.

PROBLEMS

Innovations

Smart Procurement places a premium on an innovative approach by industry to partnering MOD. So far there is little evidence that industry is taking an innovative approach to gainshare proposals, trade-offs or input in competitive phases. There is a continuation of a reactive culture in its dealings with MOD.

If MOD creates the potential for long partnering agreements spanning procurement, upgrades and in-service support, industry must reciprocate by energetic pursuit of proposals to bring major (not just minor) benefit to both sides.

Gainshare will only be made possible by industry; and by an innovative approach to it by industry.

Communications

Communications within a company, particularly large ones, are usually very poor indeed. This is inefficient and defeats attempts at transparency. No transparency means no trust. Intra-company communications must be improved.

Logistic Expertise

If MOD is to extend procurement contracts with one prime into the support phase, primes must improve their logistic expertise. While some have some expertise in some areas, none have the required expertise right across the board. That expertise must be bought in or improved in-house if MOD is to contract with primes, as primes must be able to identify and deliver year-on-year improvements in performance and reductions in cost.

Bids

Industrial bids are generally poor. They must be improved in key areas:

- Understanding the ITT.
- Coordinating the bid.
- Answering the ITT.
- Writing the bid in terms of clear language, layout, logicality and completeness.
- Management plans.
- Timeliness.

Lobbying needs to be subtler and more effective. Learning from experience (particularly from failure) is vital.

Gainshare proposals, innovative bids and innovative proposals require greater understanding, effective identification and timely submission.

SMEs

Smart Procurement is likely to be tough on SMEs, and those that do not react may well go to the wall. Those that do grab the opportunity, are likely to realise huge benefit. In particular, SMEs must:

- Concentrate on niche markets.
- Attain world class.
- Form SME clusters to achieve critical mass.
- Seek the 'right' long-term partnerships with the 'right' primes.
- Accept risk and equity sharing.
- Undertake to find more up-front funding.
- Get involved with primes and MOD.
- Put innovation and proaction at the top of the list.
- Read across lessons learned from one sector to another.

Industrial Culture

The key to industry's ability to work successfully with MOD in the new Smart Procurement world is the changes that must be made to industrial culture. These include:

- Creation of transparency and, hence, trust.
- Improved expertise, particularly in many management areas.
- Elimination of the fear/blame culture.
- Innovation, proaction and development of a stakeholder mentality.
- Better knowledge and understanding of the customer.
- Replacement of short-termism by long term planning.

None of these will be easy, none can be achieved quickly. But the longer they are left unstarted, the more industry or individual companies will be damaged.

SMART PROCUREMENT IN INDUSTRY

The Smart Procurement Initiative has, as yet, made little or no impact on vast swathes of the defence industry, except where industry has been co-opted onto IPTs, as summarised in the previous chapter. Worse, much of industry remains ignorant of, and hostile to, the changes that are being introduced. Further, there is a feeling that such things have been promised before and 'will never happen'.

Smart Procurement is a great opportunity and the potential benefits large. MOD has shown the way, although implementation is limited as yet, but cannot achieve it without the help of industry. Industry will not benefit without enthusiastic participation.